Study Guide

for use with

Financial Accounting

Fourth Edition

Robert Libby
Cornell University – Ithaca

Patricia A. Libby
Ithaca College

Daniel G. Short
Miami University – Oxford

Prepared by
Jeannie M. Folk
College of DuPage

 Irwin

Boston   Burr Ridge, IL   Dubuque, IA   Madison, WI   New York   San Francisco   St. Louis
Bangkok   Bogotá   Caracas   Kuala Lumpur   Lisbon   London   Madrid   Mexico City
Milan   Montreal   New Delhi   Santiago   Seoul   Singapore   Sydney   Taipei   Toronto

Study Guide for use with
FINANCIAL ACCOUNTING
Robert Libby, Patricia A. Libby, Daniel G. Short

Published by McGraw-Hill/Irwin, an imprint of The McGraw-Hill Companies, Inc., 1221 Avenue of the Americas, New York, NY 10020. Copyright © 1996, 1998, 2001, 2004 by The McGraw-Hill Companies, Inc. All rights reserved.

1 2 3 4 5 6 7 8 9 0 QPD/QPD 0 9 8 7 6 5 4 3 2

ISBN 0-07-247367-3

www.mhhe.com

This Study Guide was developed to help you study more effectively. It incorporates many of the accounting survival skills essential to your success. It is designed to accompany the fourth edition of *Financial Accounting* by Libby, Libby and Short, but is not a substitute for your textbook. Each chapter of the Study Guide contains the following sections: *Organization of the Chapter, Chapter Focus Suggestions; Learning Objectives; Read and Recall Questions; Chapter Take-Aways; Key Ratio; Finding Financial Information; Self-Test Questions and Exercises; Solutions to Self-Test Questions and Exercises;* and *An Idea for Your Study Team.*

AN ACCOUNTING SURVIVAL PLAN

✓ Preview
Before you read a chapter in the textbook, preview it. Start by reading the *Organization of the Chapter, Learning Objectives* and *Chapter Focus Suggestions* sections that appear at the beginning of each chapter in this Study Guide. Next, thumb through the chapter in the textbook, noting the names of each of the section headings. Finally, read the textbook chapter summary and key terms list.

✓ Read & Recall
Now that you know what to expect, start reading. As you finish reading each section of the chapter in the textbook, answer the related *Read and Recall Questions* included in the Study Guide. Check your answers by referring to the related section in your textbook. If you were not able to answer all of the questions, read the related section of the chapter in your textbook again. When you can answer the *Read and Recall Questions*, you understand and can recall what you just read. To move that information into long-term memory, you'll need to practice and apply what you have learned.

✓ Practice & Apply
After reading the *Chapter Take-Aways, Key Ratio* and *Finding Financial Information* sections of the Study Guide, practice and apply what you have learned by completing the *Self-Test Questions and Exercises*. Match the key terms with the textbook definitions, answer each of the true-false and multiple choice questions, and complete each of the exercises. Periodically, check your answers using the *Solutions to Self-Test Questions and Exercises* section..

✓ Review
Use the Study Guide daily. The *Read and Recall Questions, Chapter Take-Aways* and *Key Ratio* sections can be used to review the essential concepts covered in each chapter. The *Self-Test Questions and Exercises* are likely to be similar to the materials you will encounter on exams.

Finally, remember that you're not alone. Develop your own support system by forming a study team with three or four of your classmates. Each chapter of the Study Guide contains an *Idea for Your Study Team*. You'll learn by discussion, and develop valuable interpersonal skills.

Don't forget to use positive self-talk as you visualize your success in this accounting class. You can do it!

I would appreciate your comments and suggestions.

Jeannie M. Folk, CPA
Professor, Accounting
College of DuPage
folkje@cdnet.cod.edu

This Study Guide is dedicated to my children,
Andy, Jessie & Kevin,
Who support my efforts as a teacher and author.

TABLE OF CONTENTS

TITLE		PAGES

ORGANIZATION OF THE CHAPTER

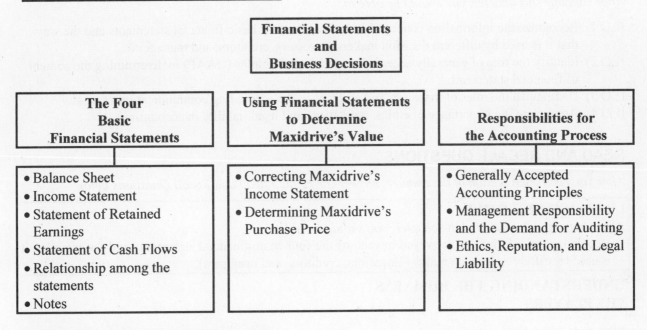

CHAPTER FOCUS SUGGESTIONS

Overview

This chapter describes the process that businesses use to communicate financial information to investors and creditors.

Terminology

If you have not yet worked in a business setting, you most likely will not be familiar with many of the terms used in this chapter. A solid understanding of the terminology used in this chapter is essential to your success. A listing of key terms appears at the end of the chapter; you should learn the definitions of each of these key terms. However, you should also make sure that you are familiar with other terms that are used in this chapter. These terms will be used throughout this course.

Financial Statement Matters

Four basic financial statements (that is, the income statement, statement of retained earnings, balance sheet and statement of cash flows) are used to communicate financial information to decision makers. This chapter provides an overview of each of the four basic financial statements. Memorize the equations for the financial statements so that you are able to easily identify the categories of items that are reported on each. Practice preparing all four financial statements. You will also be expected to understand how the financial statements are interrelated. As such, take the time to trace the common numbers from one financial statement to the next as you prepare the financial statements for a given company.

This chapter also introduces the parties involved in the communication process. Knowing which items are reported on each financial statement will help you to understand how decision makers use the financial statements.

LEARNING OBJECTIVES

After studying this chapter, you should be able to:

(LO 1) Recognize the information conveyed in each of the four basic financial statements and the way that it is used by different decision makers (investors, creditors, and managers).

(LO 2) Identify the role of generally accepted accounting principles (GAAP) in determining the content of financial statements.

(LO 3) Distinguish the roles of managers and auditors in the accounting communication process.

(LO 4) Appreciate the importance of ethics, reputation, and legal liability in accounting.

READ AND RECALL QUESTIONS

After you read each section of the chapter, answer the related Read and Recall Questions below.

LEARNING OBJECTIVE
After studying this section of the chapter, you should be able to:
1. Recognize the information conveyed in each of the four basic financial statements and the way that it is used by different decision makers (investors, creditors, and managers).

UNDERSTANDING THE BUSINESS
THE PLAYERS

What do investors hope to gain when they purchase all or part of a company? What risks do they assume? Why do creditors lend money to companies? What risks do they assume?

THE BUSINESS OPERATIONS

What must you understand before you can understand a company's financial statements?

THE ACCOUNTING SYSTEM

What functions are performed by Maxidrive's accounting system? What two major groups use the reports produced by this accounting system? How does financial accounting differ from managerial accounting? Which of the two is the focal point of this text?

THE FOUR BASIC FINANCIAL STATEMENTS – AN OVERVIEW

What did Exeter Investors (Maxidrive's new owner) and American Bank (Maxidrive's largest creditor) use to learn more about the company before making their purchase and lending decisions? What assumption did they make when they used this information to make their purchase and lending decisions?

What do the four basic financial statements summarize? When are financial statements prepared?

THE BALANCE SHEET

What is the purpose of the balance sheet? What is another name for the balance sheet?

Structure

What four significant items are found in the heading of a balance sheet? What is the time dimension of the balance sheet? What unit of measure is used to prepare financial statements of U.S. companies?

What is the basic accounting equation? What is another name for the basic accounting equation?

Elements

What is an asset? How are assets initially measured on the balance sheet? What is a liability? How do liabilities arise? What is stockholders' equity? What two items are reported in the Stockholders' Equity section of the balance sheet?

FINANCIAL ANALYSIS
INTERPRETING ASSETS, LIABILITIES, AND STOCKHOLDERS' EQUITY ON THE BALANCE SHEET

Why did American Bank and Exeter assess Maxidrive's assets? Why are assets so important?

Why were Exeter Investors and American Bank interested in Maxidrive's debts? If a company is not able to pay its debts, what action can its creditors take?

Why was the amount of Maxidrive's stockholders' equity important to American Bank? If a company goes out of business and its assets are sold, how will the proceeds be used?

THE INCOME STATEMENT – Structure

What four significant items are found in the heading of an income statement? What is the time dimension of the income statement? What is an accounting period? What is the income statement equation?

Elements

What are revenues? When should revenues be reported on the income statement? Does the receipt of cash from a customer always coincide with the recording of revenue? Why or why not?

What do expenses represent? When are expenses reported on the income statement? Is it appropriate to correlate the recording of an expense with the payment of cash for that expense? Why or why not?

What is net income? When is a net loss reported? What term is used when total revenues equal total expenses?

FINANCIAL ANALYSIS
ANALYZING THE INCOME STATEMENT: BEYOND THE BOTTOM LINE

Why do investors (such as Exeter) and creditors (such as American Bank) closely monitor a firm's net income?

STATEMENT OF RETAINED EARNINGS – Structure

What four significant items are found in the heading of a statement of retained earnings? What is the time dimension of the statement of retained earnings? Does net income increase or decrease the balance of retained earnings? Does the declaration of dividends increase or decrease the balance of retained earnings? What is the retained earnings equation?

FINANCIAL ANALYSIS
Interpreting Retained Earnings

What is an important source of financing for companies (such as Maxidrive)? Why do creditors (such as American Bank) closely monitor a firm's retained earnings statement?

STATEMENT OF CASH FLOWS–Structure

What four significant items are found in the heading of a statement of cash flows? What is the time dimension of the statement of cash flows? Why aren't reported revenues always equal to the amount of cash collected from customers? Why aren't reported expenses always equal to the cash paid out during the period? What is the statement of cash flows equation?

Elements

What are cash flows from operating activities? What are cash flows from investing activities? What are cash flows from financing activities? What is the cash flow statement equation?

FINANCIAL ANALYSIS
Interpreting the Cash Flows Statement

What do analysts believe regarding the usefulness of the statement of cash flows? Which section of the statement do bankers consider the most important? Why? Why are stockholders interested in the company's cash flows from operations?

RELATIONSHIPS AMONG THE STATEMENTS

Which line on the income statement carries through to the statement of retained earnings? Which line on the statement of retained earnings appears on the balance sheet? Which line on the balance sheet appears on the statement of cash flows?

NOTES

Why are the notes (or footnotes) to the financial statements so important? What type of information is provided by each of the three types of notes to the financial statements?

FINANCIAL ANALYSIS
Management Uses of Financial Statements

How do the managers of a company (or firm) make direct use of the firm's financial statements?

USING FINANCIAL STATEMENTS TO DETERMINE MAXIDRIVE'S VALUE – CORRECTING MAXIDRIVE'S INCOME STATEMENT

What two types of errors did Exeter find in Maxidrive's financial statements?

DETERMINING THE PURCHASE PRICE FOR MAXIDRIVE

What factors did Exeter consider when deciding on a purchase price for Maxidrive? What is one method that is used to estimate the value of a company?

What does the price/earnings (PE) ratio measure? All others things equal, what does a high P/E ratio mean? How is the P/E ratio computed? How did Exeter Investors use this ratio to estimate its loss?

LEARNING OBJECTIVE
After studying this section of the chapter, you should be able to:
2. Identify the role of generally accepted accounting principles (GAAP) in determining the content of financial statements.

RESPONSIBILITIES FOR THE ACCOUNTING COMMUNICATION PROCESS

What do decision makers need to understand before using accounting information? What is the name of the measurement rules that are used to develop accounting information?

GENERALLY ACCEPTED ACCOUNTING PRINCIPLES
How are Generally Accepted Accounting Principles Determined?

What was created when the Securities Exchange Acts of 1933 and 1934 were passed into law by Congress? What function does the Securities and Exchange Commission (SEC) perform? What group has the primary responsibility to work out the detailed rules that become generally accepted accounting principles (GAAP)?

Why is GAAP Important to Managers and External Users?

Companies incur the cost of preparing financial statements and bear the major economic consequences of their publication. What are the three major potential economic consequences?

INTERNATIONAL PERSPECTIVE – Are Generally Accepted Accounting Principles Similar in Other Counties?

Is there one set of generally accepted accounting principles in use throughout the world? What is the International Accounting Standards Board attempting to accomplish? Until their goal is reached, what must managers and users do in order to successfully interpret financial statements?

LEARNING OBJECTIVE
After studying this section of the chapter, you should be able to:
3. Distinguish the roles of managers and auditors in the accounting communication process.

MANAGEMENT RESPONSIBILITY AND THE DEMAND FOR AUDITING

Who has the primary responsibility for the information that is presented in a company's financial statements? What steps do managers take to ensure the accuracy of the company's records? What section of a company's annual report reiterates these responsibilities?

What does an audit report describe? Who can issue an audit report? What does an audit involve? What does an independent CPA do while performing an audit? What happens when an audit, the best protection available to the public, fails?

LEARNING OBJECTIVE

After studying this section of the chapter, you should be able to:

4. Appreciate the importance of ethics, reputation, and legal liability in accounting.

ETHICS, REPUTATION AND LEGAL LIABILITY

What is necessary if financial statements are to be of any value to decision makers?

Why does the American Institute of Certified Public Accountants require all of its members to adhere to a professional code of ethics and professional auditing standards?

EPILOGUE

What are the two most common forms of financial statement fraud?

CHAPTER SUPPLEMENT A *(Determine whether you are responsible for this supplement.)*

Types of Business Entities

What is a sole proprietorship? What is a partnership? What is a corporation? What are the characteristics of each of the three types of business? What is the dominant form of business organization in the United States? Why is it the dominant form?

CHAPTER SUPPLEMENT B *(Determine whether you are responsible for this supplement).*

Employment in the Accounting Profession Today

What requirements must be met before an accountant may be licensed as a Certified Public Accountant? What three types of services are performed by accounting firms?

CHAPTER TAKE-AWAYS

1. **Recognize the information conveyed in each of the four basic financial statements and the way that it is used by different decision makers (investors, creditors, and managers).**

   The *balance sheet* is a statement of financial position that reports dollar amounts for the assets, liabilities, and stockholders' equity at a specific point in time.

   The *income statement* is a statement of operations that reports revenues, expenses, and net income for a stated period of time.

   The *statement of retained earnings* explains changes to the retained earnings balance that occurred during the reporting period.

   The *statement of cash flows* reports inflows and outflows of cash for a specific period of time.

   The statements are used by investors and creditors to evaluate different aspects of the firm's financial position and performance.

2. **Identify the role of generally accepted accounting principles (GAAP) in determining the content of financial statements.**

   GAAP are the measurement rules used to develop the information in financial statements. Knowledge of GAAP is necessary for accurate interpretation of the numbers in financial statements.

3. **Distinguish the roles of managers and auditors in the accounting communication process.**

   Management has primary responsibility for the accuracy of a company's financial information. Auditors are responsible for expressing an opinion of the fairness of the financial statement presentations based on their examination of the reports and records of the company.

4. **Appreciate the importance of ethics, reputation, and legal liability in accounting.**

   Users will have confidence in the accuracy of financial statement numbers only if the people associated with their preparation and audit have reputations for ethical behavior and competence. Management and auditors can also be held legally liable for fraudulent financial statements and malpractice.

FINDING FINANCIAL INFORMATION

Balance Sheet

Assets = Liabilities + Stockholders' Equity

Income Statement

Revenues
– Expense
Net Income

Statement of Retained Earnings

Retained Earnings, beginning of the period
+ Net Income
– Dividends
Retained Earnings, end of the period

Statement of Cash Flows

+/– Cash Flow from Operating Activities
+/– Cash Flow from Investing Activities
+/– Cash Flow from Financing Activities
Net Change in Cash

SELF-TEST QUESTIONS AND EXERCISES

MATCHING

Match each of the key terms listed below with the appropriate definition found in the glossary:

____	Accounting	____	Income Statement
____	Accounting Entity	____	Notes (Footnotes)
____	Accounting Period	____	Report of Independent Accountants
____	Assurance Services	____	(Audit Report)
____	Audit	____	Report of Management
	Balance Sheet		Securities and Exchange Commission
____		____	(SEC)
____	Basic Accounting Equation	____	Statement of Cash Flows
____	Financial Accounting Standards Board (FASB)	____	Statement of Retained Earnings
____	Generally Accepted Accounting Principles		
	(GAAP)		

A. Indicates management's primary responsibility for financial statement information and the steps taken to ensure the accuracy of the company's records.

B. Reports the revenues less the expenses of the accounting period.

C. Assets = Liabilities + Stockholders' Equity.

D. Provide supplemental information about the financial condition of a company, without which the financial statements cannot be fully understood.

E. The organization for which financial data are to be collected (separate and distinct from its owners).

F. The U.S. government agency that determines the financial statements that public companies must provide to stockholders and the measurement rules that they must use in producing those statements.

G. A system that collects and processes (analyzes, measures, and records) financial information about an organization and reports that information to decision makers.

H. The private sector body given the primary responsibility to work out the detailed rules that become generally accepted accounting principles.

I. An examination of the financial reports to ensure that they represent what they claim and conform with generally accepted accounting principles.

J. Reports the financial position (assets, liabilities, and stockholders' equity) of an accounting entity at a point in time.

K. The measurement rules used to develop the information in financial statements.

L. Describes the auditors' opinion of the fairness of the financial statement presentations and the evidence gathered to support that opinion.

M. Reports inflows and outflows of cash during the accounting period in the categories of operations, investing, and financing.

N. The time period covered by the financial statements.

O. Reports the way that net income and the distribution of dividends affected the financial position of the company during the accounting period.

P. Independent professional services that improve the quality of information for decision makers.

TRUE-FALSE QUESTIONS

Enter a T or F in the blank to indicate whether each statement is true or false.

___1. (LO 1) The focus of financial accounting is on external users, whereas the focus of managerial accounting is on internal users of accounting information.

___2. (LO 1) The balance sheet is prepared to summarize the results of the company's activities over a specified period of time, such as one year.

___3. (LO 1) The basic accounting equation is often called the balance sheet equation.

___4. (LO 1) The balance sheet lists a company's assets, liabilities, revenues and expenses.

___5. (LO 1) A company's financial position can be determined, in part, by reference to the current market values of its assets as reported on the balance sheet.

___6. (LO 1) Stockholders' equity is the amount of financing provided by the company's owners.

___7. (LO 1) The revenue earned from the sale of goods to a customer is always reported in the period in which the goods are paid for by the customer

___8. (LO 1) Revenues earned from providing services are reported on the income statement in the period in which the services are provided whether or not the customers have paid for the services.

___9. (LO 1) An item is considered to be an expense as soon as the company has paid cash for it.

___10. (LO 1) Expenses reported in one accounting period may be paid for in another accounting period.

___11. (LO 1) The income statement sets forth revenues, expenses and dividends declared.

___12. (LO 1) The time dimension of the statement of cash flows is the same as the income statement and the time dimension of the statement of retained earnings is the same as the balance sheet.

___13. (LO 1) The price/earnings ratio is a measure of expected company growth.

___14. (LO 2) The FASB specifies the laws under which financial statements are prepared, and the SEC enforces these laws.

___15. (LO 2) The FASB actively solicits the input of the business community in the development of new accounting rules.

___16. (LO 2) Investors and creditors do not need to obtain an understanding of the company's operations if they are relying on financial statements that have been prepared in accordance with generally accepted accounting principles.

___17. (LO 3) If a company has implemented internal control procedures, decision makers can safely assume that no errors exist in the company's records or financial statements.

___18. (LO 3) If a company has implemented internal control procedures, its managers can safely assume that the company's assets are then safeguarded against any possibility of theft or embezzlement.

___19. (Supplement A) The owners of sole proprietorships and partners in general partnerships are personally liable for the debts of these types of businesses; as a result, the businesses cannot be treated as separate accounting entities from their owners.

___20. (Supplement A) A corporation is legally separate from its owners; as such, a corporation is a separate business entity that must be accounted for separately from its several owners.

MULTIPLE CHOICE QUESTIONS

Choose the best answer or response by placing the identifying letter in the space provided.

___1. (LO 1) When accountants refer to a "creditor" of a company, they mean the person or business that

    a. owns the company.
    b. owes the company money.
    c. loaned the company money or allowed it to buy goods and pay for them later.
    d. has reviewed the company favorably in the business press.
    e. takes care of the company's banking needs.

___2. (LO 1) Each of the following is one of the four basic financial statements except the

    a. income statement.
    b. statement of cash flows.
    c. statement of retained earnings.
    d. balance sheet.
    e. bank statement.

___3. (LO 1) The statement of financial position is another term for the

    a. income statement.
    b. statement of cash flows.
    c. company's bank statement.
    d. results of today's trading in the company's stock.
    e. balance sheet.

___4. (LO 1) An accounting period is

    a. exactly one year in length.
    b. one specific date in time.
    c. any specified time period.
    d. the time required to collect accounts receivable.
    e. the life of the entity.

___5. (LO 1) The balance sheet equation may be stated as

    a. assets = liabilities + owners' equity.
    b. assets – liabilities = owners' equity.
    c. assets – owners' equity = liabilities.
    d. assets + liabilities = owners' equity.
    e. a, b, or c above.

___6. (LO 1) All of the following items are classified on the balance sheet as assets except

    a. notes payable.
    b. inventories.
    c. land.
    d. accounts receivable.
    e. cash.

___7. (LO 1) Amounts owed by customers to the company for prior sales to these customers are reported on the balance sheet as _____, whereas amounts owed by the company to vendors or suppliers for goods or services are reported as _____.

    a. cash; cash.
    b. accounts payable; accounts receivable.
    c. accounts receivable; accounts payable.
    d. inventories; sales.
    e. sales; inventories.

___8. (LO 1) Assets are usually reported on the balance sheet at

    a. acquisition cost.
    b. market value on the balance sheet date.
    c. market value adjusted for any deterioration from storage.
    d. cost adjusted for inflation since the purchase date.
    e. expected selling price.

___9. (LO 1) Retained earnings is the amount of

    a. cash that stockholders may reasonably expect to receive as dividends in the future.
    b. earnings held for payment of executive bonuses.
    c. cash that will be left over after all of the company's liabilities have been satisfied.
    d. earnings kept, or reinvested, in the business, and thus not paid out as dividends.
    e. cash invested by the owners of the business.

___10. (LO 1) Revenues are reported on the income statement

    a. in the period in which an order is received from a customer.
    b. in the period in which the goods or services are actually provided to the customer.
    c. in the period in which cash is collected from the customer.
    d. any time the company receives cash.
    e. all of the above.

___11. (LO 1) All of the following are classified on the income statement as revenues except

    a. cash sales of goods to customers.
    b. credit sales of goods to customers.
    c. amounts earned by providing services to customers.
    d. amounts earned by renting property to others.
    e. cash received when money is borrowed from a bank.

___12. (LO 1) Expenses are reported on the income statement

    a. in the period in which an order for goods or services is placed with a vendor or supplier.
    b. in the period in which the goods or services provided by a vendor or supplier are used to generate revenues.
    c. in the period in which cash is paid to vendors or suppliers for goods or services that have been purchased.
    d. any time the company disburses (or pays out) cash.
    e. all of the above.

___13. (LO 1) All of the following items are classified on the income statement as expenses except

    a. the cost of acquiring the merchandise that was sold.
    b. wages of sales staff.
    c. the Vice President's annual bonus.
    d. the cost of a parcel of land acquired for the construction of a new store.
    e. research and development costs on a potential new product.

___14. (LO 1) If revenues are less than expenses during an accounting period,

    a. a net loss is reported.
    b. no dividends can be declared or paid during the accounting period.
    c. dividends can be declared but not paid during the accounting period.
    d. net income results.
    e. none of the above.

___15. (LO 1) Net income is often called

    a. net earnings.
    b. profit.
    c. the bottom line.
    d. all of the above.
    e. none of the above.

___16. (LO 1) The statement of retained earnings indicates the relationship between

    a. the income statement and the balance sheet.
    b. sales and cash collected.
    c. beginning and ending cash.
    d. assets, liabilities, revenues and expenses.
    e. all of the above.

___17. (LO 1) The equation for the statement of retained earnings is

    a. net income – dividends = retained earnings.
    b. beginning retained earnings + net income + dividends = ending retained earnings.
    c. beginning retained earnings + net income–dividends = ending retained earnings.
    d. beginning retained earnings – net income – dividends = ending retained earnings.
    e. none of the above.

___18. (LO 1) The statement of cash flows is divided into the following categories:

    a. cash inflows, cash outflows.
    b. current, non-current.
    c. operating, investing, financing.
    d. assets, liabilities, equity.
    e. revenues, expenses.

___19. (LO 1) The price earnings ratio (or multiplier) is computed as

   a. dividends divided by market price.
   b. market price divided by net earnings.
   c. revenues divided by expenses.
   d. stockholders' equity divided by net earnings.
   e. market price divided by dividends.

___20. (LO 1) The notes (or footnotes) that accompany the financial statements

   a. describe accounting rules applied in the preparation of the financial statements.
   b. present additional detail about particular line items listed on the financial statements.
   c. present information about certain items not reported on the financial statements.
   d. a, b, and c above.
   e. are optional, and present any information the company would like to add to its financial statements.

EXERCISES

Record your answer to each exercise in the space provided. Show your work.

Exercise 1 (LO 1)

Apply the balance sheet equation in each of the independent cases below to compute the missing amounts.

Component	Case A	Case B	Case C
Assets	(a)	$13,100	$6,500
Liabilities	$3,500	(b)	4,100
Stockholders' equity	5,900	9,600	(c)

Case A

Case B

Case C

Exercise 2 (LO 1)
Part A

The balance sheet of Exeter Corporation contains the following items (in thousands). Mark each item to identify it as an asset (A), liability (L) or stockholders' equity (SE) item.

A, L or SE	Balance Sheet Item	Amount
	Accounts payable	$350
	Accounts receivable	300
	Cash	200
	Contributed capital	275
	Inventories	175
	Plant and equipment	650
	Note payable	500
	Retained earnings	?

Part B

Determine the amount of the retained earnings at June 30, 20A.

Game Plan for Determining the Amount of Retained Earnings
Start by determining the total amount of stockholders' equity using the basic accounting equation.
Then, recalling the two components of stockholders' equity, solve for the amount of retained earnings.

Part C

Prepare a balance sheet for Exeter Corporation as of June 30, 20A.

Exeter Corporation
Balance Sheet
June 30, 20A
(in thousands of dollars)

Exercise 3 (LO 1)
Part A

The income statement of Elegance Corporation contains the following items (in thousands). Mark each item as a revenue (R) or expense (E).

R or E	Income Statement Item	Amount
	Cost of goods sold	$225
	Interest costs	40
	Provision for income taxes	20
	Research and development expense	120
	Sales revenue	550
	Selling, general and administrative expense	110

Part B

Prepare an income statement for the year ended December 31, 20A.

Elegance Corporation
Income Statement
For the year ended December 31, 20A
(in thousands of dollars)

Part C

Assume that the company had a market value of $35,000,000 at December 31, 20A. What is its P/E ratio?

Exercise 4 (LO 1)

During April, the first month of the company's operations, Landon Inc. sold $150,000 of goods to customers for cash. In addition, Landon sold $350,000 of goods on credit to customers. Payments from these customers amounted to $130,000 during April; the remaining $220,000 had not been received by April 30. How much revenue should Landon report on its income statement for April?

Exercise 5 (LO 1)

During October, the first month of the company's operations, Barbeton Corporation produced goods that cost $475,000. Goods with a cost of $375,000 were delivered to customers during October and goods amounting to $100,000 were on hand at October 31. What amount should Barbeton report as costs of goods sold on its income statement for October?

Exercise 6 (LO 1)

Apply the equation for the statement of retained earnings in each of the independent cases below to compute the missing amount for each case. Assume that it is the end of 20B, the second full year of operations, in each of the four cases.

	Case A	Case B	Case C	Case D
Retained earnings, beginning of year	$4,500	$2,300	$3,500	(d)
Net income (loss)	575	(b)	3,100	$1,275
Dividends	275	990	(c)	925
Retained earnings, end of year	(a)	$2,500	$4,000	$600

Case A

Exercise 6, continued

Case B

Case C

Case D

Exercise 7 (LO 1)

During 20A, its first year of operations, Arbor Inc. performed landscaping services for which its customers promised to pay $315,000. Customers remitted payments amounting to $250,000 by the end of the year. Arbor paid $101,000 in cash for employee wages, $29,000 in cash for rent and $68,000 in cash for landscaping materials that had been used to perform its landscaping services. At the end of the year, Arbor owed $13,000 to one of its suppliers for landscaping materials that had been used during the year. Arbor has not yet paid its income taxes for the year. Its income tax rate is 25%. On the last day of the year, Arbor declared and paid dividends of $20,000.

Part A

Determine the increase or decrease in cash during the year.

Exercise 7, continued
Part B

Prepare an income statement for Arbor's first year of operations.

Arbor Corporation
Income Statement
For the Year Ended December 31, 20A
(in thousands of dollars)

Part C

Determine the amount of retained earnings that will be reported on Arbor's balance sheet at the end of its first year of operations.

Exercise 8 (LO 1)
Part A

Faxit Corporation began the year with $67,000 in cash. The company's statement of cash flows contains the items (in thousands) listed in the following table. Mark each item as a cash flow from operating activities (O), cash flow from investing activities (I) or cash flow from financing activities (F)

O, I or F	Cash Flow Statement Item	Amount
	Cash collected from customers	$1,000
	Cash paid for dividends	125
	Cash paid for income taxes	50
	Cash paid to suppliers	250
	Cash received from bank loan	350
	Cash paid for interest	75
	Cash paid to purchase equipment	325
	Cash paid to employees	425

Part B

Prepare a statement of cash flows for the year ended September 30, 20B.

Faxit Corporation
Statement of Cash Flows
For the year ended September 30, 20B
(in thousands of dollars)

SOLUTIONS TO SELF-TEST QUESTIONS AND EXERCISES

MATCHING

G	Accounting	B	Income Statement
E	Accounting Entity	D	Notes (Footnotes)
N	Accounting Period	L	Report of Independent Accountants
P	Assurance Services		(Audit Report)
I	Audit	A	Report of Management
J	Balance Sheet	F	Securities and Exchange Commission (SEC)
C	Basic Accounting Equation	M	Statement of Cash Flows
H	Financial Accounting Standards Board (FASB)	O	Statement of Retained Earnings
K	Generally Accepted Accounting Principles (GAAP)		

TRUE-FALSE QUESTIONS

1. T
2. F – The balance sheet is prepared as of a certain date in time. The income statement and statements of retained earnings and cash flows cover a specified time period.
3. T
4. F – The balance sheet lists the company's assets, liabilities and its stockholders' equity.
5. F – Each asset is initially measured on the balance sheet by the total costs incurred to acquire it. Balance sheets do not indicate the current market values of the assets reported.
6. T
7. F – Revenues are normally reported on the income statement in the period in which the goods or services are sold. The cash may change hands in a different accounting period.
8. T
9. F – Expenses are normally reported on the income statement in the period in which goods or services are used to earn revenues. This is not necessarily the same period in which cash is paid.
10. T
11. F – Dividends declared are reported on the statement of retained earnings.
12. F – The time dimension of both the statements of cash flows and retained earnings is the same as the income statement. The balance sheet is prepared as of a certain date in time.
13. T
14. F – GAAP are standards developed by FASB; these standards are *not* laws passed by Congress.
15. T
16. F – Investors and creditors need to obtain an understanding of a company's operations in order to understand the nature of the various items reported on the financial statements.
17. F – Internal control procedures can only safeguards against errors. Some errors may not be prevented or detected by a company's internal control procedures.
18. F – Internal control procedures can only safeguards against thefts and embezzlements. Certain frauds, such as those committed by collusion, may not be prevented or detected by a company's internal control procedures.
19. F – Even though a sole proprietorship is not a separate legal entity from its owner, it is still considered to be a separate accounting entity which is accounted for separately from its owner. The same applies to partnerships.
20. T

MULTIPLE CHOICE QUESTIONS

1.	c	5.	e	9.	d	13.	d	17.	c
2.	e	6.	a	10.	b	14.	a	18.	c
3.	e	7.	c	11.	e	15.	d	19.	b
4.	c	8.	a	12.	b	16.	a	20.	d

EXERCISES

Exercise 1

The balance sheet equation is: Assets = Liabilities + Stockholders' Equity.

Case A
(a) = $3,500 + $5,900
(a) = $9,400

Case B
$13,100 = (b) + $9,600
(b) = $3,500

Case C
$6,500 = $4,100 + (c)
(c) = $2,400

Exercise 2
Part A

A, L or SE	Balance Sheet Item	Amount
L	Accounts payable	$350
A	Accounts receivable	300
A	Cash	200
SE	Contributed capital	275
A	Inventories	175
A	Plant and equipment	650
L	Note payable	500
SE	Retained earnings	?

Part B

Total amount of stockholders' equity:
Assets = Liabilities + Stockholders' Equity
$1,325 (see Part C below) = $850 (see Part C below) + SE
SE = $475

Retained earnings at June 30, 20A:
Stockholders' Equity (from above) = Contributed Capital + Retained Earnings
$475 = $275 + RE
RE = $200

Exercise 2, continued
Part C

Exeter Corporation
Balance Sheet
June 30, 20A
(in thousands of dollars)

Assets

Cash	$ 200
Accounts receivable	300
Inventories	175
Plant and equipment	650
Total assets	**$1,325**

Liabilities

Accounts payable	$350	
Notes payable	500	
Total liabilities		**$ 850**

Stockholders' equity

Contributed capital	$275	
Retained earnings *(see above)*	200	
Total stockholders' equity		475
Total liabilities and stockholders' equity		**$1,325**

Exercise 3
Part A

R or E	Income Statement Item	Amount
E	Cost of goods sold	$225
E	Interest costs	40
E	Provision for income taxes	20
E	Research and development expense	120
R	Sales revenue	550
E	Selling, general and administrative expense	110

Exercise 3, continued
Part B

Elegance Corporation
Income Statement
For the Year Ended December 31, 20A
(in thousands of dollars)

Revenues:		
Sales revenue		$550
Expenses:		
Cost of goods sold	$225	
Selling, general and administrative expense	110	
Research and development expense	120	
Interest expense	40	
Total expenses		495
Pretax income		55
Provision for income tax		20
Net income		$ 35

Part C

Price/earnings ratio = $35,000,000 ÷ $35,000 = 10

Exercise 4

Revenue is reported in the period in which goods are sold. Landon should report sales revenue of $500,000 (cash sales of $150,000 and credit sales of $350,000) on its income statement for the month of April.

Exercise 5

Cost of goods sold expense is the total cost to produce the goods that were delivered to customers during the period. Barbeton should report $375,000, the costs of goods delivered to customers, as cost of goods sold expense on its income statement for the month of October.

Exercise 6

Ending RE = Beginning RE + Net Income – Dividends
Case A
(a) = $4,500 + $575 – $275; (a) = $4,800

Case B
$2,500 = $2,300 + (b) – $990; (b) = $1,190

Case C
$4,000 = $3,500 + $3,100 – (c); (c) = $2,600

Case D
$600 = (d) + $1,275 – $925; (d) = $250

Exercise 7
Part A

Increase or decrease in cash during the year (in thousands):

Collected from customers		$ 250
Paid to/for:		
Employees	$(101)	
Rent	(29)	
Suppliers	(68)	
Dividends	(20)	
Total cash payments		(218)
Increase in cash		$ 32

Part B

Arbor Corporation
Income Statement
For the Year Ended December 31, 20A
(in thousands of dollars)

Revenues:		
Sales revenue		$315
Expenses:		
Employee wage expense	$101	
Rent expense	29	
Landscaping materials expense *(68 + 13)*	81	
Total expenses		211
Pretax income		104
Provision for income tax		26
Net income		$ 78

Part C

Ending RE = Beginning RE + Net Income – Dividends
Ending RE = $0 (no beginning RE earnings) + $78,000 – $20,000 = $58,000

Exercise 8
Part A

O, I or F	Cash Flow Statement Item	Amount
O	Cash collected from customers	$1,000
F	Cash paid for dividends	125
O	Cash paid for income taxes	50
O	Cash paid to suppliers	250
F	Cash received from bank loan	350
O	Cash paid for interest	75
I	Cash paid to purchase equipment	325
O	Cash paid to employees	425

Exercise 8, continued
Part B

Faxit Corporation
Statement of Cash Flows
For the Year Ended December 31, 20B
(in thousands of dollars)

Cash flows from operating activities:

Cash collected from customers	$1,000	
Cash paid to employees	(425)	
Cash paid to suppliers	(250)	
Cash paid for interest	(75)	
Cash paid for taxes	(50)	
Net cash flow from operating activities		$200
Cash flows from investing activities:		
Cash paid to purchase equipment	(325)	
Net cash flow used in investing activities		(325)
Cash flows from financing activities:		
Cash received from bank loan	350	
Cash paid for dividends	(125)	
Net cash flow from financing activities		225
Net increase in cash during the year		100
Cash at beginning of year		67
Cash at end of year		$167

AN IDEA FOR YOUR STUDY TEAM

Prepare a list of items that would be on the balance sheet of a typical college student. What are your assets? What are your liabilities? How would you determine your "equity?" Then, attach approximate or hypothetical values to each asset and liability listed. (Don't feel that you need to be too explicit about your own personal finances.) Compare and contrast your typical college student balance sheet with those prepared by the other members of your study team.

ORGANIZATION OF THE CHAPTER

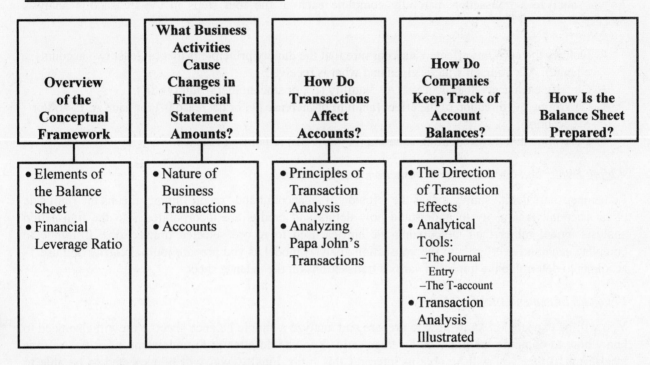

CHAPTER FOCUS SUGGESTIONS

Overview

The accounting terms and concepts set forth in chapters 2 through 4 are introduced using the Conceptual Framework that was developed and synthesized by the FASB. This chapter begins the discussion of how the accounting function collects data about business activities and processes the data to generate financial statements (that is, reports used by external decision-makers). Business activities affect both the balance sheet and income statement. However, for simplicity, chapter 2 emphasizes business activities affecting only the balance sheet. Operating activities affecting affect both the income statement and balance sheet are covered in chapters 3 and 4.

Understanding the Recording Process

As you study this chapter, you may be tempted to memorize the recording of the business transactions that are illustrated in the textbook. If you adopt this approach, you will most likely encounter transactions in assignments and on exams that differ from those you memorized. Instead, you should concentrate on **understanding** the recording process. It will be easier to remember *how* the accounting process works if you know *why* it works a certain way. A solid understanding of the recording process will come in handy as more complex transactions are covered in future chapters.

Using the Transaction Analysis Model

The accounting equation **(Assets = Liabilities + Stockholders' Equity)** was introduced in Chapter 1. It is part of the foundation of the transaction analysis model, which is used to determine how a transaction affects the entity in terms of the accounting equation. The model relies on two other important principles: (1) every transaction affects at least two accounts, and (2) the accounting equation must remain in balance after each transaction.

As you analyze a transaction, carefully complete each of the four steps in the transaction analysis process:

1. Identify the accounts affected, making sure that the duality principle is met (at least two accounts change). Ask yourself what is given and what is received.
2. Classify each account as an asset (A), liability (L), or stockholders' equity (SE).
3. Determine the direction of the effect (amount of increase [+] or decrease [−] for each A, L, and/or SE account).
4. Determine that the accounting equation (A = L + SE) remains in balance.

Adding Debits and Credits to the Transaction Analysis Model

Remember that "debit" simply means the left side of an account and "credit" simply means the right side of an account. Again, try to understand how debits and credits are incorporated into the transaction analysis model rather than memorizing the entries used to record selected transactions. Continue to complete each and every step in the transaction analysis model as you prepare journal entries and use T-accounts to determine the impact of various transactions on the balance sheet.

Financial Statement Analysis Matters

You will be expected to know how to prepare and analyze a simple balance sheet. You will also need to know how to compute the financial leverage ratio. You should attempt to understand what this ratio is measuring so that you will be able to interpret this ratio. Finally, you will be expected to be able to identify investing and financing activities and prepare the related sections of the statement of cash flows.

LEARNING OBJECTIVES

After studying this chapter, you should be able to:

(LO 1) Define the objective of financial reporting, the elements of the balance sheet, and the related key accounting assumptions and principles.

(LO 2) Compute and interpret the financial leverage ratio.

(LO 3) Identify what constitutes a business transaction and common balance sheet account titles used in business.

(LO 4) Apply transaction analysis to simple business transactions in terms of the accounting model: Assets = Liabilities + Stockholders' Equity.

(LO 5) Determine the impact of business transactions on the balance sheet using two basic tools, journal entries and T-accounts.

(LO 6) Prepare and analyze a simple balance sheet.

(LO 7) Identify investing and financing transactions and demonstrate how they are reported on the statement of cash flows.

Financial Accounting

READ AND RECALL QUESTIONS

After you read each section of the chapter, answer the related Read and Recall Questions below.

LEARNING OBJECTIVE
After studying this section of the chapter, you should be able to:
1. Define the objective of financial reporting, the elements of the balance sheet, and the related key accounting assumptions and principles.

OVERVIEW OF THE CONCEPTUAL FRAMEWORK

What group publishes the Statements of Financial Accounting Concepts that make up the conceptual framework of accounting? How does this conceptual framework relate to this *Financial Accounting* textbook?

CONCEPTS EMPHASIZED IN CHAPTER 2 – Objective of Financial Reporting

What is the primary objective of external financial reporting?

Underlying Assumptions of Accounting

What is the separate entity assumption? What is the unit-of-measure assumption? What is the continuity assumption (or going concern) assumption?

ELEMENTS OF THE BALANCE SHEET – Assets

What are assets? How are assets usually listed on the balance sheet? What are current assets?

Liabilities

What are liabilities? How are liabilities usually listed on the balance sheet? What are current liabilities?

Stockholders' Equity

What is stockholders' equity? What is contributed capital? What are retained earnings?

A Note on Ratio Analysis

Why do users of financial information compute ratios? What is one of the most common ratios? What does the current ratio measure? How is it computed?

LEARNING OBJECTIVE
After studying this section of the chapter, you should be able to:
2. Compute and interpret the financial leverage ratio.

KEY RATIO ANALYSIS: THE FINANCIAL LEVERAGE RATIO

How is the financial leverage ratio computed? What does the financial leverage ratio measure?

Why is debt financing riskier than financing with stockholders' equity? What does a financial leverage ratio near 1:1 indicate?

Basic Accounting Principle

What does the cost principle require in terms of the initial recording of all financial statement elements? How is cost measured under this principle? What is the disadvantage to this approach?

FINANCIAL ANALYSIS
UNRECORDED BUT VALUABLE ASSETS

What types of valuable assets are not listed on the balance sheet because they have no book value? What is the asset recognition rule? Why are some intangible assets listed on the balance sheet but not others?

LEARNING OBJECTIVE

After studying this section of the chapter, you should be able to:

3. Identify what constitutes a business transaction and common balance sheet account titles used in business.

WHAT BUSINESS ACTIVITIES CAUSE CHANGES IN FINANCIAL STATEMENT AMOUNTS?
Nature of Business Transactions

What is a transaction? What is an external event? What is an internal event? If an employment contract was signed when Papa John's hired a new manager, would this event be considered a transaction? Why or why not?

ACCOUNTS

What is an account? What is a chart of accounts? How is a chart of accounts usually organized? (Hint: Your reply should address each of the five types of accounts.) Why does every company have a different chart of accounts? How do the charts of accounts of most foreign companies compare to those of U.S. companies?

LEARNING OBJECTIVE

After studying this section of the chapter, you should be able to:

4. Apply transaction analysis to simple business transactions in terms of the accounting model: Assets = Liabilities + Stockholders' Equity.

HOW DO TRANSACTIONS AFFECT ACCOUNTS?

Why do business managers need to understand exactly how transactions impact the financial statements?

Principles of Transaction Analysis

What is transaction analysis? What is the basic accounting equation for a business that is organized as a corporation? What two principles underlie the transaction analysis process?

Duality of Effects

What is the duality of effects concept?

Maintaining the Accounting Equation Balance

What are the two steps that must be performed in order for systematic transaction analysis?

ANALYZING PAPA JOHN'S TRANSACTIONS

(a) Papa John's issues $2,000 of additional common stock, receiving cash from investors. Using the transaction analysis process: (1) identify and classify the accounts and effects, and (2) determine whether the accounting equation is in balance.

Assets	=	Liabilities	+	Stockholders' Equity

(b) Papa John's borrows $6,000 from its local bank, signing a note to be paid in three years. Using the transaction analysis process: (1) identify and classify the accounts and effects, and (2) determine whether the accounting equation is in balance.

Assets	=	Liabilities	+	Stockholders' Equity

(c) Papa John's purchases $10,000 of equipment, paying $2,000 in cash and signing a two-year note payable to the equipment manufacturer for the rest. Using the transaction analysis process: (1) identify and classify the accounts and effects, and (2) determine whether the accounting equation is in balance.

Assets	=	Liabilities	+	Stockholders' Equity

(d) Papa John's loans $3,000 to new franchisees who sign notes agreeing to repay the loans in five years. Using the transaction analysis process: (1) identify and classify the accounts and effects, and (2) determine whether the accounting equation is in balance.

Assets	=	Liabilities	+	Stockholders' Equity

(e) Papa John's purchases the stock of other companies as a short-term investment, paying $1,000 in cash. Using the transaction analysis process: (1) identify and classify the accounts and effects, and (2) determine whether the accounting equation is in balance.

Assets	=	Liabilities	+	Stockholders' Equity

(f) Papa John's board of directors declares and pays $3,000 in dividends to shareholders. Using the transaction analysis process: (1) identify and classify the accounts and effects, and (2) determine whether the accounting equation is in balance.

Assets	=	Liabilities	+	Stockholders' Equity

LEARNING OBJECTIVE
After studying this section of the chapter, you should be able to:
5. Determine the impact of business transactions on the balance sheet using two basic tools, journal entries
   and T-accounts.

HOW DO COMPANIES KEEP TRACK OF ACCOUNT BALANCES?

What are the two important tools that aid in reflecting the results of transaction analysis and performing other financial analysis tasks?

THE DIRECTION OF TRANSACTION EFFECTS

What does the term debit mean? What does the term credit mean? How are these two terms abbreviated?

Complete the following **Transaction Analysis Model** by inserting (1) a "+" or "−" sign and (2) a "dr" or "cr" into each side of each of the T-accounts shown below.

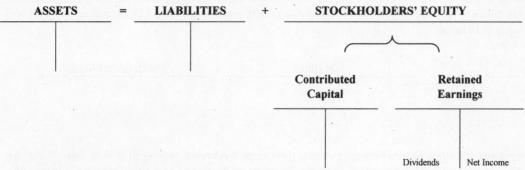

Refer to the transaction analysis model above. Do asset accounts usually have debit or credit balances? (Hint: Which is their positive, or increase, side?) Do liability accounts usually have debit or credit balances? Do stockholders' equity accounts usually have debit or credit balances?

Are credits good and debits bad? What do these terms mean to accountants? How can you remember which type of accounts increases with a debit and which types increase with a credit? What is the equality check?

ANALYTICAL TOOL: THE JOURNAL ENTRY

Where are transactions initially recorded in a bookkeeping system? What order is used to record the transactions? What is a journal entry?

ANALYTICAL TOOL: THE T-ACCOUNT

What does the bookkeeper do after the journal entries have been recorded? As a group, what are the accounts called? What is a very useful tool for summarizing transaction effects and determining balances for individual accounts? What is the T-account equation, which is used to determine an account balance?

TRANSACTION ANALYSIS ILLUSTRATED

(a) Papa John's issues $2,000 of additional common stock, receiving cash from investors. Prepare the journal entry to record this transaction:

Account	Debit	Credit

(b) Papa John's borrows $6,000 from its local bank, signing a note to be paid in three years. Prepare the journal entry to record this transaction:

Account	Debit	Credit

(c) Papa John's purchases $10,000 of equipment, paying $2,000 in cash and signing a two-year note payable to the equipment manufacturer for the rest. Prepare the journal entry to record this transaction:

Account	Debit	Credit

(d) Papa John's lengs $3,000 to new franchisees who sign notes agreeing to repay the loans in five years. Prepare the journal entry to record this transaction:

Account	Debit	Credit

(e) Papa John's purchases the stock of other companies as a short-term investment, paying $1,000 in cash. Prepare the journal entry to record this transaction:

Account	Debit	Credit

(f) Papa John's board of directors declares and pays $3,000 in dividends to shareholders. Prepare the journal entry to record this transaction:

Account	Debit	Credit

INFERRING BUSINESS ACTIVITIES FROM T-ACCOUNTS

If beginning and ending balances of Accounts Payable are $600 and $300, respectively, and purchases on account amounted to $1,500 during the period, what is the amount of cash that was paid during the period?

After studying this section of the chapter, you should be able to:
6. Prepare and analyze a simple balance sheet.

HOW IS THE BALANCE SHEET PREPARED?

When can a balance sheet be prepared? When multiple periods are presented, where are the most recent balance sheet amounts usually listed?

After studying this section of the chapter, you should be able to:
7. Identify investing and financing transactions and how they are reported on the statement of cash flows.

FOCUS ON CASH FLOWS–INVESTING AND FINANCING ACTIVITIES

What types of activities are considered investing activities? What types are considered financing activities?

CHAPTER TAKE-AWAYS

1. *Define the objective of financial reporting, the elements of the balance sheet, and the related key accounting assumptions and principles.*

   The primary objective of external financial reporting is to provide useful economic information about a business to help external parties, primarily investors and credits, make sound financial decisions. Elements of the balance sheet:
   a. Assets–probable future economic benefits owned by the entity as a result of past transactions.
   b. Liabilities–probable debts or obligations of the entity as a result of past transactions, to be paid with assets or services.
   c. Stockholders' equity–the financing provided by the owners and by business operations.

Key accounting assumptions and principles:

a. Separate-entity assumption–transactions of the business are accounted for separately from transactions of the owner.

b. Unit-of-measure assumption–financial information is reported in the national monetary unit.

c. Continuity (going-concern) assumption–a business is expected to continue to operate into the foreseeable future.

d. Historical cost principle–financial statements elements should be recorded at the cash-equivalent cost on the date of the transaction.

2. *Compute and interpret the financial leverage ratio.*

The financial leverage ratio (Average Total Assets ÷ Average Stockholders' Equity) measures the relationship between total assets and the stockholders' capital that finances the assets. The higher the ratio, the more debt is used to finance the assets. As the ratio (and thus debt) increases, risk increases.

3. *Identify what constitutes a business transaction and common balance sheet account titles used in business.*

A transaction includes:

- an exchange between a business and one or more external parties to a business.

or

- a measurable internal event such as adjustments for the use of assets in operations.

An account is a standardized format that organizations use to accumulate the dollar effects of transactions related to each financial statement item. Typical balance sheet account titles include the following:

- Assets: Cash, Accounts Receivable, Inventory, Prepaid Expenses, and Property and Equipment.
- Liabilities: Accounts Payable, Notes Payable, Accrued Liabilities, and Taxes Payable.
- Stockholders' Equity: Contributed Capital and Retained Earnings.

4. *Apply transaction analysis to simple business transactions in terms of the accounting model: Assets = Liabilities + Stockholders' Equity.*

To determine the economic effect of a transaction on the entity in terms of the accounting equation, each transaction is analyzed to determine the accounts (at least two) that are affected. In an exchange, the company receives something and gives up something. If the accounts, direction of the effects, and amounts are correctly analyzed, the accounting equation must stay in balance. The transaction analysis model is:

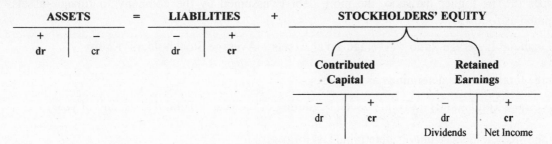

5. **Determine the impact of business transactions on the balance sheet using two basic tools, journal entries and T-accounts.**

Journal entries express the effects of a transaction on accounts in a debits-equal-credits format. The accounts and amounts to be debited are list first. Then, the accounts and amounts to be credited are listed below the debits and indented resulting in debits on the left and credits on the right.

(date or reference)   Account   xxx
                               Account   xxx

T-accounts summarize transactions effects for each account. These tools can be used to determine balances and draw inferences about a company's activities.

+	Asset	−	−	Liability and Stockholders' Equity	+
Beginning balance					Beginning balance
Increases	Decreases		Decreases		Increases
Ending balance					Ending balance

6. **Prepare and analyze a simple balance sheet.**

Classified balance sheets are structured with:

- Assets categorized as "current assets" (those to be used or turned into cash within the year, with inventory always considered a current asset) and noncurrent assets, such as long-term investments, property and equipment, and intangible assets.
- Liabilities categorized as "current liabilities" (those that will be paid with current assets) and long-term liabilities.

7. **Identify investing and financing transactions and demonstrate how they are reported on the statement of cash flows.**

A statement of cash flows reports the sources and uses of cash for the period by the type of activity that generated the cash flow: operating, investing, and financing. Investing activities are purchasing and selling long-term assets and making loans and receiving payment from loans to others. Financing activities are borrowing and repaying the principal on loans to banks, issuing and repurchasing stock, and paying dividends.

KEY RATIO

Financial leverage ratio measures the relation between total assets and the stockholders' capital that finances it. The higher the ratio, the more debt is assumed by the company to finance assets. It is computed as follows:

Financial Leverage Ratio = Average Total Assets ÷ Average Stockholders' Equity

Average total assets is determined as follows:

Average Total Assets = (Total Assets, beginning of the year + Total Assets, end of year) ÷ 2

Average stockholders' equity is determined as follows:

Average Stockholders' Equity =
(Stockholders' Equity, beginning of the year + Stockholders' Equity, end of year) ÷ 2

FINDING FINANCIAL INFORMATION

BALANCE SHEET	
Current Assets Cash Accounts and notes receivable Inventory Prepaid expenses **Noncurrent Assets** Long-term investments Property and equipment Intangibles	**Current Liabilities** Accounts payable Notes payable Accrued expenses payable Accrued liabilities payable **Noncurrent Liabilities** Long-term debt **Stockholders' Equity** Contributed capital Retained earnings

STATEMENT OF CASH FLOWS

Under Investing Activities
+ Sales of noncurrent assets for cash
– Purchases of noncurrent assets for cash
– Loans to others
+ Receipt of loan principal payments from others

Under Financing Activities
+ Borrowing from banks
– Repayment of loan principal to banks
+ Issuance of stock
– Repurchasing stock
– Payment of dividends

SELF-TEST QUESTIONS AND EXERCISES

MATCHING

Match each the key terms listed below with the appropriate textbook definition.

____ Account
____ Assets
____ Continuity (Going-Concern) Assumption
____ Contributed Capital
____ Cost Principle
____ Credits
____ Current Assets
____ Current Liabilities
____ Debits
____ Journal Entry
____ Liabilities

____ Primary Objective of External Financial Reporting
____ Retained Earnings
____ Separate-Entity Assumption
____ Stockholders' Equity (Owners' Equity or Shareholders' Equity)
____ T-Account
____ Transaction
____ Transaction Analysis
____ Unit-of-Measure Assumption

A. Short-term obligations that will be paid in cash (or other current assets) or satisfied by providing service within the coming year.
B. Results from owners providing cash (and sometimes other assets) to the business.
C. A standardized format that organizations use to accumulate the dollar effects of transactions on each financial statement item.
D. The process of studying a transaction to determine its economic effect on the business in terms of the accounting equation.
E. An accounting method for expressing the effects of a transaction on accounts in a debits-equal-credits format.
F. States that accounting information should be measured and reported in the national monetary unit.
G. A tool for summarizing transaction effects for each account, determining balances, and drawing inferences about a company's activities.

H. Provides useful economic information about a business to help external parties make sound financial decisions.

I. Probable future economic benefits owned by the entity as a result of past transactions.

J. States that businesses are assumed to continue to operate into the foreseeable future.

K. Requires assets to be recorded at the historical cash-equivalent cost, which on the date of the transaction is cash paid plus the current dollar value of all noncash considerations also given in the exchange.

L. Assets that will be used or turned into cash within one year; inventory is always considered a current asset regardless of the time needed to produce or sell it.

M. The right side of an account.

N. States that business transactions are separate from the transactions of the owners.

O. Cumulative earnings of a company that are not distributed to the owners and are reinvested in the business.

P. (1) An exchange between a business and one or more external parties or (2) a measurable internal event such as an adjustment for the use of an asset in operations.

Q. The financing provided by the owners and the operations of the business.

R. Probable debts or obligations of the entity that result from past transactions, which will be paid with assets or services.

S. The left side of an account.

TRUE-FALSE QUESTIONS

For each of the following, enter a T or F in the blank to indicate whether the statement is true or false.

___1. (LO 1) Assets are owned or controlled by the entity as a result of past transactions and have probable future benefit to the entity.

___2. (LO 1) For simplicity of presentation, individual asset categories reported on the balance sheet often include a number of assets with smaller balances which total the amount presented; the same is true for individual liability categories.

___3. (LO 1) Assets should be listed alphabetically when a balance sheet is prepared.

___4. (LO 1) Liabilities are listed on the balance sheet in order of maturity.

___5. (LO 1) Probable debts or obligations that result from past transactions are recorded as liabilities on the balance sheet only if the related amounts can be reasonably estimated.

___6. (LO 1) Contributed capital results when owners purchase stock from the company with no expectation of a return on the funds invested.

___7. (LO 1) Earnings that are not distributed to owners and are reinvested in the business by management are called retained earnings.

___8. (LO 1) Assets are recorded at cost based on an arm's-length exchange with an external party, and, as such, the balance sheet always reflects the market value of assets.

___9. (LO 3) At times, important events that have an economic impact on the entity are not recorded in the entity's financial statements.

___10. (LO 3) All publicly held companies must use the standardized chart of accounts developed by the FASB.

___11. (LO 4) The accounting equation must be in balance at the end of the accounting period, but does not necessarily need to be in balance after each individual transaction is recorded.

___12. (LO 5) Debit means the left side of an account and credit means the right.

___13. (LO 5) As a group, the accounts are called a journal.

___14. (LO 5) A T-account is a simplified representation of a ledger account and can be used as a tool for summarizing the effects of transactions and determining balances for individual accounts.

___15. (LO 6) If a company has a financial leverage ratio near 1:1, it is not enhancing the return to its stockholders.

___16. (LO 7) Financing with stockholders' equity is considered more risky than debt financing because dividends must be paid to the company's stockholders on a quarterly basis.

___17. (LO 7) The buying and selling of noncurrent assets are categorized as financing activities.

___18. (LO 7) Transactions must be measured precisely and objectively to ensure that the accounting results reported in the financial statements reflect exactly what happened.

___19. (LO 7) Accounting requires considerable professional judgment on the part of the accountant.

___20. (LO 7) Because they spend most of the day recording repetitive, uncomplicated transactions, the work performed by accountants tends to be routine and clerical in nature.

MULTIPLE CHOICE QUESTIONS
Choose the best answer or response by placing the identifying letter in the space provided.

___1. (LO 1) Providing external parties with economic information about a business so that they can make sound financial decisions is the primary objective of

    a. the Wall Street Journal.
    b. external financial reporting.
    c. news releases.
    d. financial analysts.
    e. external auditors.

___2. (LO 1) Under the separate-entity concept, a business must be accounted for separately from

    a. its owners.
    b. its owners, but only if the entity is a corporation.
    c. its owners, other persons, and other entities.
    d. other business entities only.
    e. other related businesses.

___3. (LO 1) The continuity, or going-concern, assumption holds that a business will continue to operate

    a. at least until the end of the current fiscal year.
    b. for the life (lives) of its owner(s).
    c. into the foreseeable future.
    d. long enough to meet contractual commitments and plans.
    e. c and d above.

___4. (LO 2) The financial leverage ratio is computed as follows:

    a. total assets divided by stockholders' equity.
    b. stockholders' equity divided by total assets.
    c. average total assets divided by average stockholders' equity.
    d. average stockholders' equity divided by average total assets.
    e. none of the above.

___5. (LO 3) An event with an economic impact on the entity that is recorded as part of the accounting process is known as a(n)

    a. account.
    b. asset.
    c. external event.
    d. exchange.
    e. transaction.

___6. (LO 3) A transaction that is an external event can best be described as

    a. any event that happens outside of the business.
    b. any event that occurs outside the principal location of the business.
    c. any event that has an economic impact on the entity.
    d. anything involving persons not owning or employed by the business.
    e. an exchange of assets and liabilities between the business and one or more other parties.

___7. (LO 4) The duality (or duality of effects) concept states that

    a. there is more than one way of looking at any situation.
    b. there are two entities involved in every transaction.
    c. every transaction has at least two effects on the accounting equation.
    d. every transaction must be recorded twice; once in the ledger and once in the journal.
    e. every transaction has both good and bad aspects.

___8. (LO 4) Which accounts are affected if a company purchases equipment by signing a promissory note agreeing to pay the purchase price in one year?

    a. Notes payable and notes receivable.
    b. Notes payable and cash.
    c. Notes payable and property and equipment.
    d. Notes receivable and property and equipment.
    e. No accounts are affected because a transaction has not yet taken place.

___9. (LO 4) If a company makes a payment on a promissory note, which types of accounts would be affected and what are the directional effects?

    a. Decrease an asset and decrease a liability.
    b. Decrease an asset and increase a liability.
    c. Increase an asset and decrease a liability.
    d. Increase an asset and increase a liability.
    e. None of the above.

___10. (LO 4) If a company purchases equipment, makes a cash down payment and signs a promissory note for the balance, which accounts are affected and in what direction?

a. Increase cash, increase property and equipment, and increase notes payable.
b. Decrease cash, increase property and equipment, and increase accounts payable.
c. Decrease cash, increase property and equipment, and increase notes payable.
d. Decrease cash, decrease property and equipment and decrease notes payable.
e. None of the above.

___11. (LO 5) Increases to accounts on the left side of the accounting equation are recorded on the
_____ side of the account; increases to accounts on the right side of the accounting equation are
recorded on the _____ side of the account.

a. left; right
b. left; left
c. right; left
d. right; right

___12. (LO 5) Which of the following is not true?

a. A debit increases asset accounts.
b. A debit decreases liability and stockholders' equity accounts.
c. A credit increases liability and stockholders' equity accounts.
d. A credit decreases asset accounts.
e. All accounts are increased with debits and decreased with credits.

___13. (LO 5) Which are the usual balances of assets, liabilities and stockholders' equity, respectively?

a. debit, debit and debit
b. debit, debit and credit
c. debit, credit and credit
d. credit, debit and debit
e. credit, debit and credit

___14. (LO 5) Journal entries are recorded in the journal in

a. account order
b. alphabetical order
c. balance sheet order
d. chronological order
e. no particular order

___15. (LO 5) A T-account is a simplified form of a

a. balance sheet.
b. customer invoice.
c. journal entry.
d. ledger account.
e. purchase order.

____16. (LO 7) Investing activities include all of the following except:

    a. lending cash to others.
    b. borrowing cash from banks.
    c. purchasing long-term assets.
    d. both a and b.
    e. none of the above.

EXERCISES

Record your answer to each exercise in the space provided. Show your work.

Exercise 1 (LO 4 and 5)

The following table sets forth a partial listing of items recently reported on Microsoft's balance sheet. (Some of the account titles have been reworded.) Indicate the type of account and its usual balance by placing an "X" in the appropriate columns. The first has been completed as an example.

Account	Type of Account			Usual Balance	
	Asset	Liability	Stockholders' Equity	Debit	Credit
Accounts payable		X			X
Accounts receivable					
Accrued compensation (owed to employees)					
Cash					
Contributed capital					
Income taxes payable					
Investments					
Other current assets					
Other long-term assets					
Property and equipment					
Retained earnings					
Unearned revenue (similar to Papa John's unearned franchise fees)					

Exercise 2
Part A (LO 3 and 4)

Complete the follow table by indicating the amount and direction (+ or −) of the effect of each transaction on each of the three components of the accounting equation. The first has been completed as an example.

	Transaction	Assets	Liabilities	Stockholders' Equity
A	Issued stock for cash of $14,000.	+ $14,000		+ $14,000
B	Borrowed $15,000 from a local bank and signed a six-month promissory note.			

Exercise 2, Part A, continued

	Transaction	Assets	Liabilities	Stockholders' Equity
C	Purchased office supplies for cash of $2,500.			
D	Placed an order for $8,300 of inventory for delivery next month.			
E	Purchased equipment for $15,000, paying $7,500 cash and signing a note for the remaining balance.			
F	Loaned $375 to an employee who agreed to repay the loan by signing a note repayable in one month.			
G	Made $8,000 payment on the promissory note owed to the local bank.			
H	Collected $375 on loan made to the employee.			
I	Major stockholder of company purchases a computer for $2,500 for personal use from one of the company's vendors.			
J	Purchased $5,000 of stock in another company as an investment			
	Ending Balances			

Part B (LO 5)

Prepare journal entries for each of the transactions set forth above.

Transaction	Account	Debit	Credit
A			
B			
C			

Exercise 2, Part B, continued

Transaction	Account	Debit	Credit
D			
E			
F			
G			
H			
I			
J			

Strategy Suggestion for Exercises 3, 4 and 5
Use the T-account equation to determine the ending account balance.

Exercise 3 (LO 5)

Rice Lake, Inc. purchases equipment by signing notes payable to the manufacturers of the equipment. At the beginning of the year, the balance in Rice Lake's notes payable account was $5,000. During the year, Rice Lake purchased equipment in the amount of $13,000 by signing notes payable. In addition, Rice Lake made payments on the notes payable in the amount of $6,800. What is the balance in Rice Lake's notes payable account at the end of the year?

Exercise 4 (LO 5)

During the year, Douglas Corporation's cash receipts amounted to $53,900 and the company made cash payments totaling $50,700. Douglas had $9,300 of cash on hand at the end of the year. How much cash did the company have on hand at the beginning of the year?

Exercise 5 (LO 4)

What does the entry for $2,000,400 in the T-account shown below most likely represent? What transaction is most likely represented by the entry for $1,950,400? What is the balance in the account at 12/31?

	Notes Receivable		
1/1	$ 300,000		
	2,000,400	$1,950,400	
12/31	$?		

Exercise 6

Lisa and Charlie operate a yacht maintenance service that they incorporated as Reliable Yacht Repair, Inc. On April 30, 20A, the business had the following accounts and balances, in alphabetical order. All accounts have usual normal balances (debit or credit).

Cash	$5,000
Contributed capital	6,800
Notes payable	5,000
Notes receivable	2,000
Property and equipment	8,000
Retained earnings	3,200

Part A (LO 3 and 4)

Perform transaction analysis for each of the business events that Reliable Yacht Repair participated in during the month of May 20A, the beginning of the boating season.

Strategy Suggestion for Part A

As you analyze a transaction, complete each of the four steps in the transaction analysis process:
1. *Identify the accounts affected, making sure that the duality principle is met (at least two accounts change).*
2. *Classify each account as an asset (A), liability (L), or stockholders' equity (SE).*
3. *Determine the direction of the effect (amount of increase [+] or decrease [–] for each account).*
4. *Determine that the accounting equation (A = L + SE) remains in balance.*

Exercise 6, Part A, continued

	Transaction	Assets	=	Liabilities +	Stockholders' Equity
A	Reliable issues $2,500 of additional common stock to new investors for cash.				
B	Reliable borrows $12,000 from a local bank, signing a note to be paid in one year.				
C	Reliable purchases a new outboard motor for $2,000, paying $500 and signing a note for the balance (to be paid in one year).				
D	Reliable collects $1,000 on notes receivable.				
E	Reliable repays $500 on notes payable.				
F	Reliable signs a contract to repair a yacht; the work will be performed during May.				

Part B (LO 5)

Prepare journal entries for each of the transactions identified and analyzed above.

Transaction	Account	Debit	Credit
A			
B			
C			
D			
E			
F			

Exercise 6, continued
Part C (LO 5)

Enter the beginning balances in the T-accounts, post the journal entries to the T-accounts and determine the ending account balances.

Cash	Notes Receivable	Property and Equipment	Notes Payable	Contributed Capital	Retained Earnings

Part D (LO 6)

Prepare a balance sheet for Reliable Yacht Repair as of May 31, 20A.

Reliable Yacht Repair, Inc.
Balance Sheet
May 31, 20A

Exercise 6, continued
Part E (LO 2)

Assume that Reliable did not enter into any transactions during the month of April 20A. Further, assume that the May transactions described and analyzed in the exercises above all took place on May 16, 20A. Compute Reliable's financial leverage ratio as of April 30 and May 31, 20A, and interpret the results.

April 30, 20B

May 31, 20B

Interpretation

Part F (LO 7)

Prepare the investing and financing sections of the statement of cash flows for Reliable Yacht Repair for the month ended May 31, 20A.

Reliable Yacht Repair, Inc.
Statement of Cash Flows
For the month ended May 31, 20A

Exercise 7 (LO 7)

The following is a partial list of Papa John's transactions. For purposes of classifying the transaction for inclusion on the company's statement of cash flows, label each transaction as an (1) investing or financing activity and (2) inflow or outflow of cash.

(1) Investing or Financing Activity	(2) Inflow or Outflow of Cash	Transaction
		Issued additional stock to investors for cash.
		Borrowed money from a local bank.
		Purchased stock to be held as an investment.
		Lent money to a franchisee that signed a note.
		Collected on the note signed by the franchisee.
		Made a payment on the amount borrowed from the bank.
		Declared and paid a cash dividend.

SOLUTIONS TO SELF-TEST QUESTIONS AND EXERCISES

MATCHING

C	Account		H	Primary Objective of External Financial Reporting
I	Assets			
J	Continuity (Going-Concern) Assumption		O	Retained Earnings
B	Contributed Capital		N	Separate-Entity Assumption
K	Cost Principle		Q	Stockholders' Equity (Owners' Equity or Shareholders' Equity)
M	Credits			
L	Current Assets		G	T-Account
A	Current Liabilities		P	Transaction
S	Debits		D	Transaction Analysis
E	Journal Entry		F	Unit-of-Measure Assumption
R	Liabilities			

TRUE-FALSE QUESTIONS

1.   T
2.   T
3.   F – Assets should be listed in order of liquidity.
4.   T
5.   T
6.   F – Investors do expect (or hope) to receive two types of cash flows: dividends and gains from selling their stock in the company.
7.   T
8.   F – A disadvantage of the cost principle is that the continued use of historical cost on the balance sheet does not reflect any changes in the market value of assets owned or controlled by the company.
9.   T
10. F – Each company would develop its own unique chart of accounts which conforms to the nature of its operations.

11. F – The accounting equation must be in balance after each individual transaction is recorded; as a result, it will be in balance at the end of the accounting period.
12. T
13. F – As a group, the accounts are called a ledger.
14. T
15. T
16. F – Interest must be paid on amounts borrowed; generally, there is no legal obligation to pay dividends to common stockholders. As a result, debt financing is more risky.
17. F – The buying and selling of productive assets are categorized as investing activities.
18. F – Not all transactions can be measured precisely and objectively; estimates often must be used.
19. T
20. F – The work performed by bookkeepers involves the routine, clerical part of accounting; accounting requires considerable professional judgment on the part of the accountants when complex transactions are analyzed.

MULTIPLE CHOICE QUESTIONS

1.	b	5.	e	9.	a	13.	c
2.	c	6.	e	10.	c	14.	d
3.	c	7.	c	11.	a	15.	d
4.	c	8.	c	12.	e	16.	b

EXERCISES

Exercise 1

Account	Type of Account			Usual Balance	
	Asset	Liability	Stockholders' Equity	Debit	Credit
Accounts payable		X			X
Accounts receivable	X			X	
Accrued compensation (owed to employees)		X			X
Cash	X			X	
Contributed capital			X		X
Income taxes payable		X			X
Investments	X			X	
Other current assets	X			X	
Other long-term assets	X			X	
Property and equipment	X			X	
Retained earnings			X		X
Unearned revenue (similar to Papa John's unearned franchise fees)		X			X

Exercise 2
Part A

	Transaction	Assets	Liabilities	Stockholders' Equity
A	Issued stock for cash of $14,000.	+ $14,000		+ $14,000
B	Borrowed $15,000 from a local bank and signed a six-month promissory note.	+ 15,000	+$15,000	
C	Purchased office supplies for cash of $2,500.	+ 2,500 − 2,500		
D	Placed an order for $8,300 of inventory for delivery next month.	Not a transaction	Not a transaction	Not a transaction
E	Purchased equipment for $15,000, paying $7,500 cash and signing a note for the remaining balance.	+ 15,000 − 7,500	+ 7,500	
F	Loaned $375 to an employee who agreed to repay the loan by signing a note repayable in one month.	+ 375 − 375		
G	Made $8,000 payment on the promissory note owed to the local bank.	− 8,000	− 8,000	
H	Collected $375 on loan made to the employee.	+ 375 − 375		
I	Major stockholder of company purchases a computer for $2,500 for personal use from one of the company's vendors.	Not a transaction	Not a transaction	Not a transaction
J	Purchased $5,000 of stock in another company as an investment	+ 5,000 − 5,000		
	Ending balances	$28,500	$14,500	$14,000

Part B

Transaction	Account	Debit	Credit
A	Cash	14,000	
	Contributed capital		14,000
B	Cash	15,000	
	Note payable		15,000
C	Office supplies	2,500	
	Cash		2,500
D	No entry		

©The McGraw-Hill Companies, Inc., 2004

Exercise 2, Part B, continued

Transaction	Account	Debit	Credit
E	Equipment	15,000	
	Cash		7,500
	Note payable		7,500
F	Notes receivable	375	
	Cash		375
G	Notes payable	8,000	
	Cash		8,000
H	Cash	375	
	Notes receivable		375
I	No entry		
J	Investments	5,000	
	Cash		5,000

Exercise 3

The ending balance in Rice Lake's notes payable account is $11,200 computed as follows:
Beginning balance + Effects on the increase side - Effects on the decrease side = Ending balance
Let X = the Ending balance
$5,000 + $13,000 - $6,800 = X
$11,200 = X

Exercise 4

Douglas Corporation had $6,100 of cash on hand at the beginning of the year computed as follows:
Beginning balance + Effects on the increase side - Effects on the decrease side = Ending balance
Let X = the Beginning balance
X + $53,900 - $50,700 = $9,300
X = $6,100

Exercise 5

The entry for $2,000,400 most likely represents a loan made to someone who signs a note agreeing to repay the loan in a predetermined amount of time. The entry for $1,950,400 most likely represents cash collected on the note receivable from the borrower.

The ending balance in the notes receivable account is $350,000 computed as follows:
Beginning Balance + Effects on the Increase Side - Effects on the Decrease Side = Ending Balance
Let X = the Ending balance
$300,000 + $2,000,400 - $1,950,400 = X
$350,000 = X

Exercise 6
Part A

	Transaction	Assets	=	Liabilities	Stockholders'

		Assets	+	Equity
A	Reliable issues $2,500 of additional common stock to new investors for cash.	Cash + 2,500		Contributed capital + 2,500
B	Reliable borrows $12,000 from a local bank, signing a note to be paid in one year.	Cash + 12,000	Notes payable + 12,000	
C	Reliable purchases a new outboard motor for $2,000, paying $500 and signing a note for the balance (to be paid in one year).	Property and equipment + 2,000 Cash − 500	Notes payable + 1,500	
D	Reliable collects $1,000 on notes receivable.	Cash + 1,000 Notes receivable − 1,000		
E	Reliable repays $500 on notes payable.	Cash − 500	Notes payable − 500	
F	Reliable signs a contract to repair a yacht; the work will be performed during May.	Not a transaction.	Not a transaction.	Not a transaction.

Part B

Transaction	Account	Debit	Credit
A	Cash	2,500	
	Contributed capital		2,500
B	Cash	12,000	
	Notes payable		12,000
C	Property and equipment	2,000	
	Cash		500
	Notes payable		1,500
D	Cash	1,000	
	Notes receivable		1,000
E	Notes payable	500	
	Cash		500

Exercise 6, Part B, continued

Transaction	Account	Debit	Credit
F	No entry		

Part C

		Cash		
5/1	5,000			
(A)	2,500	(C)		500
(B)	12,000			
(D)	1,000	(E)		500
5/31	19,500			

		Notes Receivable		
5/1	2,000			
		(D)		1,000
5/31	1,000			

		Property and Equipment	
5/1	8,000		
(C)	2,000		
5/31	10,000		

		Notes Payable		
		5/1		5,000
		(B)		12,000
(E)	500	(C)		1,500
		5/31		18,000

	Contributed Capital		
	5/1		6,800
	(A)		2,500
	5/31		9,300

	Retained Earnings		
	5/1		3,200
	5/31		3,200

Part D

Reliable Yacht Repair, Inc.
Balance Sheet
May 31, 20A

Assets	
Cash	$19,500
Notes receivable	1,000
Property and equipment	10,000
Total assets	**$30,500**
Liabilities	
Notes payable	$18,000
Stockholders' equity	
Contributed capital	9,300
Retained earnings	3,200
Total stockholders' equity	**12,500**
Total liabilities and stockholders' equity	**$30,500**

Exercise 6, continued
Part E

April 30, 20A

Compute average total assets and average total stockholders' equity. (Recall assumption that no transactions took place during April. Thus, monthly averages would be the same as the month-end totals.) Divide average total assets by average total stockholders' equity to get the financial leverage ratio.

$(5,000 + 2,000 + 8,000) \div (6,800 + 3,200) = 15,000 \div 10,000 = 1.5 : 1$

May 31, 20A

Compute average total assets and average total stockholders' equity. (Recall that the May transactions took place on the 16th, the middle of the month. Compute the averages by adding the respective totals at April 30, 20A and May 31, 20A, and then divide by two to get the average.) Divide average total assets by average total stockholders' equity to get the financial leverage ratio.

$[(15,000 + 30,500) \div 2] \div [(10,000 + 12,500) \div 2] = 22,750 \div 11,250 = 2 : 1$

Interpretation

The financial leverage ratio measures the relation between total assets and the stockholders' equity that finances the assets. At May 31, 20A, the financial leverage ratio was higher; a higher proportion of assets was financed by debt. Increasing the financial leverage ratio increases the amount of assets the company employs to earn income for stockholders, which increases the chances of earning higher income. However, debt financing is riskier than financing with stockholders' equity because periodic interest payments are legally required on debt, whereas dividends on stock are not. But, as long as the additional income generated by the assets exceeds the additional interest on debt, using debt to acquire assets will enhance stockholders' earnings.

Part F

Reliable Yacht Repair, Inc.
Statement of Cash Flows
For the month ended May 31, 20A

Operating Activities:	
[None in this problem]	
Investing Activities:	
Purchased equipment	$ (500)
Received payment on notes receivable	1,000
Net cash provided by investing activities	500
Financing Activities:	
Issued common stock for cash	2,500
Proceeds from borrowing from bank	12,000
Payments on borrowing	(500)
Net cash provided by financing activities	14,000
Change in cash	14,500
Beginning cash balance	5,000
Ending cash balance	$19,500

Exercise 7

(1) Investing or Financing Activity	(2) Inflow or Outflow of Cash	Transaction
Financing	Inflow	Issued additional stock to investors for cash.
Financing	Inflow	Borrowed money from a local bank.
Investing	Outflow	Purchased stock to be held as an investment.
Investing	Outflow	Lent money to a franchisee who signed a note.
Investing	Inflow	Collected on the note signed by the franchisee.
Financing	Outflow	Made a payment on the amount borrowed from the bank.
Financing	Outflow	Declared and paid a cash dividend.

AN IDEA FOR YOUR STUDY TEAM

Imagine that the members of your study team meet for lunch ten years from now and decide to go into business together. First, with the other members of your study team, decide what type of business you would operate. Then, individually, prepare a chart of accounts for your business. (Include only balance sheet accounts at this point.) Finally, get together with the other members of your study team and compare and contrast your charts of accounts.

ORGANIZATION OF THE CHAPTER

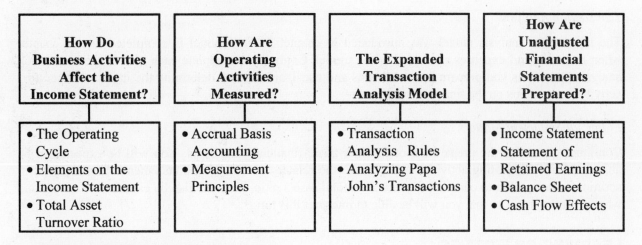

How Do Business Activities Affect the Income Statement?	How Are Operating Activities Measured?	The Expanded Transaction Analysis Model	How Are Unadjusted Financial Statements Prepared?
• The Operating Cycle • Elements on the Income Statement • Total Asset Turnover Ratio	• Accrual Basis Accounting • Measurement Principles	• Transaction Analysis Rules • Analyzing Papa John's Transactions	• Income Statement • Statement of Retained Earnings • Balance Sheet • Cash Flow Effects

CHAPTER FOCUS SUGGESTIONS

Overview

Chapter 3 continues the discussion of how the accounting function collects and processes data to provide periodic financial statements. Emphasis is placed on concepts relating to the measurement of revenues and expenses and analyzing transactions that affect the income statement.

Elements of the Income Statement

After a typical operating cycle is overviewed, each of the major elements of the income statement (that is, revenues, gains, expenses and losses) is discussed. You should become familiar with each major element.

Cash Basis and Accrual Basis

When the cash basis of accounting is used, revenues are recorded when cash is received from customers and expenses are recorded when cash is disbursed to vendors and suppliers. The cash basis of accounting is not appropriate for most companies; make sure that you should understand the underlying reasons.

GAAP requires the use of the accrual basis for financial reporting. The revenue principle governs the recording of revenues; four conditions must be met. The matching principle governs the recording of expenses; all resources consumed in generating the revenues earned during the accounting period should be recorded in the same accounting period. Essentially, revenues are recognized when earned and expenses when incurred. *Remember that the timing of cash receipts and payments does not control the recording of revenues and expenses when the accrual basis is used.* Cash may be received before, when, or after a service is provided or goods are sold; the revenue is recorded when the four conditions for revenue recognition are met. Similarly, cash may be paid before, when, or after a resource is consumed; the expense is recorded when incurred.

When cash is *received before* revenues are earned or *paid before* expenses are incurred, entries are often required at the end of the accounting period to properly recognize (or record) the revenue earned or expense incurred during the period. Also, when cash is *received after* revenues are earned or *paid after* expenses are incurred, entries are often necessary at the end of the period to recognize the related revenues earned and expenses incurred during the period. The entries that must be made at the end of the accounting period are covered in Chapter 4.

Transaction Analysis

The transaction analysis model was introduced in chapter 2. This model is completed in this chapter when revenues and expenses are added to the model. Continue to complete each step in the transaction analysis process as you prepare journal entries and use T-accounts to determine the impact of operating activity transactions on the financial statements.

Financial Statement Matters

Continue to practice the preparation of the four basic financial statements. You will be expected to be able to identify operating activities and prepare the related sections of the statement of cash flows. In addition to being able to compute the return on total assets ratio, you will also be expected to understand what it is measuring so that you will be able to interpret this ratio.

LEARNING OBJECTIVES

After studying this chapter, you should be able to:

(LO 1) Describe a typical business operating cycle and explain the necessity for the time period assumption.
(LO 2) Explain how business activities affect the elements of the income statement.
(LO 3) Compute and interpret the total asset turnover ratio.
(LO 4) Explain the accrual basis of accounting and apply the revenue and matching principles to measure income.
(LO 5) Apply transaction analysis to examine and record the effects of operating activities on the financial statements.
(LO 6) Prepare unadjusted financial statements.

READ AND RECALL QUESTIONS

After you read each section of the chapter, answer the related Read and Recall Questions below.

LEARNING OBJECTIVE
After studying this section of the chapter, you should be able to:
1. Describe a typical business operating cycle and explain the necessity for the time period assumption.

WHAT BUSINESS ACTIVITIES AFFECT THE FINANCIAL STATEMENTS?
THE OPERATING CYCLE

What is the long-term objective for any business? What must happen in the long run for a company to stay in business?

What is the operating cycle? How would you determine the length of time for a company's operating cycle?

What is assumed by the time period assumption? What are two issues that arise in reporting periodic income to the users of financial statements?

LEARNING OBJECTIVE
After studying this section of the chapter, you should be able to:
2. Explain how business activities affect the elements of the income statement.

ELEMENTS ON THE INCOME STATEMENT
Revenues

What are revenues? How are assets and/or liabilities affected when revenues are recorded?

Costs and Expenses

What is the difference between an expenditure and an expense? How are assets and/or liabilities affected when expenses are recorded?

Other Revenues, Gains, Expenses, and Losses

What are peripheral transactions? What is investment income? What is interest expense? How do gains result? How do losses result?

Income Tax Expense

How is a company's income tax expense calculated?

Earnings Per Share

What does the earnings per share ratio measure? How is the earnings per share ratio computed?

LEARNING OBJECTIVE

After studying this section of the chapter, you should be able to:

3. Compute and interpret the total asset turnover ratio.

KEY RATIO ANALYSIS: THE TOTAL ASSET TURNOVER RATIO

How is the total asset turnover ratio computed? What does it measure?

What does a high total asset turnover ratio signify? How do creditors and securities analysts use the total asset turnover ratio? Are fluctuations expected? Why or why not? What will happen to this ratio prior to a heavy sales season? Why? How do the resulting high sales then impact the ratio during the heavy sales season?

LEARNING OBJECTIVE

After studying this section of the chapter, you should be able to:

4. Explain the accrual basis of accounting and apply the revenue and matching principles to measure income.

HOW ARE OPERATING ACTIVITIES RECOGNIZED AND MEASURED?

What is the cash basis of accounting? How is financial performance measured when the cash basis of accounting is used? What types of businesses use the cash basis of accounting?

ACCRUAL ACCOUNTING

Why aren't cash basis financial statements very useful? What basis of accounting is required by GAAP for financial reporting purposes? When are revenues and expenses recognized when accrual basis accounting is used?

The Revenue Principle

What four conditions normally must be met for revenue to be recognized (recorded) under the revenue principle? When do these conditions normally occur?

When a company (such as Papa John's) receives cash *before* it provides services to its customers (or franchisees), is revenue recorded at that time? Why or why not? What account is used to record (keep track of) monies received before services are provided? What does this deferred or unearned revenue account balance represent?

When a company receives cash *after* it earns the related revenue, what type of account is created? What does this receivable account represent? When is the receivable account reduced?

QUESTION OF ETHICS – MANAGEMENT'S INCENTIVES TO VIOLATE THE REVENUE PRINCIPLE

Who establishes earnings expectations for publicly held companies? Why are managers motivated to produce earnings that meet or exceed expectations? What might the managers be tempted to do if the company's earnings are not expected to meet expectations?

The Matching Principle

What does the matching principle require?

Sometimes, goods (such as food and paper product supplies) or services (such as rent) are acquired or paid for prior to their use. The asset must then be allocated to a related expense account over time as it is used. What type of account is used to record (keep track of) these goods or services? When should the related expenses be recorded?

Sometimes resources are used to generate resources prior to the related cash outlay. In such cases, when should the expenses (that is, relating to the use of the resources) be recorded?

LEARNING OBJECTIVE

After studying this section of the chapter, you should be able to:

5. Apply transaction analysis to examine and record the effects of operating activities on the financial statements.

THE EXPANDED TRANSACTION ANALYSIS MODEL
TRANSACTION ANALYSIS RULES

What account is used to accumulate all past revenues and expenses minus any income distributed as dividends to stockholders? Does net income increase or decrease that account balance?

FINANCIAL ANALYSIS – THE FEEDBACK VALUE OF ACCOUNTING INFORMATION AND STOCK MARKET REACTION

When might the stock market react negatively to a company? Does a net loss need to occur to cause a negative reaction? Why or why not?

How do revenues impact stockholders' equity? What is the normal balance of a revenue account? How do expenses impact stockholders' equity? What is the normal balance of an expense account?

Complete the transaction analysis model by inserting (1) a "+" or "–" sign and (2) a "dr" or "cr" into each side of each of the T-accounts shown below.

ASSETS	LIABILITIES	STOCKHOLDERS' EQUITY ACCOUNTS	REVENUES AND GAINS	EXPENSES AND LOSSES

(a) Papa John's restaurants sold pizza to customers for $36,000 cash. In addition, Papa John's commissaries sold $30,000 in supplies to restaurants, receiving $21,000 cash with the rest due on account. First, prepare the journal entry to record this transaction. Then, determine the effect on the accounting equation:

Account	Debit	Credit

_____ Assets _____ = _____ Liabilities _____ + _____ Stockholders' Equity _____

(b) The cost of the dough, sauce, cheese, and other ingredients for the restaurant sales in (a) was $10,000. The cost of the equipment and supplies for the commissary sales in (a) was $20,000. First, prepare the journal entry to record this transaction. Then, determine the effect on the accounting equation:

Account	Debit	Credit

_____ Assets _____ = _____ Liabilities _____ + _____ Stockholders' Equity _____

(c) Papa John's sold new franchises for $400 cash. The company earned $100 immediately by performing services for franchisees; the rest will be earned over the next several months. First, prepare the journal entry to record this transaction. Then, determine the effect on the accounting equation:

Account	Debit	Credit

_____ Assets _____ = _____ Liabilities _____ + _____ Stockholders' Equity _____

(d) In January, Papa John's paid $7,000 for utilities, repairs, and fuel for delivery vehicles, all considered general and administrative expenses. First, prepare the journal entry to record this transaction. Then, determine the effect on the accounting equation:

Account	Debit	Credit

_____ Assets _____ = _____ Liabilities _____ + _____ Stockholders' Equity _____

(e) Papa John's commissaries ordered and received $29,000 in supplies inventories, paying $9,000 in cash and owing the rest on account to suppliers. First, prepare the journal entry to record this transaction. Then, determine the effect on the accounting equation:

Account	Debit	Credit

_____ Assets _____ = _____ Liabilities _____ + _____ Stockholders' Equity _____

(f) Papa John's paid $14,000 cash to employees for their work in January. First, prepare the journal entry to record this transaction. Then, determine the effect on the accounting equation:

Account	Debit	Credit

_____ Assets _____ = _____ Liabilities _____ + _____ Stockholders' Equity _____

(g) At the beginning of January, Papa John's paid the following: $2,000 for insurance covering the next four months beginning January 1, $6,000 for renting space in shopping centers over the next three months beginning January 1, and $1,000 for advertising to be run in February, all considered prepaid expenses when paid. First, prepare the journal entry to record this transaction. Then, determine the effect on the accounting equation:

Account	Debit	Credit

_____ Assets _____ = _____ Liabilities _____ + _____ Stockholders' Equity _____

(h) Papa John's sold land with an historical cost of $1,000 for $4,000 cash. First, prepare the journal entry to record this transaction. Then, determine the effect on the accounting equation:

Account	Debit	Credit

_____ Assets _____ = _____ Liabilities _____ + _____ Stockholders' Equity _____

LEARNING OBJECTIVE

After studying this section of the chapter, you should be able to:

6. Prepare unadjusted financial statements.

HOW ARE UNADJUSTED FINANCIAL STATEMENTS PREPARED?

Why are some financial statements called *unadjusted*?

FINANCIAL ANALYSIS – REPORTING FINANCIAL INFORMATION BY GEOGRAPHIC AND OPERATING SEGMENTS

What is a multinational? What additional information is provided in the footnotes to the financial statements of multinationals?

FOCUS ON CASH FLOWS—OPERATING ACTIVITIES

What types of cash flows are reported in the operating activities section of the statement of cash flows?

Is net income on an accrual basis equivalent to the change in cash? Why or why not?

Chapter Take-Aways

1. Understand a typical business operating cycle.

- The operating cycle, or cash-to-cash cycle, is the time needed to purchase goods or services from suppliers, sell the goods or services to customers, and collect cash from customers.
- Time period assumption—to measure and report financial information periodically, we assume the long life of a company can be cut into shorter periods.

2. Explain how business activities affect the elements of the income statement.

Elements on the income statement:
a. Revenues—increases in assets or settlements of liabilities from ongoing operations.
b. Expenses—decreases in assets or increases in liabilities from ongoing operations.
c. Gains—increases in assets or settlements of liabilities from peripheral activities.
d. Losses—decreases in assets or increases in liabilities from peripheral activities.

3. Compute and interpret total asset turnover.

The total asset turnover ratio (Sales ÷ Average Total Assets) measures the sales generated per dollar of assets used. The higher the ratio, the more efficient the company is at managing assets.

4. Explain the accrual basis of accounting and apply the revenue and matching principles to measure income.

In accrual basis accounting, revenues are recognized when earned and expenses are recognized when incurred.
- Revenue principle—recognize revenues when (1) delivery has occurred, (2) there is persuasive evidence of an arrangement for customer payment, (3) the price is fixed or determinable, and (4) collection is reasonably assured.
- Matching principle—recognize expenses when they are incurred in generating revenue.

5. Apply transaction analysis to examine and record the effects of operating activities on the financial statements.

The expanded transaction analysis model includes revenues and expenses:

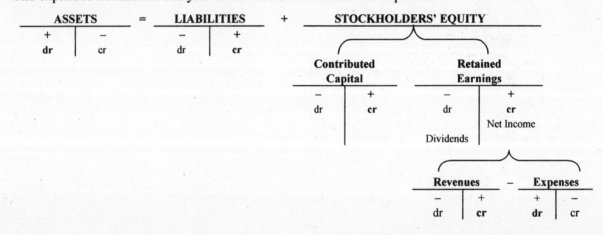

6. *Prepare unadjusted financial statements.*

Until the accounts are updated for all revenues earned and expenses incurred in a period (due to a difference in the time when cash is received or paid), the financial statements are titled "unadjusted:"
- Unadjusted income statement
- Unadjusted statement of retained earnings
- Unadjusted balance sheet
- Unadjusted statement of cash flows

KEY RATIO

Total asset turnover measures the sales generated per dollar of assets. A high ratio suggests that the company is managing its assets (resources used to generate revenues) efficiently. It is computed as follows:

Total Asset Turnover = Sales ÷ Average Total Assets

Average total assets is determined as follows:

Average Total Assets = (Total Assets, beginning of the year + Total Assets, end of year) ÷ 2

FINDING FINANCIAL INFORMATION

BALANCE SHEET		INCOME STATEMENT

Current Assets
  Cash
  Accounts and notes
  receivable
  Inventory
  Prepaid expenses
Noncurrent Assets
  Long-term investments
  Property and equipment
  Intangibles
	Current Liabilities
	  Accounts payable
	  Notes payable
	  Accrued liabilities
	  payable
	Noncurrent Liabilities
	  Long-term debt
	Stockholders' Equity
	  Contributed capital
	  Retained earnings
		Revenues
		  Sales (from various operating activities)
		Expenses
		  Cost of sales (used inventory)
		  Rent, wages, interest, depreciation,
		    insurance, etc.
		Operating Income
		Other Items
		  Interest expense
		  Investment income
		  Gains on sale of assets
		  Losses on sale of assets
		Pretax Income
		  Income tax expense
		Net Income
		Earnings per Share

STATEMENT OF CASH FLOWS	NOTES

Under operating activities
  + Cash from customers
  + Cash from investments
  − Cash to suppliers
  − Cash to employees
  − Interest paid
  − Income taxes paid
	Under summary of significant accounting policies
	Description of the company's revenue recognition policy.

SELF-TEST QUESTIONS AND EXERCISES

MATCHING

Match each of the key terms listed below with the appropriate textbook definition:

____ Accrual Basis Accounting   ____ Matching Principle
____ Cash Basis Accounting   ____ Operating Cycle (Cash-to-Cash Cycle)
____ Expenses   ____ Revenue Principle
____ Gains   ____ Revenues
____ Losses   ____ Time-Period Assumption

A. Increases in assets or decreases in liabilities from peripheral transactions.
B. Increases in assets or settlements of liabilities from ongoing operations.
C. Records revenues when cash is received and expenses when paid.
D. The long life of a company can be reported in shorter time periods.
E. Decreases in assets or increases in liabilities to generate revenues during the period.
F. Requires that expenses recorded when incurred in earning revenue.
G. Records revenues when earned and expenses when incurred, regardless of cash receipts or payments.
H. Decreases in assets or increases in liabilities from peripheral transactions.
I. Revenues are recognized (recorded) when the earnings process is complete or nearly complete, an exchange has taken place, and collection is probable.
J. The time it takes for a company to purchase goods or services from suppliers, sell those goods or services to customers, and collect cash from customers.

TRUE-FALSE QUESTIONS

For each of the following, enter a T or F in the blank to indicate whether the statement is true or false.

____1. (LO 1) The length (of time) of a company's operating cycle cannot be changed.

____2. (LO 1) Publicly traded companies are required to present three years of income statement information to help users assess trends over time.

____3. (LO 2) A company's effective tax rate is computed by dividing its income tax expense by its income before income taxes.

____4. (LO 2) Gains from peripheral transactions are not related to the central operations of the company and, as such, are not reported in the other income category on the income statement.

____5. (LO 3) Differences in operating strategy may cause a company's total asset turnover ratio to be different from that of its competitors.

____6. (LO 4) Many small businesses use the cash basis of accounting.

____7. (LO 4) Only publicly held companies must use accrual basis accounting.

____8. (LO 4) A company can only receive cash from a customer after it has completed delivery of a product or service to that customer.

____9. (LO 4) An exchange transaction has taken place if the customer promises to pay for the service performed by the company.

____10. (LO 4) The three criteria for revenue recognition are met by most businesses at the point of delivery of goods or services.

____11. (LO 4) Deferred or unearned revenue results when a customer pays in advance and the account balance represents the amount of goods or services owed to the customer or the refund due if the customer cancels the order.

___12. (LO 4) The resources that are used to earn revenues are called expenses.

___13. (LO 4) The time-period principle requires that all of the resources consumed in earning revenues should be recorded in the same period as those revenues.

___14. (LO 5) When expenses exceed revenues, a net loss results, which decreases retained earnings and increases stockholders' equity.

___15. (LO 5) If a company receives cash from a customer and, in exchange for the cash received, provides some services to the customer immediately and promises to provide additional services in the future, cash is increased as is fees earned (or the related revenue account).

___16. (LO 5) A deferred or unearned revenue (such as unearned franchise royalties and development fees) is a liability account that is reported on the balance sheet.

___17. (LO 6) Financial statements are called unadjusted if the accounts have not been updated for revenues earned and expenses incurred during the accounting period, where the receipt or payment of cash is at a different time.

___18. (LO 6) If an income statement is unadjusted, income tax expense is not reported on the income statement.

___19. (LO 6) Net income on an accrual basis can never be the same as cash flow from operations.

MULTIPLE CHOICE QUESTIONS

Choose the best answer or response by placing the identifying letter in the space provided.

___1. (LO 1) The time it takes a company to purchase goods or services from suppliers, sell them to customers, and collect cash from customers is

    a. one month.
    b. one year.
    c. the operating cycle.
    d. the accounting cycle.
    e. either c or d.

___2. (LO 2) The concept that recognizes the fact that decision makers require periodic information about the financial condition and performance of a business is the

    a. continuity assumption.
    b. dual-aspect assumption.
    c. interim assumption.
    d. separate-entity assumption.
    e. time-period assumption.

___3.   (LO 2) Revenues are _____ from ongoing operations.

    a.   increases in cash
    b.   increases in assets
    c.   settlements of liabilities
    d.   contra-expenses
    e.   either b or c

___4.   (LO 2) Expenses are _____ from ongoing operations.

    a.   decreases in cash
    b.   decreases in assets
    c.   increases in liabilities
    d.   contra-revenues
    e.   either b or c

___5.   (LO 2) Gains are similar to _____ and losses are similar to _____.

    a.   revenues; expenses
    b.   expenses; revenues
    c.   debits; credits
    d.   credits; debits
    e.   assets; liabilities

___6.   (LO 2) *When* revenues or expenses should be recognized is a _____ issue; *what amounts* should be recognized is a _____ issue.

    a.   cost-benefit; materiality
    b.   matching; full-disclosure
    c.   primary; secondary
    d.   time-period; conservatism
    e.   timing; measurement

___7.   (LO 7) The total asset turnover ratio

    a.   is computed by dividing average stockholders' equity by average total assets.
    b.   is computed by dividing net income by average total assets.
    c.   is computed by dividing the markup on a product by its sales price.
    d.   measures a company's financial condition.
    e.   measures how effective management is in generating sales from assets (resources).

___8.   (LO 4) The _____ basis of accounting recognizes revenues and expenses when cash changes hands; the _____ basis recognizes revenues when earned and expenses when incurred.

    a.   proprietorship; corporate
    b.   American; international
    c.   cash; accrual
    d.   conservative; liberal
    e.   financial; managerial

___9. (LO 4) The earnings process is considered complete when

   a. the company has a written purchase order from the customer.
   b. the company has shipped the goods to its warehouse in the customer's town.
   c. the customer has given the company a deposit on the promised goods or services.
   d. the company has the goods on hand, or has begun the service promised.
   e. the company has delivered the promised goods or services to the customer.

___10. (LO 4) Under the revenue principle, revenue is recorded as long as the earnings process is substantially complete, there has been payment or a promise to pay, and

   a. collection is reasonably assured.
   b. the check is in the mail.
   c. the company does not permit returns of its product.
   d. the customer is satisfied with the product or service.
   e. the sale has been recorded on the customer's books.

___11. (LO 4) Assume that you worked 30 hours during the week ending December 31st, but will not be paid until January 7th. Your employer recorded your earned wages as an expense in December, rather than in January. This is an example of

   a. income manipulation.
   b. the matching principle.
   c. the time-period assumption.
   d. the conservatism principle.
   e. the continuity assumption

___12. (LO 4) Revenues are measured at the cash or cash-equivalent value of the assets received from customers in accordance with the

   a. cash basis.
   b. historical cost principle.
   c. matching principle.
   d. revenue recognition principle.
   e. unit-of-measure assumption.

___13. (LO 5) Revenues _____ retained earnings, and normally have a _____ balance; expenses _____ retained earnings, and normally have a _____ balance.

   a. increase; debit; decrease; credit
   b. increase; credit; decrease; debit
   c. decrease; debit; increase; credit
   d. decrease; credit; increase; debit
   e. increase; credit; decrease; credit

___14. (LO 6) Financial statements that are prepared to reflect operating activities *before* accounts have been updated for revenues earned or expenses incurred during the accounting period where the receipt or payment of cash is at a different time are called unadjusted financial statements because

    a. total debits will not equal total credits.

    b. all of the required financial statements have not yet been prepared.

    c. dividends have not been taken into account.

    d. they have not been prepared using the accrual basis and are not in accordance with generally accepted accounting principles.

    e. the revenue and expense accounts are up-to-date but the asset and liability accounts are not.

EXERCISES

Record your answer to each exercise in the space provided. Show your work.

Exercise 1 (LO 4)

The following economic events relate to a corporation that operates as a law firm. Indicate whether or not the events would result in recording a revenue on the company's income statement. If a revenue would be recorded, indicate an appropriate account title and amount. Then, indicate the other accounts affected.

Event	Accounts Affected and Type of Account	Amount of Revenue Earned in Current Month OR Revenue Criteria Not Met
The law firm completes legal work relating to a real estate transaction and is paid $5,500 when the papers are signed.		
Legal work in the amount of $26,000 is performed on account for customers.		
A customer makes a payment of $2,500 on account for legal services that were performed last month.		
A new client calls to request assistance in filing the documents for a patent; a fee of $3,000 is paid and the parties agree that the work will commence next month.		
A client pays a retainer of $15,000 for legal work; one-third of the work is performed in the current month and the remainder will be provided over the next two months.		
The law firm borrows $10,000 from a local bank.		

Exercise 2 (LO 4)

The following economic events relate to a corporation that operates a clothing store. Indicate whether or not the events would result in recording an expense on the company's income statement. If an expense would be recorded, indicate an appropriate account title and amount. Then, indicate the other accounts affected.

Event	Accounts Affected and Type of Account	Amount of Expense Incurred in Current Month OR Why an Expense is Not Incurred
Wages earned by employees of $33,000 are paid in cash.		
At the end of the month, the company acquires equipment on account of $55,000.		
In the current month, the cost of clothing sold to customers was $18,000.		
Payment of $375 made on account to a consulting firm for services received last month.		
Payment of $12,000 made at the beginning of the month for six month's of rent; period covered begins this month.		
Utility bills in the amount of $125 arrive in the mail; the bills will not be paid until next month.		

Exercise 3
Part A (LO 5)

Complete the following table by indicating the amount and effect of each transaction (+ or -) on the accounting equation.

Transaction	Assets	Liabilities	Stockholders' Equity
A. Issued stock for $25,000 of cash.			
B. Borrowed $50,000 from local bank in exchange for a promissory note due in one year.			
C. Signed a lease and made a payment of $4,500 to the landlord comprised of the current month's rent of $1,500 and the required $3,000 security deposit.			
D. Purchased equipment on account for $35,000.			
E. Purchased supplies for $6,500 on account and used them immediately.			
F. Performed services and received cash of $57,000.			

Exercise 3, Part A, continued,

Transaction	Assets	Liabilities	Stockholders' Equity
G. Performed services on account for $28,000.			
H. Received a payment of $24,000 for services to be performed in the future.			
I. Collected $14,000 from customers on account.			
J. Paid employees cash of $11,000.			
K. Made a $35,000 payment on account for equipment that was purchased above.			
L. Made a payment of $6,500 on account for the supplies purchased above.			
M. Purchased supplies on account for $10,700.			
N. Received bills for the current month from telephone and electricity companies totaling $3,800; payments will be made next month.			
Ending balances			

Part B (LO 5)

Prepare journal entries for the transactions set forth above.

Transaction	Account	Debit	Credit
A			
B			
C			
D			
E			

Exercise 3, Part B, continued

Transaction	Account	Debit	Credit
F			
G			
H			
I			
J			
K			
L			
M			
N			

Exercise 4 (LO 4)

Carl's Catering just completed its first year of operations. During the year, customer payments in the amount of $64,000 were received at the time the catering services were performed. Another $35,000 of catering services were performed on account for customers; payments amounting to $6,000 have been received from those customers.

On the last day of the year, a local company paid Carl $3,000 for catering services to be performed in 30 days. Employee wages totaled $25,000 and were paid in cash. The food, beverages, and supplies that were used to perform the catering services were paid for in cash and amounted to $26,000. Unpaid bills for truck rentals during the year in the amount of $1,000 were on hand at the end of the year. On the last day of the year, Carl paid $12,000 in advance for rent on some office space.

What was the net income for Carl's Catering on a cash basis? What was the net income on an accrual basis?

Exercise 5

Lisa and Charlie operate a yacht maintenance service that they incorporated as Reliable Yacht Repair, Inc. On June 1, 20A, the business had the following accounts and balances, in alphabetical order. (Note that these are the May 31, 20A balances in the related exercise that you completed in chapter 2.) All accounts have normal balances (debit or credit).

Cash	$19,500
Contributed capital	9,300
Property, plant and equipment	10,000
Notes payable	18,000
Notes receivable	1,000
Retained earnings	3,200

Part A (LO 5)

Using the transaction analysis process outlined in the text [(1) identify the accounts affected, (2) classify each account as an asset (A), liability (L) or stockholders' equity (SE), (3) determine the amount and direction of the effect (increase (+) or decrease (-) on each A, L and/or SE) and (4) determine that the accounting equation remains in balance], perform transaction analysis for each of the transactions entered into by Reliable Yacht Repair during June 20A.

Exercise 5, Part A, continued

Transaction	Assets	=	Liabilities	+	Stockholders' Equity
(1) Lisa and Charlie remove the winter cover from a yacht, and perform maintenance to prepare it for the season. They mail a bill for $800 to the owner of the yacht.					
(2) The owner of another yacht presents Lisa with a check for $200 as an advance payment to paint his boat. He will send a check for the other $800 when the job is complete.					
(3) Charlie stops by the marina to buy $125 of supplies on account.					
(4) Charlie refinishes the trim on a boat and the owners of the boat pay him $150.					
(5) Lisa opens the mail and finds a telephone bill for $175 and a bill in the amount of $300 for insurance coverage for the three-month period beginning July 1st. The phone bill is not due for another 30 days, so she sets it aside. She pays the insurance bill.					

Part B (LO 5)

Prepare journal entries for each of the transactions that you analyzed above.

Transaction	Account	Debit	Credit
(1)			
(2)			
(3)			
(4)			
(5)			

Exercise 5, continued
Part C (LO 5)

Enter the beginning balances in the T-accounts, post the journal entries and determine the ending balances.

Cash	Accounts Receivable	Notes Receivable	Maintenance Supplies

Prepaid Expenses	Property, Plant, and Equipment	Accounts Payable	Unearned Revenue

Notes Payable	Contributed Capital	Retained Earnings	Maintenance Revenue

Refinishing Revenue	Maintenance Supplies Expense	Utilities Expense

Exercise 5, continued
Part D (LO 6)

Prepare an unadjusted income statement for Reliable Yacht Repair, Inc. for the month of June 20A.

Reliable Yacht Repair, Inc.
Unadjusted Income Statement
for the month ended June 30, 20A

Exercise 6 (LO 3)

Pixar was formed when Steve Jobs purchased the computer division of Lucasfilm in 1986 and then incorporated it as a separate company. In 1991, Pixar agreed to develop and produce up to three animated feature films to be marketed and distributed by Disney. In 1997, Pixar agreed to produce five computer animated feature-length motion pictures distributed by Disney over the next ten years. Pixar also produces jointly with Disney related products such as merchandise and sound tracks.

The selected financial information set forth below was taken from the statements of operations (income statements) and balance sheets included in the Forms 10-K that were filed by Pixar with the SEC for fiscal 2001 (year ending December 29, 2001), fiscal 2000 (year ending December 30, 2001) and fiscal 1999 (year ending January 1, 2000). All dollar amounts shown below are in thousands.

	Fiscal 2001	Fiscal 2000	Fiscal 1999
Year ended			
Total revenues	$ 70,223,000	$172,267,000	
Net income (see below)	36,006,000	78,027,000	
As of the end of the year			
Total assets	523,294,000	476,603,000	$374,905,000
Total shareholders' equity	505,686,000	435,720,000	344,443,000

The net income amounts reported above are described as net income from continuing operations in Pixar's statements of operations.

Exercise 6, continued

Compute Pixar's total asset turnover for fiscal 2001 and 2000 using the information set forth above and interpret the results.

Fiscal 2001:

Fiscal 2000:

Interpretation:

SOLUTIONS TO SELF-TEST QUESTIONS AND EXERCISES
MATCHING

G	Accrual Basis Accounting	F	Matching Principle
C	Cash Basis Accounting	J	Operating Cycle (Cash-to-Cash Cycle)
E	Expenses	I	Revenue Principle
A	Gains	B	Revenues
H	Losses	D	Time-Period Assumption

TRUE-FALSE QUESTIONS

1. F – The length of a company's operating cycle depends on the nature and current operations of the business.
2. T
3. T
4. F – Because gains from peripheral transactions are not related to the central operations of the company, they are reported in the other income category on the income statement.
5. T
6. T
7. F – Any company that prepares its financial statements in accordance with GAAP must use the accrual basis of accounting.
8. F – A company can receive cash before, at the same time as, or after it has completed delivery of a product or service to a customer.
9. T
10. T
11. T
12. T
13. T

14. F – When expenses exceed revenues, a net loss results, which decreases retained earnings and stockholders' equity.

15. F – If a company receives cash from a customer and, in exchange for the cash received, provides some services and promises to provide additional services in the future, three accounts are increased: cash, unearned revenues and fees earned (or the related revenue account).

16. T

17. T

18. T

19. F – Net income on an accrual basis *could be* the same as cash flow from operations if the company was not required to make any adjusting entries; that is, if it always received cash at the time revenues were earned and paid cash at the time expenses were incurred. It is also possible that net income on an accrual basis could be the same as cash flow from operations if the net effect of all of the adjusting entries on the company's net income was zero.

MULTIPLE CHOICE QUESTIONS

1. c	5. a	9. e	13. b
2. e	6. e	10. a	14. d
3. e	7. e	11. b	
4. e	8. c	12. d	

EXERCISES

Exercise 1

Event	Accounts Affected and Type of Account	Amount of Revenue Earned in Current Month OR Revenue Criteria Not Met
The law firm completes legal work relating to a real estate transaction and is paid $5,500 when the papers are signed.	Cash (A) Legal Fees (R)	$5,500 earned.
Legal work in the amount of $26,000 is performed on account for customers.	Accounts Receivable (A) Legal Fees (R)	$26,000 earned.
A customer makes a payment of $2,500 on account for legal services that were performed last month.	Cash (A) Accounts Receivable (A)	No revenue in current month; cash collection relates to earnings in prior accounting period (that is, last month).
A new client calls to request assistance in filing the documents for a patent; a fee of $3,000 is paid and the parties agree that the work will commence next month.	Cash (A) Unearned Revenue (L)	Earnings process not complete; cash collection relates to earnings in future accounting periods.

Exercise 1, continued

Event	Accounts Affected and Type of Account	Amount of Revenue Earned in Current Month OR Revenue Criteria Not Met
A client pays a retainer of $15,000 for legal work; one-third of the work is performed in the current month and the remainder will be provided over the next two months.	Cash (A) Unearned Revenue (L) Legal Fees (R)	$5,000 earned; $10,000 deferred as earnings process not yet complete.
The law firm borrows $10,000 from a local bank.	Cash (A) Notes payable (L)	Financing transaction; no revenue earned.

Exercise 2

Event	Accounts Affected and Type of Account	Amount of Expense Incurred in Current Month OR Why an Expense is Not Incurred
Wages earned by employees of $33,000 are paid in cash.	Cash (A) Wages (or salaries) expense (E)	$33,000 incurred.
At the end of the month, the company acquires equipment on account of $55,000.	Equipment (A) Accounts Payable (L)	No expense incurred until equipment is placed in service (that is, used).
In the current month, the cost of clothing sold to customers was $18,000.	Inventory (A) Cost of sales (E)	$18,000 incurred (matched with related revenue that was earned when the clothing was sold).
Payment of $375 made on account to a consulting firm for services received last month.	Cash (A) Accounts Payable (L)	Expense incurred last month; paid in current month.
Payment of $12,000 made at the beginning of the month for six month's of rent; period covered begins this month.	Cash (A) Prepaid Expense (A) Rent Expense (E)	$2,000 incurrent in current month; $10,000 not yet incurred (to be incurred in the next five months).
Utility bills in the amount of $125 arrive in the mail; the bills will not be paid until next month.	Accounts Payable (L) Utility expense (E)	$125 incurred in current month; to be paid next month.

Exercise 3
Part A

Transaction	Assets	Liabilities	Stockholders' Equity
A. Issued stock for $25,000 of cash.	+ 25,000		+ 25,000
B. Borrowed $50,000 from local bank in exchange for a promissory note due in one year.	+ 50,000	+ 50,000	

Exercise 3, Part A, continued

C.	Signed a lease and made a payment of $4,500 to the landlord comprised of the current month's rent of $1,500 and the required $3,000 security deposit.	+ 3,000 − 4,500		− 1,500
D.	Purchased equipment on account for $35,000.	+ 35,000	+ 35,000	
E.	Purchased supplies for $6,500 on account and used them immediately.		+ 6,500	− 6,500
F.	Performed services and received cash of $57,000.	+ 57,000		+ 57,000
G.	Performed services on account for $28,000.	+ 28,000		+ 28,000
H.	Received a payment of $24,000 for services to be performed in the future.	+ 24,000	+ 24,000	
I.	Collected $14,000 from customers on account.	+ 14,000 − 14,000		
J.	Paid employees cash of $11,000.	− 11,000		− 11,000
K.	Made a $35,000 payment on account for equipment that was purchased above.	− 35,000	− 35,000	
L.	Made a payment of $6,500 on account for the supplies purchased above.	− 6,500	− 6,500	
M.	Purchased supplies on account for $10,700.	+ 10,700	+ 10,700	
N.	Received bills for the current month from telephone and electricity companies totaling $3,800; payments will be made next month.		+ 3,800	− 3,800
Ending balances		$175,700	$88,500	$87,200

Part B

Transaction	Account	Debit	Credit
A	Cash	25,000	
	Contributed capital		25,000
B	Cash	50,000	
	Notes payable		50,000
C	Prepaid expense (or security deposit)	3,000	
	Rent expense	1,500	
	Cash		4,500
D	Equipment	35,000	
	Accounts payable		35,000
E	Supplies expense	6,500	
	Accounts payable		6,500

Exercise 3, Part B, continued

Transaction	Account	Debit	Credit
F	Cash	57,000	
	Legal fees (or legal revenue)		57,000
G	Accounts receivable	28,000	
	Legal fees		28,000
H	Cash	24,000	
	Unearned revenue		24,000
I	Cash	14,000	
	Accounts receivable		14,000
J	Wage expense	11,000	
	Cash		11,000
K	Accounts payable	35,000	
	Cash		35,000
L	Accounts payable	6,500	
	Cash		6,500
M	Supplies	10,700	
	Accounts payable		10,700
N	Utility expense	3,800	
	Accounts payable		3,800

Exercise 4

Cash basis net income can be computed as follows:

Cash Receipts
Catering service revenue ($64,000 + $6,000 + $3,000) $73,000
Cash Payments
Employee wage expense $25,000
Cost of food, beverage and supplies   26,000
Rent expense   12,000
  Total cash payments   63,000
  Cash basis net income $10,000

Accrual basis net income can be computed as follows:

Revenues
Catering service revenue ($64,000 + $35,000) $99,000
Expenses
Employee wage expense $25,000
Cost of food, beverage and supplies   26,000
Truck rental expense   1,000
  Total expenses   52,000
  Accrual basis net income $47,000

Exercise 5
Part A

Transaction	Assets	=	Liabilities	+	Stockholders' Equity
(1) Lisa and Charlie remove the winter cover from a yacht, and perform maintenance to prepare it for the season. They mail a bill for $800 to the owner of the yacht.	Accounts receivable + 800				Maintenance revenue + 800
(2) The owner of another yacht presents Lisa with a check for $200 as an advance payment to paint his boat. He will send a check for the other $800 when the job is complete.	Cash + 200		Unearned revenue + 200		
(3) Charlie stops by the marina to buy $125 of supplies on account.	Maintenance supplies + 125		Accounts payable + 125		
(4) Charlie refinishes the trim on a boat and the owners of the boat pay him $150.	Cash + 150				Refinishing revenue + 150
(5) Lisa opens the mail and finds a telephone bill for $175 and a bill in the amount of $300 for insurance coverage for the three-month period beginning July 1st. The phone bill is not due for another 30 days, so she sets it aside. She pays the insurance bill.	Prepaid expense + 300 Cash − 300		Accounts payable + 175		Utilities expense − 175

Part B

Transaction	Account	Debit	Credit
(1)	Accounts receivable	800	
	Maintenance revenue (or fees)		800
(2)	Cash	200	
	Unearned revenue		200
(3)	Maintenance supplies	125	
	Accounts payable		125
(4)	Cash	150	
	Refinishing revenue (or fees)		150
(5)	Utilities expense	175	
	Accounts payable		175
	Prepaid expenses	300	
	Cash		300

Exercise 5, continued
Part C

	Cash			
6/1	19,500			
(2)	200			
(4)	150	(5)	300	
6/30	19,550			

	Accounts Receivable		
6/1	0		
(1)	800		
6/30	800		

	Notes Receivable		
6/1	1,000		
6/30	1,000		

	Maintenance Supplies		
6/1	0		
(3)	125		
6/30	125		

	Prepaid Expenses		
6/1	0		
(5)	300		
6/30	300		

	Property, Plant and Equipment		
6/1	10,000		
6/30	10,000		

	Accounts Payable		
		6/1	0
		(3)	125
		(5)	175
		6/30	300

	Unearned Revenue		
		6/1	0
		(2)	200
		6/30	200

	Note Payable		
		6/1	18,000
		6/30	18,000

	Contributed Capital		
		6/1	9,300
		6/30	9,300

	Retained Earnings		
		6/1	3,200
		6/30	3,200

	Maintenance Revenue		
		6/1	0
		(1)	800
		6/30	800

	Refinishing Revenue		
		6/1	0
		(4)	150
		6/30	150

	Maintenance Supplies Expense		
6/1	0		
6/30	0		

	Utilities Expense		
6/1	0		
(5)	175		
6/30	175		

Exercise 5, continued
Part D

Reliable Yacht Repair, Inc.
Unadjusted Income Statement
for the month ended June 30, 20A

Revenues		
Maintenance revenue	$800	
Refinishing revenue	<u>150</u>	
Total revenues		$950
Expenses		
Utilities expense		<u>175</u>
Net income		<u>$775</u>

Exercise 6

Total revenue (or sales) ÷ [(Total assets, beginning of the year + Total assets, end of year) ÷ 2]

Fiscal 2001:
$70,223,000 ÷ [($476,603,000 + $523,294,000) ÷ 2] = $70,223,000 ÷ $499,948,500 = 14.0%

Fiscal 2000:
$172,267,000 ÷ [($374,905,000 + $476,603,000) ÷ 2] = $172,267,000 ÷ $425,754,000 = 40.5%

Interpretation
The total asset turnover ratio measures the sales (or, in this case, revenues) generated per dollar of assets. On the average, Pixar generated $14.00 of revenues for each dollar invested in total assets during fiscal 2001 and $40.50 of revenues per dollar invested in total assets during fiscal 2000. Generally, a decreasing total asset turnover ratio appears to signify less efficient management of Pixar's assets in 2001 compared to 2000.

A company's products and business strategy contribute significantly to its resulting ratio. The total asset turnover ratio will also decline from increases in assets and/or decreases in revenues (both of which were experienced by Pixar during fiscal 2001). A detailed analysis of the changes in key components of assets will provide additional information on the nature of the total asset turnover ratio change and thus management's decisions. Further information about such changes may be obtained from Pixar's Annual Report.

AN IDEA FOR YOUR STUDY TEAM

Make a list of companies or industries that might have exceptionally long operating cycles with the members of your study team. For each, estimate the length of its operating cycle. Is there a limit on the length of an operating cycle? How do you think that these companies might recognize revenue? How would these companies apply the matching principle to recognize expenses?

ORGANIZATION OF THE CHAPTER

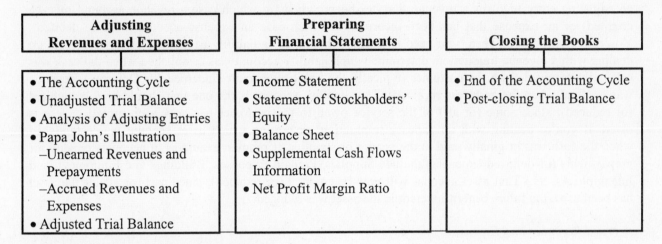

Adjusting Revenues and Expenses	Preparing Financial Statements	Closing the Books

• The Accounting Cycle
• Unadjusted Trial Balance
• Analysis of Adjusting Entries
• Papa John's Illustration
  –Unearned Revenues and Prepayments
  –Accrued Revenues and Expenses
• Adjusted Trial Balance
	• Income Statement
	• Statement of Stockholders' Equity
	• Balance Sheet
	• Supplemental Cash Flows Information
	• Net Profit Margin Ratio
		• End of the Accounting Cycle
		• Post-closing Trial Balance

CHAPTER FOCUS SUGGESTIONS

Overview

In chapter 3, you learned that cash does not always change hands at the same time a revenue is earned or an expense is incurred. When these situations arise, adjustments are often required to properly report the revenues earned and expenses incurred. This chapter covers the adjustment process, an important step in the accounting cycle. Chapter 4 also covers the closing process, the final step in the accounting cycle.

The Adjustment Process

Chapter 4 covers the adjustment process that is used to record these adjusting entries. As you analyze transactions that require adjustments, note that *every adjusting entry must include either a credit to a revenue account or a debit to an expense account*. This rule makes sense if you understand the purpose of adjusting entries. The adjustment process ensures that *all revenues earned* during the period *are recorded* (revenue accounts are credited to record increases) and *all expenses incurred* to generate those revenues *are recorded* (expense accounts are debited to record increases). Pay particular attention to the time period covered by an adjusting entry when calculating the dollar amount to be used in the entry.

Unearned Revenues and Prepayments

A customer may pay cash to a company *before* the related revenue is earned (that is, in advance). Revenue cannot be recognized (or recorded) at the time of the cash receipt, because the company has not yet earned the revenue. This situation is considered a "deferral" because the recording of the revenue is deferred (or postponed) until such time as the revenue is actually earned. Alternatively, the company may pay cash to a vendor *before* the related expense is incurred; this situation may be described as a "prepayment." Expense cannot be recognized (or recorded) at the time of the cash payment, because the company has not yet used the goods or services (that is, the company has not incurred the expense).

You analyzed and recorded such cash receipt and cash payment transactions in Chapter 3. Now, imagine that some time has passed, and the revenue has been earned (that is, the service has been provided to the customer) or the expense incurred (that is, the company has used the goods or services). Typically, adjusting entries must be prepared to record the related revenues (previously unearned) that were earned and expenses (previously prepaid) that were incurred during this accounting period.

Remember the rule (stated above) that **each adjusting entry must include either a credit to a revenue account or a debit to an expense account**. Start by deciding whether the transaction that now requires an adjusting entry involves a revenue that has been earned (in which case a revenue account must be credited) or an expense that has been incurred (in which case an expense account must be debited). You're halfway there! Then, you need to decide what asset or liability account is affected. If you are dealing with a revenue transaction, determine which liability account was established when the cash was originally received from the customer (typically the liability account Unearned (or Deferred) Revenue was credited when the cash was received). That liability account is the one that should now be debited (or reduced); since some (or all) of the service owed to the customer has now been provided, less is owed. If you're dealing with an expense transaction, determine which asset account was established when the cash was originally paid to the vendor or supplier. (Common examples of accounts created for prepayments (of deferred expenses) include Supplies, Prepaid Expenses, Buildings and Equipment, and Intangible Assets.) That asset account will now be credited (or reduced); since part (or all) of the asset has been used, the future benefit inherent in the asset was reduced.

Accrued Revenues and Expenses

A customer may remit cash to a company *after* the related revenue is earned. Revenue must be recognized during the accounting period in which the service is performed. Alternatively, the company may disburse cash to a vendor *after* the related expense is incurred. The expense must be recognized during the accounting period in which the goods or services have been used. Often, the company's accounting system will record these transactions in the correct accounting period. However, if the accounting system has not recorded all revenues earned and all expenses incurred during the period, adjustments must be made. This is often the case towards the end of the accounting period. For example, a service may be performed just before the end of the month that is not yet recorded. Or, there might be a delay in the receipt of the invoice from a vendor. Care must be taken to ensure that all revenues earned and expenses incurred are identified and recorded.

Again, remember the rule that each adjusting entry must include either a credit to a revenue account or a debit to an expense account. Start by figuring out whether the adjusting entry involves a revenue transaction (in which case a revenue account must be credited) or an expense transaction (in which case an expense account must be debited). Again, you're halfway there! Than, you need to decide what asset or liability account should be included in the adjusting entry. If you're dealing with a revenue, recall the company has not been paid; as such, a receivable must now be created with a debit. If you're dealing with an expense; recall that the company has not yet paid; as such, a payable must now be recorded with a credit.

Financial Statement Matters

Financial statements are usually prepared after the adjusting entries have been recorded. Pay special attention to the interrelationships between the financial statements (that is, how they relate to each other). You will also need to know how to compute the net profit margin ratio. You should attempt to understand what this ratio is measuring so that you will be able to interpret this ratio.

Closing Process

This chapter concludes the coverage of the accounting cycle with the closing process. Entries made during the closing process close the revenue and expense accounts (the temporary accounts) and transfer their balances to retained earnings. After the closing entries are posted, the retained earnings account balance will agree to that reported on the balance sheet and the temporary accounts will be ready to accumulate the following year's revenues and expenses.

LEARNING OBJECTIVES

After studying this chapter, you should be able to:

(LO 1) Explain the purpose of a trial balance.
(LO 2) Analyze the adjustments necessary at the end of the period to update balance sheet and income statements accounts.
(LO 3) Present an income statement with earnings per share, statement of stockholders' equity, balance sheet, and supplemental cash flow information.
(LO 4) Compute and interpret net profit margin.
(LO 5) Explain the closing process.

READ AND RECALL QUESTIONS

After you read each section of the chapter, answer the related Read and Recall Questions below.

BUSINESS BACKGROUND

What are the two characteristics of high quality financial information? Why must adjustments be made at the end of an accounting period?

ADJUSTING REVENUES AND EXPENSES – THE ACCOUNTING CYCLE

What are the fundamental steps in the accounting cycle (as set forth in Exhibit 4.1)?

LEARNING OBJECTIVE
After studying this section of the chapter, you should be able to:
1. Explain the purpose of a trial balance.

UNADJUSTED TRIAL BALANCE

What is a trial balance and what does it reflect? Why are the debit and credit columns of the trial balance totaled?

ANANYSIS OF ADJUSTING ENTRIES

Why are adjusting entries necessary?

Unearned Revenues and Prepayments

When the company receives cash from a customer in advance (that is, before the related service is performed), what account is used to keep track of the prepayment? What type of account is it? What does the balance in that account represent at any point in time? Why does this account balance need to be adjusted as time passes? What other type of account is involved in the adjusting entry?

When the company pays for its goods or services from a vendor or supplier (such as insurance coverage) before it uses those goods or services to generate revenues, what type of account is used to keep track of the prepayment? What does the balance in that account represent at any point in time? Why does this account balance need to be adjusted as time passes? What other type of account is involved in the adjusting entry?

Accrued Revenues and Expenses

What are accrued revenues? Why is an adjusting entry needed in this regard at the end of the accounting period? What two types of accounts appear in this adjusting entry?

What are accrued expenses? Why is an adjusting entry needed in this regard at the end of the accounting period? What two types of accounts appear in this adjusting entry?

The Adjustment Process

What three steps should be performed to identify and calculate adjusting entries?

PAPA JOHN'S ILLUSTRATION – UNEARNED REVENUES AND PREPAYMENTS
Inventories

(a) Inventories include food, paper products, and equipment for sale to franchisees by the commissaries. At the end of the month, Papa John's counted $13,000 in inventories on hand, but the Inventories account indicated a balance of $17,000. First, prepare the necessary adjusting entry. Then, determine the effect on the accounting equation:

Account	Debit	Credit

Assets _____ = _____ Liabilities _____ + _____ Stockholders' Equity _____

Prepaid Expenses

(b) Prepaid Expenses includes $2,000 for insurance coverage over four months. One month has expired and there remains three months of future insurance benefits. First, prepare the necessary adjusting entry. Then, determine the effect on the accounting equation:

Account	Debit	Credit

Assets _____ = _____ Liabilities _____ + _____ Stockholders' Equity _____

(c) Prepaid Expenses also includes $6,000 for rental of space at shopping centers over the next three months. One month has expired and two months of future rental benefits remain. First, prepare the necessary adjusting entry. Then, determine the effect on the accounting equation:

Account	Debit	Credit

Assets _____ = _____ Liabilities _____ + _____ Stockholders' Equity _____

Property, Plant, and Equipment (and Accumulated Depreciation)

When buildings and equipment are used over time to generate revenues, what does the matching principle require? What is depreciation expense? What does *depreciation* simply describe? What is the contra-account Accumulated Depreciation used for? As Accumulated Depreciation increases, what happens to the net book value reported on the balance sheet? What is *net book value*?

(d) Property and equipment have an historical cost of $338,000 at the end of the month. The accumulated depreciation of $83,000 is the used-up portion of the historical cost prior to this month. The depreciation is estimated to be $30,000 per year or $2,500 per month. First, prepare the necessary adjusting entry. Then, determine the effect on the accounting equation:

Account	Debit	Credit

_____ Assets _____ = _____ Liabilities _____ + _____ Stockholders' Equity _____

Unearned Revenues

(e) Papa John's performed $100 in additional services in January to new franchisees who had previously paid Papa John's. First, prepare the necessary adjusting entry. Then, determine the effect on the accounting equation:

Account	Debit	Credit

_____ Assets _____ = _____ Liabilities _____ + _____ Stockholders' Equity _____

Receivables

(f) Papa John's franchisees reported that they will pay Papa John's in February $900 in royalties for sales the franchisees made in the last week of January. First, prepare the necessary adjusting entry. Then, determine the effect on the accounting equation:

Account	Debit	Credit

_____ Assets _____ = _____ Liabilities _____ + _____ Stockholders' Equity _____

Accrued Expenses Payable (such as Salaries, Utilities, and Interest)

(g) Papa John's owed its employees salaries and benefits for working four days at the end of January at $500 per day. The employees will be paid during the first week in February. First, prepare the necessary adjusting entry. Then, determine the effect on the accounting equation:

Account	Debit	Credit

_____ Assets _____ = _____ Liabilities _____ + _____ Stockholders' Equity _____

(h) Papa John's received a $600 utility bill at the end of January for gas and electricity used in January. The company categorizes Utilities Expense as general and administrative expenses on the income statement. The bill will be paid during the first week in February. First, prepare the necessary adjusting entry. Then, determine the effect on the accounting equation:

Account	Debit	Credit

_____ Assets _____ = _____ Liabilities _____ + _____ Stockholders' Equity _____

(i) Papa John's borrowed $6,000 at the beginning of January, signing a note payable due in three years at 12 percent interest per year with interest to be paid at the end of each year. Note that the principal was recorded properly in the past. However, interest expense is incurred over time as the bank's money is used. First, prepare the necessary adjusting entry. Then, determine the effect on the accounting equation:

Account	Debit	Credit

_____ Assets _____ = _____ Liabilities _____ + _____ Stockholders' Equity _____

Income Taxes Payable

Why are income taxes considered an accrued expense? How is the amount of income taxes payable computed?

QUESTION OF ETHICS – ADJUSTMENTS AND INCENTIVES

Who is most directly affected by the information presented in financial statements? Why might these parties be tempted to manipulate the year-end adjustments? What do SEC enforcement actions most often relate to?

LEARNING OBJECTIVE

After studying this section of the chapter, you should be able to:

3. Present an income statement with earnings per share, statement of stockholders' equity, balance sheet, and supplemental cash flow information.

PREPARING FINANCIAL STATEMENTS

Which set of columns in Exhibit 4.3 would be used to prepare financial statements?

INCOME STATEMENT

What is the income statement formula? Why is the income statement prepared first? How is the amount of earnings per share computed?

Statement of Stockholders' Equity

What amount(s) from the income statement is (are) carried forward to the statement of stockholders' equity?

Balance Sheet

What amount(s) from the statement of stockholders' equity is (are) carried forward to the balance sheet? How is the contra-asset account Accumulated Depreciation shown on the balance sheet? How are current assets and current liabilities ordered on the balance sheet?

FOCUS ON CASH FLOWS–DISCLOSURE

What does the statement of cash flows explain? How are transactions categorized on the statement of cash flows? (Hint: There are three categories.) What additional information must be provided on the statement itself or in the notes to the financial statements? (Hint: There are three types of supplemental disclosures.)

FINANCIAL ANALYSIS – CASH FLOWS FROM OPERATIONS, NET INCOME, AND THE QUALITY OF EARNINGS

What do analysts look for when they attempt to predict future period's earnings? What is a useful warning sign? When do certain users consider earnings to be of higher quality?

LEARNING OBJECTIVE
After studying this section of the chapter, you should be able to:
4. Compute and interpret net profit margin.

KEY RATIO ANALYSIS: NET PROFIT MARGIN

How is the net profit margin ratio computed? What does the net profit margin ratio measure? What does a rising net profit margin ratio signal? What do financial analysts expect of well-run businesses?

LEARNING OBJECTIVE
After studying this section of the chapter, you should be able to:
5. Explain the closing process.

CLOSING THE BOOKS
END OF THE ACCOUNTING CYCLE

Which types of accounts are considered to be permanent (or real) accounts? What happens to the balances in these accounts at the end of the accounting period? Which types of accounts are considered to be temporary (or nominal) accounts? What happens to the balances in these accounts at the end of the accounting period?

What are the two purposes of closing entries? What accounts are closed? Why? How are temporary accounts with credit balances closed? How are temporary accounts with debit balances closed? What is the other account affected by these closing entries?

POST-CLOSING TRIAL BALANCE

What is the name of the trial balance that is prepared after the closing entries have been recorded? What types of accounts appear on this trial balance?

FINANCIAL ANALYSIS – JUDGING EARNINGS QUALITY

As noted in your text, certain adjustments (discussed in later chapters) involve difficult and complex estimates about the future. What type of estimates do firms that follow *conservative* financial reporting strategies make? How do experienced analysts react to financial reports prepared by such firms? Why are earnings numbers reported by these companies often said to be of "higher quality?"

When are firms judged to be *aggressive* in terms of estimates made? How do analysts react to such firms?

CHAPTER TAKE-AWAYS

1. *Explain the purpose of a trial balance.*

   A trial balance is a list of all accounts with their debit or credit balances indicated in the appropriate column to provide a check on the equality of the debits and credits. The trial balance may be
   • Unadjusted—before adjustments are made.
   • Adjusted—after adjustments are made.
   • Post-closing—after revenues and expenses are closed to Retained Earnings.

2. **Analyze the adjustments necessary at the end of the period to update balance sheet and income statements accounts.**

   - Adjusting entries are necessary at the end of the accounting period to measure income properly, correct errors, and provide for adequate valuation of balance sheet accounts. The analysis involves
     (1) Identifying deferred accounts (created in the past when cash was received or paid before being earned or incurred) and accruals (revenues earned and expenses incurred before cash is to be received or paid in the future).
     (2) Drawing a timeline and setting up T-accounts along with any computations.
     (3) Recording the adjusting entry needed to obtain the appropriate ending balances in the accounts.
   - Recording adjusting entries has no effect on the Cash account.

3. **Present an income statement with earnings per share, statement of stockholders' equity, balance sheet, and supplemental cash flow information.**

   Adjusted account balances are used in preparing the following financial statements:
   - Income Statement: Revenues - Expenses = Net Income (including earnings per share computed as net income available to the common stockholders divided by the weighted-average number of shares of common stock outstanding during the period).
   - Statement of Stockholders' Equity: (Beginning Contributed Capital + Stock Issuances - Stock Repurchases) + (Beginning Retained Earnings + Net Income - Dividends) = Ending Total Stockholders' Equity.
   - Balance Sheet: Assets = Liabilities + Stockholders' Equity.
   - Supplemental cash flow information: Interest paid, income taxes paid, and significant noncash transactions.

4. **Compute and interpret the net profit margin.**

   Net profit margin (Net Income ÷ Net Sales) measures how much of every dollar of sales generated during the period is profit. A rising net profit margin signals more efficient management of sales and expenses.

5. **Explain the closing process.**

   Temporary accounts (revenues, expenses, gains, and losses) are closed to a zero balance at the end of the accounting period to allow for the accumulation of income items in the following period. To close these accounts, debit each revenue and gain account, credit each expense and loss account, and record the difference (equal to net income) to Retained Earnings.

KEY RATIO

Net profit margin measures how much of every sales dollar generated during the period is profit. A high or rising ratio suggests that the company is managing its sales and expenses efficiently. It is computed as follows:

Net Profit Margin = Net Income ÷ Net Sales

FINDING FINANCIAL INFORMATION

Balance Sheet	
Current Assets	*Current Liabilities*
Accruals include:	Accruals include:
Interest receivable	Interest payable
Rent receivable	Wages payable
Deferrals include:	Utilities payable
Inventory	Income taxes
Prepaid expenses	payable
Noncurrent Assets	Deferrals include:
Deferrals include:	Deferred revenue
Property and	
equipment	
Intangibles	

Income Statement

Revenues
  Increased by adjusting entries
Expenses
  Increased by adjusting entries
Pretax Income
  Income tax expense
Net Income

Statement of Cash Flows

Adjusting Entries do not Affect Cash
  Interest paid
  Income taxes paid
  Significant noncash transactions

Notes

In Various Notes if not on the Balance Sheet
  Details of accrued expenses payable
  Interest paid, income taxes paid, significant
   noncash transactions (if not reported on the
   statement of cash flows)

SELF-TEST QUESTIONS AND EXERCISES

MATCHING

Match each of the key terms listed below with the appropriate textbook definition:

_____ Accrued Revenues and Expenses   _____ Post-Closing Trial Balance
_____ Adjusting Entries   _____ Prepayments (or Deferred Expenses)
_____ Book Value (Net Book Value, Carrying Value)   _____ Temporary (Nominal) Accounts
_____ Closing Entries   _____ Trial Balance
_____ Contra-Account   _____ Unearned (or Deferred) Revenues
_____ Permanent (Real) Accounts

A. Made at the end of the accounting period to transfer balances in temporary accounts to Retained Earnings and to establish a zero balance in each of the temporary accounts.

B. The balance sheet accounts that carry their ending balances into the next accounting period.

C. An account that is an offset to, or reduction of, the primary account.

D. Previously recorded liabilities and revenues that need to be adjusted at the end of the period to reflect earned revenues.

E. Previously recorded assets and expenses that need to be adjusted at the end of the period to reflect incurred expenses.

F. Should be prepared as the last step in the accounting cycle to check that debits equal credits and all temporary accounts have been closed.

G. Acquisition cost of the asset less accumulated depreciation, or amortization.

H. Entries necessary at the end of the accounting period to measure income properly, correct errors, and provide for adequate valuation of balance sheet accounts.

I. Income statement (and sometimes dividends declared) accounts that are closed to retained earnings at the end of the accounting period.

J. Revenues that have been earned and expenses that have been incurred by the end of the current accounting period but that will not be collected or paid until a future accounting period.

K. A list of all accounts with their balances to provide a check on the equality of the debits and credits.

TRUE-FALSE QUESTIONS

For each of the following, enter a T or F in the blank to indicate whether the statement is true or false.

___1. (LO 1) A trial balance is considered one of the most useful financial statements because it provides detailed information to external users.

___2. (LO 1) A trial balance is prepared to give an accountant assurance that all the work done up to the point of adjusting entries was done correctly.

___3. (LO 2) Depreciation is recorded to reflect declines in the market values of long-lived assets.

___4. (LO 2) The cost of a long-lived asset less the accumulated depreciation on that asset is the net market value of the asset.

___5. (LO 2) The net book value, or carrying value, of an asset does not represent the current market value of the asset.

___6. (LO 2) Nearly all asset and liability accounts need to be analyzed and adjusted at year-end.

___7. (LO 2) When a payment is made before an expense is recognized, the asset recorded is known as a deferral (or prepaid expense).

___8. (LO 2) Previously recorded assets, liabilities, revenues, or expenses that need to be adjusted at the end of the period to properly recognize revenue or expenses are referred to as deferrals.

___9. (LO 2) An accrual results when a company earns revenue after cash has been exchanged.

___10. (LO 2) When an accrual exists, either another entity owes something to the company or the company owes something to another entity.

___11. (LO 2) The difference between an accrual adjusting entry and a deferral (an unearned or prepayment) adjusting entry is in the timing of the cash payment or receipt that gives rise to that entry.

___12. (LO 3) The flow of information from one statement to the next dictates that the balance sheet should be the first statement prepared.

___13. (LO 3) The net cash flows that result from operating activities is usually not equivalent to the amount of net income reported by the company on the income statement.

___14. (LO 4) A rising net profit margin ratio indicates that the company is becoming less efficient in managing the company's sales and expenses.

___15. (LO 5) Temporary or nominal accounts are those used to accumulate data from the current accounting period only.

___16. (LO 5) Closing entries reduce the balances of income statement accounts to zero and transfer their balances to the retained earnings account.

MULTIPLE CHOICE QUESTIONS

Choose the best answer or response by placing the identifying letter in the space provided.

___1. (LO 1) A trial balance is prepared to provide assurance that:

    a. journal entries were prepared correctly.
    b. the correct accounts have been debited and credited.
    c. all accounts have been updated.
    d. the total of the debit account balances equals the total of the credit account balances.
    e. all of the above.

___2. (LO 2) A contra-asset is an account that is

    a. really a liability which is directly related to a primary asset account.
    b. an incorrectly entered asset account balance.
    c. an offset to an asset account.
    d. a reduction of the primary asset account.
    e. c and d.

___3. (LO 2) The book value of a long-lived asset

    a. is not meant to represent its market value.
    b. is equal to the difference between an asset's acquisition cost and its accumulated depreciation.
    c. is also referred to as its net book value or carrying value.
    d. results from a cost allocation process.
    e. all of the above.

___4. (LO 2) An example of a deferral would be

    a. the payment of a premium on an insurance policy before the coverage period.
    b. interest owed on a loan.
    c. interest earned but not yet collected on a loan made to a franchisee.
    d. wages earned by employees but not yet paid.
    e. all of the above.

___5. (LO 2) An example of an accrual would be

    a. rent collected in advance of occupancy from a tenant.
    b. an insurance premium paid in advance of the start of coverage.
    c. a customer deposit for services to be provided in the future.
    d. interest owed on a promissory note.
    e. none of the above.

___6. (LO 2) Depreciation for each accounting period is computed using the straight-line method by

    a. dividing the cost of the asset by its useful life.
    b. dividing the residual value of the asset by its cost.
    c. dividing the difference between the cost of the asset and its residual value by its useful life.
    d. dividing the cost of the asset by two.
    e. any of the above.

___7. (LO 2) The difference between the cost of a long-lived asset and its related accumulated depreciation is its

    a. market value.
    b. net book value.
    c. current cost.
    d. selling price.
    e. salvage value.

___8. (LO 3) When preparing financial statements, it is best to start with the:

    a. balance sheet.
    b. statement of cash flows.
    c. income statement.
    d. statement of stockholders' equity.
    e. any of the above.

___9. (LO 3) SEC enforcement sanctions most often relate to:

    a. accrual of revenues and receivables that should be deferred to future periods.
    b. bonuses that have been paid to managers.
    c. deferral of expenses which have been incurred to future periods.
    d. overstatements of the book values of long-lived assets.
    e. unexpected increases in the book value of the company's stock.

___10. (LO 5) Accounts are closed by transferring their balances to:

    a. the temporary accounts.
    b. the permanent accounts.
    c. the balance sheet accounts.
    d. contributed capital.
    e. retained earnings.

___11. (LO 5) Accounts that are closed include the:

    a. assets accounts.
    b. liabilities accounts.
    c. revenue and expense accounts.
    d. all stockholders' equity accounts.
    e. all of the above.

EXERCISES

Record your answer to each exercise in the space provided. Show your work.

Exercise 1 (LO 1)

You may recall that Lisa and Charlie operate a yacht maintenance service that they incorporated as Reliable Yacht Repair, Inc. They recently talked to their banker about obtaining a loan. The banker sounded interested, but wants to see last month's income statement. She reminded them that the bank only accepts financial statements that are prepared in accordance with GAAP. Lisa and Charlie ask you for advice.

Exercise 1, continued

Charlie prepared the following trial balance shown below on May 31, 20B. He carefully put the company's accounts in alphabetical order (it seemed like a logical approach to him). All of the company's accounts have normal balances (debit or credit).

Accounts payable	$ 300
Accounts receivable	800
Cash	19,500
Contributed capital	9,300
Maintenance revenue	800
Maintenance supplies	125
Maintenance supplies	50
Notes payable	18,000
Notes receivable	1,000
Prepaid expenses	300
Property, plant and	10,000
Refinishing revenue	150
Retained earnings	3,200
Unearned revenue	200
Utilities expense	175

Prepare an unadjusted trial balance for Reliable Yacht Repair, Inc. as of May 31, 20B.

Exercise 2 (LO 2)

Review the unadjusted trial balance you prepared in Exercise 1. Identify the accounts that might require adjustment at June 30, 20B, and describe what information you would need to determine the nature and amount of the adjusting entry for each of the accounts identified.

Exercise 3 (LO 2)

Prepare adjusting entries, dated September 30, 20B, for each of the following transactions described below. Assume that you are adjusting the related accounts as of the end of the year and that no adjustments have been made since the dates given below.

> **Strategy Suggestion for Parts A through D** – *Deferred Revenues and Expenses*
>
> *Remember that a deferral results when cash is received from a customer before the revenue is earned. The amount is initially recorded as a liability when the company receives the prepayment because the company owes something to its customer. (Debit cash and credit the liability.) As time passes, an adjusting entry is used to record the revenue as it is earned and reduce the liability to the customer. (Debit the liability and credit revenue.) On the other hand, a deferral (or prepayment) also results when cash is paid to a vendor, supplier or other entity before the related expense is incurred (that is, before the goods or services provided by the vendor are actually used). The amount is initially recorded as an asset when the company makes the payment because the company will realize a benefit in the future. (Debit the asset and credit cash.) As time passes, an adjusting entry is used to record the expense as it is incurred and reduce the asset that is being used up. (Debit the expense and credit the asset.)*

Part A

The company had $4,000 of office supplies on hand on October 1, 20A, purchased $6,300 of supplies during the year, and had $1,200 of supplies were on hand on September 30, 20B.

Transaction	Account	Debit	Credit

Exercise 3, continued
Part B

On December 1, 20A, a three-year insurance premium of $27,000 was paid for coverage beginning on that date. The payment was recorded in the prepaid insurance account.

Transaction	Account	Debit	Credit

Part C

A delivery truck was purchased for $33,000 on January 1, 20A. The truck's residual value is estimated at $3,000 at the end of its useful life of 5 years and will be depreciated using the straight-line basis.

Transaction	Account	Debit	Credit

Part D

The company rents some of its unused factory space to a small manufacturer. The lease required an advance payment of $18,000 for six months' rent. The advance payment received from the tenant was recorded as unearned revenue upon receipt on August 1, 20B.

Transaction	Account	Debit	Credit

Strategy Suggestion for Parts E and F – *Accrued Revenues and Expenses*

Remember that an accrual results when a revenue is earned before the cash is received. Depending on the company's accounting system, a routine journal entry to recognize this revenue may not have been recorded. If so, an adjusting entry must be used to record the revenue earned and create the related receivable. (Debit a receivable and credit revenue.) Later, when cash is received, the receivable is reduced. (Debit cash and credit receivable.) On the other hand, an accrual also results when an expense is incurred (that is, a resource obtained is used to generate revenues) before the cash is paid. Again, depending on the company's accounting system, a routine journal entry to recognize this expense may not have been recorded. If so, an adjusting entry must be used to record the expense incurred and create the related liability. (Debit the expense and credit a liability.) Later, when cash is paid, the liability is reduced. (Debit the liability and credit cash.)

Exercise 3, continued
Part E

Employees work five days per week and are paid $75,000 every other Friday. The last payday during the company's fiscal year was Friday, September 26, 20B. The employees continued to work through September 30, 20B, but they will not be paid until Friday, October 10, 20B.

Transaction	Account	Debit	Credit

Part F

The Accounting Department sends bills to customers every Friday and records the revenue earned at that time. The last bills were sent on Friday, September 26, 20B. Services performed on September 29 and 30, 20B, amounted to $29,000. This amount has not been recorded.

Transaction	Account	Debit	Credit

Exercise 4 (LO 2)

Assume that the accountant neglected to analyze the company's accounts and did not prepare any adjusting entries at the end of the year. For each overlooked adjusting entry, first complete the "current year" columns by indicating the effect of the error on the company's assets (A), liabilities (L) and stockholders' equity (SHE) at the end of the year and its net income (NI) for the year. Indicate whether the effect of the error was to overstate (write "over") or understate (write "under") or have no effect (leave blank) on each of the financial statement totals. Then, do the same for the "next year" columns. Assume that the company recorded only "routine" entries during the next year; no one recorded the current year adjustments.

Transaction	Current Year				Next Year			
	A	L	SHE	NI	A	L	SHE	NI
The current year's depreciation on the building, furniture, equipment, delivery vehicles and equipment was not recorded.								
A customer payment made in advance for three months of services during the last month of the year was properly recorded; but no adjustment was made at year-end.								

Exercise 4, continued

Transaction	Current Year				Next Year			
	A	L	SHE	NI	A	L	SHE	NI
The premium paid on a three-month insurance policy during the last month of the current year was properly recorded; no adjustment was made at year-end.								
The entry to record employee wages during the last few days of the year was not recorded; the employees were paid during the next year.								

Exercise 5

You were introduced to Pixar in chapter 3 of this Study Guide. The selected financial information set forth below was taken from the statements of operations (income statements) and balance sheets included in the Forms 10-K that were filed by Pixar with the SEC for fiscal 2001 (year ending December 29, 2001), fiscal 2000 (year ending December 30, 2000) and fiscal 1999 (year ending January 1, 2000). All dollar amounts shown below are in thousands.

	Fiscal 2001	Fiscal 2000	Fiscal 1999
Year ended			
Total revenues	$ 70,223,000	$172,267,000	
Net income (see below)	36,006,000	78,027,000	
As of the end of the year			
Total assets	523,294,000	476,603,000	$374,905,000
Total shareholders' equity	505,686,000	435,720,000	344,443,000

The net income amounts reported above are described as "net income from continuing operations" in Pixar's statements of operations. As reported on Pixar's fiscal 2001 Statement of Operations, the number of shares used in computing "basic net income per share" (or earnings per share) for 2001 and 2000 were 48,276,000 and 47,280,000 respectively.

Part A (LO 3)

Compute Pixar's earnings per share for fiscal 2001 and 2000 using the information set forth above.

Fiscal 2001:

Fiscal 2000:

Exercise 5, continued
Part B (LO 4)

Compute Pixar's net profit margin for fiscal 2001 and 2000 using the information set forth above and interpret the results.

Fiscal 2001:

Fiscal 2000:

Interpretation

Exercise 6 (LO 5)

Assume that Charlie (once again) prepared a trial balance in alphabetical order for Reliance Yacht Repair, Inc. on September 30, 20B, the end of the company's fiscal year.

Accounts payable	$1,500
Accounts receivable	6,000
Accumulated depreciation	2,000
Cash	6,900
Contributed capital	7,800
Insurance expense	500
Interest expense	80
Maintenance revenue	7,500
Maintenance supplies	1,500
Maintenance supplies expense	2,500
Notes payable	2,500
Notes receivable	5,500
Prepaid expenses	500
Property, plant and equipment	4,000
Retained earnings	2,180
Refinishing revenue	3,500
Unearned revenue	2,000
Utilities expense	1,500

Exercise 6, continued
Part A

Prepare closing entries for the company.

Transaction	Account	Debit	Credit

Part B

Post the entries to the retained earnings account.

Retained Earnings

	10/1 2,180

Part C

Prepare a post-closing trial balance.

SOLUTIONS TO SELF-TEST QUESTIONS AND EXERCISES

MATCHING

J	Accrued revenues and expenses	F	Post-Closing Trial Balance
H	Adjusting Entries	E	Prepayments (or Deferred Expenses)
G	Book Value (Net Book Value, Carrying Value)	I	Temporary (Nominal) Accounts
A	Closing Entries	K	Trial Balance
C	Contra-Account	D	Unearned (or Deferred) Revenues
B	Permanent (Real) Accounts		

TRUE-FALSE QUESTIONS

1. F – A trial balance is not a financial statement that is provided to external users; it is simply a tool used by accountants.
2. F – Certain errors (that is, those which do not affect the equality of debits and credits) will not be detected by the preparation of a trial balance.
3. F – Depreciation is a cost allocation process; the amount of depreciation recorded does not represent the decline in the market value of the asset.
4. F – Cost less accumulated depreciation is referred to as the book value, net book value or carrying value of the asset; it does not represent the market value of the asset.
5. T
6. T
7. T
8. T
9. F – A deferral results when a company earns revenue after cash has been exchanged. An accrual results when a company earns revenue before cash has been exchanged.
10. T
11. T
12. F – The income statement should be prepared first.
13. T
14. F – A rising net profit margin ratio indicates that the company is becoming more efficient in managing the company's sales and expenses.
15. T
16. T

MULTIPLE CHOICE QUESTIONS

1.	d	4.	a	7.	b	10.	e
2.	e	5.	d	8.	c	11.	c
3.	e	6.	c	9.	a		

EXERCISES

Exercise 1

Reliable Yacht Repair, Inc.
Unadjusted Trial Balance
at May 31, 20B

Cash	$19,500	
Accounts receivable	800	
Notes receivable	1,000	
Maintenance supplies	125	
Prepaid expenses	300	
Property, plant and equipment	10,000	
Accounts payable		$ 300
Unearned revenue		200
Notes payable		18,000
Contributed capital		9,300
Retained earnings		3,200
Maintenance revenue		800
Refinishing revenue		150
Maintenance supplies expense	50	
Utilities expense	175	
Totals	$31,950	$31,950

Exercise 2

Accounts which might require adjustment and information needed:

- Accounts receivable and maintenance and/or refinishing revenue – Amount of any maintenance and refinishing services that have been performed but not billed or recorded.
- Accumulated depreciation and depreciation expense – Estimated residual values and lives of the property, plant and equipment.
- Maintenance supplies and maintenance supplies expense – Supplies on hand at year-end.
- Prepaid expenses and related expense account(s) – Date of prepayment and length of time until prepayment expires.
- Accounts payable and related expense account(s) – Nature and amount of any unpaid bills and estimates of any unbilled amounts that have not been recorded at year-end.
- Interest payable and expense – Date of note(s), principal amount(s), and interest rate(s).
- Unearned revenue and maintenance and/or refinishing revenue – Amount and type of work performed to date for customer(s) who paid in advance.

Exercise 3

Transaction	Account	Debit	Credit
A	Supplies expense	9,100	
	Supplies		9,100
	$4,000 on hand at beginning of year + $6,300 of supplies purchased – $1,200 on hand at end of period		

Exercise 3, continued

B	Insurance expense	7,500	
	Prepaid insurance		7,500
	$27,000 (premium) x (10 months (Dec. through Sept.) ÷ 36 months (policy term))		
C	Depreciation expense	4,500	
	Accumulated depreciation		4,500
	($33,000 cost − $3,000 residual value) x (9 months (Jan. though Sept.) ÷ 60 months(life in months))		
D	Unearned revenue	6,000	
	Rental revenue		6,000
	$18,000 x (2 months (Aug. and Sept.) ÷ 6 months (term of lease))		
E	Wage expense	15,000	
	Wages payable		15,000
	$75,000 x (2 days (Mon. the 29th and Tues. the 30th) ÷ 10 days (in work week))		
F	Accounts receivable	29,000	
	Service revenue		29,000

Exercise 4

Transaction	Current Year				Next Year			
	A	L	SHE	NI	A	L	SHE	NI
The current year's depreciation on the building, furniture, equipment, delivery vehicles and equipment was not recorded.	Over		Over	Over	Over		Over	
A customer payment made in advance for three months of services during the last month of the year was properly recorded; but no adjustment was made at year-end.		Over	Under	Under		Over	Under	
The premium paid on a three-month insurance policy during the last month of the current year was properly recorded; no adjustment was made at year-end.	Over		Over	Over	Over		Over	

Exercise 4, continued

Transaction	Current Year				Next Year			
	A	L	SHE	NI	A	L	SHE	NI
The entry to record employee wages during the last few days of the year was not recorded; the employees were paid during the next year.		Under	Over	Over				Under

Exercise 5 – Part A

EPS = Net income ÷ Weighted average shares outstanding

Fiscal 2001
$36,006,000 ÷ 48,276,000 = $0.74
Fiscal 2000
$78,027,000 ÷ 47,280,000 = $1.65

Part B

Net Profit Margin = Net income ÷ Net sales
(Since Pixar did not report Net Sales, Total Revenues was used instead.)

Fiscal 2001
$36,006,000 ÷ $70,223,000 = 51.3%
Fiscal 2000
$78,027,000 ÷ $172,267,000 = 45.3%

Interpretation
The net profit margin ratio measures how much of every sales dollar generated during the period is profit. Pixar's increasing net profit margin ratio suggests that the company was more efficient during fiscal 2001 in its management of sales and expenses. Additional analysis of the ratio will provide information about trends in each component of revenues and expenses. A common-sized income statement (in which each line is divided by net sales) would be a useful tool in such analysis. Further information about such changes may be obtained from Pixar's Annual Report.

Exercise 6
Part A

Transaction	Account	Debit	Credit
(1)	Maintenance revenue	7,500	
	Refinishing revenue	3,500	
	Retained earnings		11,000
(2)	Retained earnings	4,580	
	Insurance expense		500
	Interest expense		80
	Maintenance supplies expense		2,500
	Utilities expense		1,500

Exercise 6, continued
Part B

	Retained earnings		
		10/1	2,180
		(1)	11,000
(2)	4,580		
		9/30	8,600

Part C

Reliance Yacht Repair, Inc.
Post-Closing Trial Balance
at September 30, 20B

	Debit	Credit
Cash	$ 6,900	
Accounts receivable	6,000	
Notes receivable	5,500	
Maintenance supplies	1,500	
Prepaid expenses	500	
Property, plant and equipment	4,000	
Accumulated depreciation		$ 2,000
Accounts payable		1,500
Unearned revenue		2,000
Notes payable		2,500
Contributed capital		7,800
Retained earnings		8,600
Totals	$24,400	$24,400

AN IDEA FOR YOUR STUDY TEAM

Get together with the other members of your study team. Each person should select a well-known company from a different industry (such as fast food, airlines, publishing, manufacturing, etc.). Individually, think of two or three transactions that your company might enter into which fall into each of the four adjustment categories listed below:

- **Prepayments** – Pay cash now, record expense later

- **Deferred revenues** – Receive cash now, record revenues later

- **Accrued expenses** – Record expense now, pay cash later

- **Accrued revenues** – Record revenue now, receive cash later

Get back together with the other members of your study team and compare your transactions. Were all of the transactions that you thought of correctly categorized?

CHAPTER 5
COMMUNICATING AND INTERPRETING ACCOUNTING INFORMATION

ORGANIZATION OF THE CHAPTER

Players in the Accounting Communication Process	The Disclosure Process	A Closer Look at Financial Statement Formats and Notes	ROE Analysis: A Framework for Evaluating Company Performance
• Managers (CEO, CFO, and Accounting Staff) • Auditors • Information Intermediaries: Analysts and Information Services • Government Regulators • Users: Institutional and Private Investors, Creditors, and Others • Guiding Principles for Communicating Useful Information	• Press Releases • Annual Reports • Quarterly Reports • SEC Reports – 10K, 10Q, 8K	• Classified Balance Sheet • Classified Income Statement • Statement of Stockholders' Equity • Statement of Cash Flows • Notes to Financial Statements • Voluntary Disclosures • Constraints of Accounting Measurement	• ROE Profit Driver Analysis • Profit Drivers and Business Strategy

CHAPTER FOCUS SUGGESTIONS

Overview

The conceptual framework of accounting underlies and guides the coverage in this chapter. After contrasting the roles of preparers and users of financial information, the various methods of disclosing accounting information are described. Then, after detailing the components of each of the four financial statements, general overviews of the nature of the notes to the financial statements and other voluntary disclosures are provided. The chapter concludes with an in-depth discussion of the use of the return on equity ratio to assess performance.

Accounting Communication Process

As you read about the various players involved in the accounting communication process, pay attention to the roles that each group plays and the standards that provide guidance to these groups. Note that accounting information must be relevant and reliable to be useful to any of the user groups. Both of these characteristics are important. Accounting information provided to users is relevant if it is capable of influencing decisions made by users. Accounting information is reliable if it is accurate, unbiased and verifiable. Users may make bad decisions if the accounting information that is used during the decision-making process is not relevant and/or is unreliable. The disclosure process is the process by which accounting information is provided to user groups. As you read about the various methods used to provide accounting information, note which methods are required and which are optional.

Financial Statement Formats and Notes

You may be surprised to discover that different financial statement and disclosure formats are in use. Note, however, that the various formats are indeed consistent with the broad principles discussed in this chapter. The classified balance sheet and classified income statement are covered in detail in this chapter. Make sure that you understand the criteria used to classify assets and liabilities on the balance sheet. You should practice preparing the portion of the income statement that relates to continuing operations using the multiple-step format. In addition to gaining an understanding of the terminology that relates to the other three sections of the income statement (that is, discontinued operations, extraordinary items and cumulative effects of changes in accounting method), you should know how to incorporate such items into a classified income statement. This section of the chapter also provides an overview of the notes (footnotes) to the financial statements. The notes provide additional details about the information set forth in the financial statements and facilitate analysis. Familiarize yourself with each of the three categories of notes.

Financial Statement Analysis Matters

In addition to knowing how to compute the return on equity (ROE) ratio, you should able to define and calculate each of its three components: net profit margin, asset turnover (efficiency) and financial leverage. Take the time to gain an understanding of what is being measured by the ROE ratio and each of its three factors. You will be expected to explain the results and make recommendations for improvement.

LEARNING OBJECTIVES

After studying this chapter, you should be able to:

(LO 1) Recognize the people involved in the accounting communication process (managers, auditors, information intermediaries, government regulators, and users), their roles in the process, and the guidance they receive from legal and professional standards.

(LO 2) Identify the steps in the accounting communication process, including the issuance of press releases, annual reports, quarterly reports, and SEC filings as well as the role of electronic information services in this process.

(LO 3) Recognize and apply the different financial statement and disclosure formats used by companies in practice.

(LO 4) Analyze a company's performance based on return on equity and its components.

READ AND RECALL QUESTIONS

After you read each section of the chapter, answer the related Read and Recall Questions below.

BUSINESS BACKGROUND

Why do Callaway Golf executives value integrity in the communication of financial results? What benefits are realized?

LEARNING OBJECTIVE

After studying this section of the chapter, you should be able to:

1. Recognize the people involved in the accounting communication process (managers, auditors, information intermediaries, government regulators, and users), their roles in the process, and the guidance they receive from legal and professional standards.

PLAYERS IN THE ACCOUNTING COMMUNICATION PROCESS
MANAGERS (CEO, CFO, AND ACCOUNTING STAFF)

Which two officers of the company are primarily responsible for the information in the financial statements and related disclosures? What is their legal responsibility with regards to financial reporting? What do the members of the accounting staff do and what is their responsibility in this regard?

AUDITORS

When a CPA firm signs an unqualified, or clean, audit opinion, what responsibility does the CPA firm assume with regards to the financial statements that were audited? Why is the risk to the private investors and financial institutions lowered when a company's financial statements are audited? What benefits does the company realize?

INFORMATION INTERMEDIARIES: ANALYSTS AND INFORMATION SERVICES
Financial Analysts

How do financial analysts analyze the information that they gather about a given company? What predictions do they make? What decisions do they make based on these predictions? What information is normally included in reports written by financial analysts?

Information Services

How do companies file forms with the SEC? How can users easily retrieve these forms?

FINANCIAL ANALYSIS
INFORMATION SERVICES: USES IN MARKETING, CLASSWORK, AND JOB SEARCH

How might sales representatives use the information provided by electronic information services? How might students make use of such information? How would this information be useful in a job interview?

GOVERNMENT REGULATORS

What government agency sets additional reporting standards for firms with publicly traded debt or equity securities? What functions does this agency perform with regards to reports filed by such companies?

USERS: INSTITUTIONAL AND PRIVATE INVESTORS, CREDITORS, AND OTHERS

What groups are considered to be institutional investors? How do private investors differ from institutional investors? What is the primary external user group for financial statements of private companies?

QUESTION OF ETHICS
CONFLICTING INTERESTS OF MANAGERS, STOCKHOLDERS, AND CREDITORS

How do the economic interests of managers, stockholders and creditors differ? How are these differing interests kept in check?

Why do customers, suppliers and competitors make use of financial information about a company? What is the cost-benefit constraint?

GUIDING PRINCIPLES FOR COMMUNICATING USEFUL INFORMATION

What is *relevant* information? What is *reliable* information? What is meant by *consistent* information? What is meant by *comparable* information?

LEARNING OBJECTIVE

After studying this section of the chapter, you should be able to:

2. Identify the steps in the accounting communication process, including the issuance of press releases, annual reports, quarterly reports, and SEC filings as well as the role of electronic information services in
    this process.

THE DISCLOSURE PROCESS
PRESS RELEASES

Why do companies use press releases? What are unexpected earnings? How does the stock market react when actual earnings are published?

ANNUAL REPORTS

What are the three components of annual reports issued by privately held companies? What types of information are included in the *nonfinancial* section of the annual reports of public companies?

What are the eight principal components of the *financial* section of the annual reports of public companies? What information is set forth in the Management Discussion and Analysis section of such reports?

QUARTERLY REPORTS

How do quarterly reports differ from annual reports?

SEC REPORTS – 10-K, 10-Q, 8-K

What reports must be filed by public companies with the SEC? How does a Form 10-K differ from an annual report? What is a Form 10-Q Quarterly Report? What is reported on a Form 8-K Current Report?

LEARNING OBJECTIVE

After studying this section of the chapter, you should be able to:

3. Recognize and apply the different financial statement and disclosure formats used by companies in practice.

A CLOSER LOOK AT FINANCIAL STATEMENT FORMATS AND NOTES
CLASSIFIED BALANCE SHEET

How does a classified balance sheet differ from one that is not classified? How are assets ordered on a classified balance sheet? How are liabilities ordered?

What are the characteristics of assets that are categorized as property, plant and equipment? How is book value (or net book value) determined? What are intangible assets? What types of intangible assets are *not* reflected on the balance sheet? Why aren't these intangible assets reported on the balance sheet?

What is expected if the Deferred Taxes account is classified as an asset? What if it is classified as a liability?

What are the two accounts that often comprise a company's contributed capital?

What is par value? What does par value establish? When a corporation (such as Callaway Golf) issues stock at the market price, what amount is reported as Common Stock? What account is used to keep track of the difference between the issuance price and the par value of the stock issued? What other names are used for this account?

What are the three additional types of gains or losses that are included in the account Other Accumulated Comprehensive Income?

FINANCIAL ANALYSIS
BALANCE SHEET RATIOS AND DEBT CONTRACTS

How is the current ratio computed? What does the current ratio measure? How is a company's debt-to-equity ratio determined? What does the debt-to-equity ratio measure?

CLASSIFIED INCOME STATEMENT

What are two common titles for the income statement? What are the five major sections of a multiple step income statement?

Continuing Operations

What is cost of goods sold? How is gross profit (or gross margin) determined?

What are operating expenses? How is Income from Operations (or Operating Income) determined?

What are nonoperating (other) items? How is Income before Income Taxes (or Pretax Earnings) determined?

Non-Recurring Items

What are discontinued operations? What are extraordinary items? What is presented by the Cumulative Effects of Changes in Accounting Methods?

Earnings per Share

How is the amount of earnings per share computed (assuming a simple capital structure)? What must be displayed when non-recurring items are reported on the income statement?

FINANCIAL ANALYSIS
ACCOUNTING-BASED EXECUTIVE BONUSES

How does Callaway Golf compensate its five executive officers?

STATEMENT OF STOCKHOLDERS' EQUITY

What is reported on the statement of stockholders' equity?

STATEMENT OF CASH FLOWS

What are the three classifications of cash flows on the statement of cash flows? What are the two methods for reporting cash from operations?

FOCUS ON CASH FLOWS–OPERATING ACTIVITIES (INDIRECT METHOD)

Why is the amount of net income reported usually different than the amount of cash flows from operations? What information is provided when the indirect method is used to prepare the cash flows from operations section of the statement of cash flows?

NOTES TO FINANCIAL STATEMENTS

What are the three categories of notes (footnotes) to the financial statements?

FINANCIAL ANALYSIS
ALTERNATIVE ACCOUNTING METHODS AND GAAP

When more than one acceptable accounting method exists, what does GAAP permit? How is the task of a user of financial statements complicated as a result?

Additional Detail Supporting Reported Numbers

What are some of the types of data reported as supplemental information in the financial statements?

Relevant Financial Information not Disclosed on the Statements

What other types of information impacts the company financially but is not shown on the financial statements?

VOLUNTARY DISCLOSURES

Do companies, such as Callaway, tend to disclose only the minimum level of required financial disclosures?

CONSTRAINTS OF ACCOUNTING MEASUREMENT

How do accountants decide if an item is material or immaterial? What is required by the conservatism constraint? What does this guideline attempt to offset? How might the industry that a company operates in affect its reporting requirements?

LEARNING OBJECTIVE
After studying this section of the chapter, you should be able to:
4. Analyze a company's performance based on return on equity and its components.

RETURN ON EQUITY ANALYSIS: A FRAMEWORK FOR EVALUATING COMPANY PERFORMANCE
KEY RATIO ANALYSIS: RETURN ON EQUITY

What are two other names for the return on equity (ROE) ratio? How is return on equity (ROE) computed? What does this ratio measure? In the long run, with all other things equal, what is expected with regards to firms with higher ROE? If a company stops its investment in research and development or fails to modernize its plant equipment, how would its ROE be affected? What might be the long-term consequences of such a strategy?

ROE PROFIT DRIVER ANALYSIS

What analysis method is used to break down ROE into its three factors? What are the three factors? Why are these factors called profit drivers or profit levers?

What does the net profit margin ratio measure? How is it computed? What does the asset turnover (efficiency) ratio measure? How is it computed? What does the financial leverage ratio measure? How is it computed?

ROE Profit Driver Analysis
Exhibit 5.7

Complete top row of boxes by: (1) inserting the names of each of the three ROE factors in the top row of boxes and (2) writing out the related formulas in the bottom row of boxes.

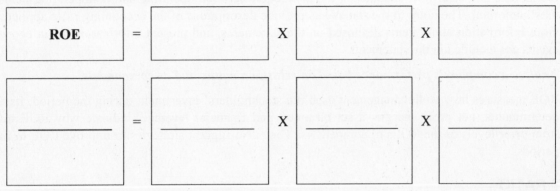

PROFIT DRIVERS AND BUSINESS STRATEGY

What are the two business strategies followed by successful manufacturers?

CHAPTER TAKE-AWAYS

1. *Recognize the people involved in the accounting communication process (managers, auditors, information intermediaries, government regulators, and users), their roles in the process, and the guidance they receive from legal and professional standards.*

   Management of the reporting company must decide on the appropriate format (categories) and level of detail to present in its financial reports. Independent audits increase the credibility of the information. Financial statement announcements from public companies usually are first transmitted to users through electronic information services. The SEC staff reviews public financial reports for compliance with legal and professional standards, investigates irregularities, and punishes violators. Analysts play a major role in making financial statement and other information available to average investors through their stock recommendations and earnings forecasts.

2. *Identify the steps in the accounting communication process, including the issuance of press releases, annual reports, quarterly reports, and SEC filings as well as the role of electronic information services in this process.*

   Earnings are first made public in press releases. Companies follow these announcements with annual and quarterly reports containing statements, notes, and additional information. Public companies must file additional reports with the SEC, including the 10-K, 10-Q, and 8-K, which contain more details about the company. Electronic information services are the key source of dissemination of this information to sophisticated users.

3. **Recognize and apply the different financial statement and disclosure formats used by companies in practice.**

Most statements are classified and include subtotals that are relevant to analysis. On the balance sheet, the most important distinctions are between current and noncurrent assets and liabilities. On the income and cash flow statements, the distinction between operating and nonoperating items are most important. The notes to the statements provide descriptions of the accounting rules applied, add more information about items disclosed on the statements, and present information about economic events not included in the statements.

4. **Analyze a company's performance based on return on equity and its components.**

ROE measures how well management used the stockholders' investment during the period. Its three determinants, net profit margin, asset turnover, and financial leverage, indicate why ROE differs from prior levels or the ROEs of competitors. They also suggest strategies to improve ROE in future periods.

KEY RATIO

Return on equity (ROE) measures how much the firm earned for each dollar of stockholders' investment. It is computed as follows:

Return on Equity = Net income ÷ Average Stockholders' Equity

Average stockholders' equity is determined as follows:

Average Stockholders' Equity =
  (Stockholders' Equity, beginning of the year + Stockholders' Equity, end of year) ÷ 2

FINDING FINANCIAL INFORMATION

Balance Sheet
Key Classifications
Current and non-current assets and liabilities
Contributed capital and retained earnings

Income Statement
Key Subtotals
Gross profit
Income from operations
Net income
Earnings per share

Statement of Cash Flows
Under Operating Activities (Indirect Method)
Net income
± Differences between net income and cash provided by operating activities
= Cash provided by operating activities

Notes
Key Classifications
Descriptions of accounting rules applied in the statements
Additional detail supporting reported numbers
Relevant financial information not disclosed on the statements

SELF-TEST QUESTIONS AND EXERCISES

MATCHING

This table sets forth the key terms introduced in this chapter. Match each key term with the appropriate definition by inserting the letter that corresponds to that definition.

____ Accumulated Other Comprehensive
     Information
____ Comparable Information
____ Conservatism
____ Consistent Information
____ Cost-Benefit Constraint
____ Cumulative Effects of Changes in Accounting
     Methods
____ Discontinued Operations
____ Earnings Forecasts
____ Extraordinary Items
____ Form 8-K
____ Form 10-K
____ Form 10-Q

____ Gross Profit (Gross Margin)
____ Income before Income Taxes (Pretax
     Earnings)
____ Income From Operations (Operating Income)
____ Institutional Investors
____ Lenders (Creditors)
____ Material Amounts
____ Paid-in Capital
____ Par Value
____ Press Release
____ Private Investors
____ Relevant Information
____ Reliable Information
____ Unqualified (Clean) Audit Opinion

A. Suggests that the benefits of accounting for and reporting information should outweigh the costs.
B. Gains and losses that are both unusual in nature and infrequent in occurrence; they are reported net of tax on the income statement.
C. The amount of contributed capital less the par value of the stock; also called Additional Paid-in Capital, Contributed Capital in Excess of Par, Paid-in Capital.
D. Suppliers and financial institutions that lend money to companies.
E. Predictions of earnings for future accounting periods.
F. Financial results from the disposal of a major segment of the business and are reported net of income tax effects.
G. Information that can be compared across businesses because similar accounting methods have been applied.
H. The annual report that publicly traded companies must file with the SEC.
I. Information that can be compared over time because similar accounting methods have been applied.
J. Net unrealized gains or losses on securities, net minimum pension liability adjustments, and net foreign currency translation adjustment, which are directly credited or debited to the stockholders' equity account.
K. The report used by publicly traded companies to disclose any material event not previously reported.
L. Information that is accurate, unbiased, and verifiable.
M. Suggests that care should be taken not to overstate assets and revenues or understate liabilities and expenses.
N. The quarterly report that publicly traded companies must file with the SEC.
O. Auditors' statement that the financial statements are fair presentations in all material respects in conformity with GAAP.
P. Net sales less cost of goods sold.
Q. Individuals who purchase shares in companies.

R. Revenues less all expenses except income tax expense.

S. Amounts that are large enough to influence a user's decision.

T. Equals net sales less cost of goods sold and other operating expenses.

U. A legal amount per share established by the board of directors; it establishes the minimum amount a stockholder must contribute and has no relationship to the market price of the stock.

V. A written public news announcement that is normally distributed to major news services.

W. Amounts reflected on the income statement for adjustments made to balance sheet accounts when applying different accounting principles.

X. Information that can influence a decision; it is timely and has predictive and/or feedback value.

Y. Managers of pension, mutual, endowment, and other funds that invest on the behalf of others.

TRUE-FALSE QUESTIONS

For each of the following, enter a T or F in the blank to indicate whether the statement is true or false.

___1. (LO 1) The primary responsibility for the information presented in a company's financial statements lies with the company's auditors.

___2. (LO 1) Only public companies go to the expense of having audited financial statements prepared.

___3. (LO 1) Institutional investors usually employ their own analysts; private investors often rely on the advice of information intermediaries or turn their money over to institutional investors.

___4. (LO 1) Each year, Congress updates the "additional reporting standards" for public companies.

___5. (LO 2) The annual reports of public companies are significantly more elaborate than those of private companies solely as a result of additional SEC reporting requirements.

___6. (LO 2) Any material event not previously reported in the 10-Q or 10-K is reported on the 8-K.

___7. (LO 3) Assets classified as property, plant and equipment, like most other assets, are usually held for resale or investment and will eventually be turned into cash.

___8. (LO 3) Intangible assets have no tangible substance and are not reported on the balance sheet.

___9. (LO 3) Capital in excess of par is also referred to as additional paid-in capital, contributed capital in excess of par, or paid-in capital.

___10. (LO 3) There is no difference in the individual revenue, expense, gain, and loss items reported using each of the two different formats available to present the results of continuing operations.

___11. (LO 3) Gross profit is calculated by subtracting the cost of providing services to customers from the revenues earned by providing those services.

___12. (LO 3) The results of all segments of the business disposed of prior to the beginning of the year covered by the income statement must be separately reported, net of tax, on the income statement.

___13. (LO 3) GAAP often permits more than one accounting method for use in the computation of the amount reported for selected line items on the financial statements.

___14. (LO 3) A change in accounting principles results in an inconsistent application of accounting methods; as such, footnote disclosure is necessary.

___15. (LO 3) Information may be relevant but not reliable.

___16. (LO 3) Immaterial amounts do not have to conform to GAAP or be separately reported because such amounts would not influence users' decisions.

___17. (LO 3) Conservative accountants tend to choose accounting methods that understate assets and revenues and overstate liabilities and expenses.

___18. (LO 4) In the long run, companies with higher ROE are expected to have higher stock prices than companies with lower ROE, all other things equal.

___19. (LO 4) Strategies that increase ROE in the short run may result in future declines in ROE.

___20. (LO 4) Net profit margin measures how many sales dollars are generated per dollar of assets.

___21. (LO 4) Successful companies following a low-cost strategy usually produce high ROE with higher asset turnover and higher leverage to make up for lower net profit margin.

MULTIPLE CHOICE QUESTIONS

Choose the best answer or response by placing the identifying letter in the space provided.

___1. (LO 1) The primary responsibility for the information reported by a company rests with

    a. the company's auditors.
    b. accountants who prepared the information.
    c. SEC.
    d. company's management.
    e. the Board of Directors.

___2. (LO 1) Many privately owned companies have their financial statements audited because

    a. it is required by the SEC.
    b. they will eventually be public companies.
    c. the audit opinion lends credibility to the information presented.
    d. lenders and private investors often require this.
    e. both (c) and (d).

___3. (LO 1) The government regulatory agency that sets and enforces reporting standards for public companies is the

    a. SEC.
    b. Congress.
    c. FASB.
    d. Senate.
    e. AICPA.

___4. (LO 1) The cost to produce and report financial information must not exceed

    a. the benefit gained from the disclosure.
    b. a certain percentage of net income.
    c. the company's revenues.
    d. an amount set by the FASB.
    e. none of the above; all information must be reported.

___5. (LO 1) To be useful, information must be:

    a. relevant.
    b. reliable.
    c. extraordinary.
    d. comprehensive.
    e. both a and b above.

___6. (LO 1) Relevant information is information

   a. that people want to know.
   b. about current activities only.
   c. capable of influencing decisions.
   d. that management feels is necessary to disclose.
   e. approved for release by the Board of Directors.

___7. (LO 1) Accurate, unbiased and verifiable information is information that is

   a. audited
   b. reliable
   c. relevant
   d. public
   e. consistent

___8. (LO 1) Similar accounting methods must be applied by businesses in order for their respective financial information to be

   a. publishable.
   b. reliable.
   c. relevant.
   d. comparable.
   e. cost beneficial.

___9. (LO 1) Consistent information is information that

   a. can be compared across businesses.
   b. is capable of influencing decisions.
   c. can be compared over time within a company.
   d. is accurate, unbiased, and verifiable.
   e. never changes.

___10. (LO 2) Firms with publicly traded debt or equity securities are required to file the following reports with the SEC:

   a. Form 8-Q Current Report.
   b. Form 10-K Annual Report.
   c. Form 10-Q Quarterly Report.
   d. both (b) and (c).
   e. all of the above.

___11. (LO 3) Net book value or carrying value:

   a. is computed by subtracting accumulated depreciation from the initial cost of the operational asset.
   b. measures the current market value of the operational asset.
   c. represents the cost that has been apportioned to expense.
   d. represents the historical cost of the company's fixed assets.
   e. All of the above.

___12. (LO 3) The par value of stock is

    a. what the first person who bought the shares paid for them.
    b. an arbitrary number set by the company meaning nothing to accountants.
    c. the approximate amount the company expects to realize for newly issued stock.
    d. a legal term, setting a value below which the stock cannot be sold.
    e. equal to contributed capital.

___13. (LO 3) Gross profit, or gross margin, is

    a. the same as net income.
    b. equal to income before taxes.
    c. another word for revenues
    d. equal to income before extraordinary items.
    e. sales less cost of goods sold.

___14. (LO 3) Information relating to a company's sales to customers in Europe would most likely

    a. not be found in the annual report.
    b. be disclosed in a footnote to the financial statements.
    c. be reported on the income statement.
    d. be discussed only in the management discussion and analysis section of the annual report.
    e. be reported on the balance sheet.

___15. (LO 3) The _____ constraint requires that care be taken to avoid overstating revenues and assets.

    a. materiality
    b. cost-benefit
    c. relevancy
    d. conservatism
    e. full disclosure

___16. (LO 4) Return on equity (ROE) may be calculated as:

    a. net income divided by average stockholders' equity.
    b. net income divided by net sales times net sales divided by average total assets times average total assets divided by average stockholders' equity.
    c. net profit margin times asset turnover times financial leverage.
    d. both (b) and (c) above.
    e. all of the above.

EXERCISES

Record your answer to each exercise in the space provided. Show your work.

Exercise 1 (LO 3)

The following is a list of financial statement items and amounts from a recent income statement and balance sheet of Basic Corporation. Assume that the cumulative effect of change in accounting principle shown below caused the company's net income to be higher than it would have otherwise been this year. All of the other items have normal debit and credit balances. The company closed its books on December

31, 20A. For each financial statement item listed, indicate whether it appears on the income statement or balance sheet. The first item has been completed as an example.

Financial Statement Item	Amount	Income Statement	Balance Sheet
Accounts payable	$ 41,000		X
Accounts receivable	262,000		
Accrued expenses payable	37,000		
Accumulated depreciation	128,000		
Bonds payable	51,000		
Cash and cash equivalents	125,000		
Common stock	150,000		
Contributed capital in excess of par	20,000		
Cost of goods sold	350,000		
Cumulative effect of change in accounting principle, net of income tax	11,000		
Extraordinary gain, net of income tax	32,000		
General and administrative expenses	75,000		
Interest income	10,000		
Intangible assets	85,000		
Inventory	167,000		
Lease obligations	124,000		
Net sales	900,000		
Notes and mortgages payable	258,000		
Other assets	15,000		
Other current assets	5,000		
Other short-term liabilities	89,000		
Prepaid expenses	31,000		
Property, plant and equipment	312,000		
Provision for income taxes	32,000		
Research and development costs	250,000		
Retained earnings	161,000		
Selling expenses	125,000		
Short-term investments	57,000		

Exercise 2 (LO 3)

Using the information provided in Exercise 1, prepare in good form a multiple-step income statement (showing gross profit, income from operations and income from continuing operations) for the year ended December 31, 20A.

Exercise 3 (LO 3)

Using the information provided in Exercise 1, prepare in good form a classified balance sheet as of December 31, 20A.

Exercise 4 (LO 3)

Review the income statement and balance sheet that you prepared in Exercises 2 and 3. What other disclosures are commonly made on the face of these financial statements?

Exercise 5 (LO 4)

Basic's total assets and total stockholders' equity at the beginning of 20A were $876,000 and $152,000, respectively. Using this information and the income statement that you prepared in Exercise 2, compute Basic's ROE. Then, interpret the meaning of Basic's ROE by comparison to that of Microsoft, the company featured in the Demonstration Problem at the end of Chapter 5 in the textbook.

Strategy Suggestion for Exercise 5

The ROE ratio can be used to evaluate how well management has used the stockholders' investment during the period. ROE profit driver analysis indicates the sources of a company's ROE by breaking down ROE into three factors. Your interpretation of Basic's ROE will be more meaningful if you use the information provided by this approach. Accordingly, you should perform the ROE profit driver analysis as part of your calculation of Basic's ROE.

Calculations:

Interpretation:

Exercise 6 (LO 3)

Determine the missing amounts in each of the following independent cases.

	Case A	Case B	Case C	Case D
Administrative expenses	$ 25,000	$ 90,000	$?	$?
Cost of goods sold	50,000	?	55,000	125,000
Gross margin	?	300,000	100,000	?
Income before income taxes	?	100,000	?	?
Income tax expense	15,000	?	?	10,000
Net income	?	70,000	35,000	?
Total operating expenses	?	?	50,000	100,000
Sales revenue	125,000	600,000	?	250,000
Selling expenses	10,000	?	15,000	35,000

Strategy Suggestion for Exercise 6

Instead of using equations to determine the unknown amounts, reorganize the table so that it more closely resembles a multi-step income statement.

SOLUTIONS TO SELF-TEST QUESTIONS AND EXERCISES

MATCHING

_J_	Accumulated Other Comprehensive Information	_P_	Gross Profit (Gross Margin)
_G_	Comparable Information	_R_	Income before Income Taxes (Pretax Earnings)
_M_	Conservatism	_T_	Income From Operations (Operating Income)
_I_	Consistent Information	_Y_	Institutional Investors
_A_	Cost-Benefit Constraint	_D_	Lenders (Creditors)
_W_	Cumulative Effects of Changes in Accounting Methods	_S_	Material Amounts
		_C_	Paid-in Capital
_F_	Discontinued Operations	_U_	Par Value
_E_	Earnings Forecasts	_V_	Press Release
_B_	Extraordinary Items	_Q_	Private Investors
_K_	Form 8-K	_X_	Relevant Information
_H_	Form 10-K	_L_	Reliable Information
_N_	Form 10-Q	_O_	Unqualified (Clean) Audit Opinion

TRUE-FALSE QUESTIONS

1. F – The primary responsibility for the information presented in a company's financial statements lies with *management* as represented by the highest officer in the company and the highest officer associated with the financial and accounting side of the business.

2. F – While companies with publicly traded debt or equity securities are required to file audited financial statements with the SEC, many privately owned companies choose to have their financial statements audited.

3. T

4. F – The *SEC* sets additional reporting standards for firms with publicly traded debt or equity securities.

5. F – The annual reports of public companies are significantly more elaborate, both because of additional SEC reporting requirements *and* the fact that many companies use their annual reports as public relations tools to communicate nonaccounting information to shareholders, customers, the press, and others.

6. T

7. F – The property, plant and equipment asset category includes tangible assets that are acquired for use in operating the business; such assets are not usually held for resale or investment.

8. F – Although internally developed intangible assets are not reported on the balance sheet of a company because there is no identifiable transaction (not because there is no tangible substance to these assets), material intangible assets purchased from others *are* reported on the balance sheet.

9. T

10. T

11. F – Merchandisers and manufacturers (not service providers) report gross profit as the difference between net sales and cost of goods sold.

12. F – The results of all segments of the business that were disposed of *during* the accounting period covered by the income statement must be separately reported, net of tax, on the face of the income statement.

13. T

14. T
15. T
16. T
17. T
18. T
19. T
20. F – Net profit margin measures how much of every sales dollar is profit; asset turnover (efficiency) measures how much of every sales dollar the company generates with each dollar of assets.
21. T

MULTIPLE CHOICE QUESTIONS

1. d	5. e	9. c	13. e
2. e	6. c	10. d	14. b
3. a	7. b	11. a	15. d
4. a	8. d	12. d	16. e

EXERCISES

Exercise 1

Financial Statement Item	Amount	Income Statement	Balance Sheet
Accounts payable	$ 41,000		X
Accounts receivable	262,000		X
Accrued expenses payable	37,000		X
Accumulated depreciation	128,000		X
Bonds payable	51,000		X
Cash and cash equivalents	125,000		X
Common stock	150,000		X
Contributed capital in excess of par	20,000		X
Cost of goods sold	350,000	X	
Cumulative effect of change in accounting principle, net of income tax	11,000	X	
Extraordinary gain, net of income tax	32,000	X	
General and administrative expenses	75,000	X	
Interest income	10,000	X	
Intangible assets	85,000		X
Inventory	167,000		X
Lease obligations	124,000		X
Net sales	900,000	X	
Notes and mortgages payable	258,000		X
Other assets	15,000		X
Other current assets	5,000		X
Other short-term liabilities	89,000		X
Prepaid expenses	31,000		X

Exercise 1, continued

Financial Statement Item	Amount	Income Statement	Balance Sheet
Property, plant and equipment	312,000		X
Provision for income taxes	32,000	X	
Research and development costs	250,000	X	
Retained earnings	161,000		X
Selling expenses	125,000	X	
Short-term investments	57,000		X

Exercise 2

Basic Corporation
Income Statement
for the year ended December 31, 20A

Net sales	$900,000
Cost of goods sold	350,000
Gross profit (or gross margin)	550,000
Operating expenses:	
General and administrative expenses	75,000
Selling expenses	125,000
Research and development costs	250,000
Total operating expenses	450,000
Income from operations	100,000
Nonoperating income and expenses:	
Interest income	10,000
Income before income taxes	110,000
Provision for income taxes	32,000
Income from continuing operations	78,000
Extraordinary gain, net of income tax	32,000
Income before cumulative effect of change in accounting principle, net of income tax	110,000
Cumulative effect of change in accounting principle, net of income tax	11,000
Net income	$121,000

Exercise 3

Basic Corporation
Balance Sheet
December 31, 20A

Assets

Current assets:

Cash and cash equivalents		$125,000
Short-term investments		57,000
Accounts receivable		262,000
Inventory		167,000
Prepaid expenses		31,000
Other current assets		5,000
Total current assets		647,000
Property, plant and equipment	$312,000	
Less accumulated depreciation	128,000	184,000
Intangible assets		85,000
Other assets		15,000
Total Assets		$931,000

Liabilities

Current liabilities:

Accounts payable	$ 41,000	
Accrued expenses payable	37,000	
Other short-term liabilities	89,000	
Total current liabilities		$167,000
Notes and mortgages payable		258,000
Lease obligations		124,000
Bonds payable		51,000
Total liabilities		600,000

Stockholders' equity

Common stock		150,000
Contributed capital in excess of par		20,000
Retained earnings		161,000
Total stockholders' equity		331,000
Total liabilities and stockholders' equity		$931,000

Exercise 4

The following disclosures are commonly found on the face of the income statement and balance sheet:

- Earnings per share should follow net income on the income statement.
- Any company that reports discontinued operations, extraordinary items, or cumulative effect of changes in accounting methods must also display these effects on a per share basis on the income statement.
- Information about the par value of the common stock, the number of shares that the company is authorized to issue and the number of shares issued and outstanding is commonly disclosed on the face of the balance sheet.

Exercise 5

	Basic	**Microsoft***
Detailed Calculations for Basic Corporation:		

Net Profit Margin

Net Income ÷ Net Sales
$121,000 ÷ $900,000 → 0.13 | 0.29

x Asset Turnover (Efficiency)

Net Sales ÷ Average Total Assets
$900,000 ÷ [($931,000 + $876,000) ÷ 2] → 1.00 | 0.46

x Financial Leverage

Average Total Assets ÷ Average Stockholders' Equity
[($931,000 + $876,000) ÷ 2] ÷ [($331,000 + $152,000) ÷ 2] → 3.74 | 1.25

= Return on Investment (ROE)

Net Income ÷ Average Stockholders' Equity
$121,000 ÷ [($331,000 + $152,000) ÷ 2] → 0.50 | 0.17

* Ratios are from Part 2 of the Suggested Solution to Demonstration Case at the end of Chapter 5 in your textbook.

Interpretation

ROE measures how well management used the stockholders' investment during the year. For the year ended December 31, 20A, Basic's stockholders earned a ROE of 50%. For the year ended June 30, 2001, Microsoft's shareholders earned a ROE of 17%. Basic earned 50¢ of net income for every dollar of stockholders' equity while Microsoft earned only 17¢ per dollar of stockholders' equity. While Basic's ROE is indeed higher than Microsoft's, a ROE profit driver analysis reveals additional information.

Basic generated a much lower net profit margin than Microsoft. Basic earned 13¢ of net income for every dollar of sales while Microsoft earned 29¢ on the sales dollar. Basic could improve its net profit margin by increasing sales volume, increasing sales price and/or decreasing expenses.

Basic achieved a higher asset turnover (efficiency) compared to Microsoft. Basic generated $1 of sales per dollar of assets, whereas Microsoft generated $0.46 of sales for each dollar invested in assets. Microsoft could improve its asset turnover (efficiency) by increasing sales volume and/or decreasing its less productive assets.

Finally, Basic's financial leverage ratio indicates that its capital is primarily debt based; it employs $3.74 of assets for each dollar of stockholders' investment. Microsoft's capital is primarily equity based; it has $1.25 of assets for each dollar of stockholders' equity. Basic relies heavily on financial leverage. If the company reduces its financial leverage (by decreasing its borrowings or issuing stock), the risk to stockholders would be reduced if Basic experiences a particularly bad year in the future.

Note: To better understand Basic's business strategy, a comparison of this year's profit drivers with those of the last two to three years should also be performed.

Exercise 6

	Case A	Case B	Case C	Case D
Sales revenue	$125,000	$600,000	**$155,000**	$250,000
Cost of goods sold	50,000	**300,000**	55,000	125,000
Gross margin	**75,000**	300,000	100,000	**125,000**
Administrative expenses	25,000	90,000	**35,000**	65,000
Selling expenses	10,000	**110,000**	15,000	35,000
Total operating expenses	**35,000**	**200,000**	50,000	100,000
Income before income taxes	**40,000**	100,000	**50,000**	25,000
Income tax expense	15,000	**30,000**	**15,000**	10,000
Net income	**$ 25,000**	**$ 70,000**	$ 35,000	**$ 15,000**

AN IDEA FOR YOUR STUDY TEAM

Arrange a tour of your school's library or learning resource center for the members of your study team. Determine which types of electronic information services are available and how you might use these services.

ORGANIZATION OF THE CHAPTER

Accounting for Sales Revenue	Measuring and Reporting Receivables	Reporting and Safeguarding Cash
• Credit Card Sales to Consumers • Sales Discounts to Businesses • Sales Returns and Allowances • Reporting Net Sales	• Classifying Receivables • Accounting for Bad Debts • Reporting Accounts Receivable and Bad Debts • Estimating Bad Debts • Receivables Turnover Ratio • Control over Accounts Receivable	• Cash and Cash Equivalents Defined • Cash Management • Internal Control of Cash • Reconciliation of Cash Accounts and Bank Statements

CHAPTER FOCUS SUGGESTIONS

Overview

Chapter 6 begins an in-depth discussion of various items reported on the financial statements. Initially, emphasis is placed on income statement transactions that involve revenue. Credit card sales, sales on account, sales discounts, trade discounts and sales returns are analyzed. A variety of reporting issues relating to sales revenues, accounts receivable and cash are addressed, as are the computation and interpretation of the gross profit percentage and receivables turnover ratio. An overview of the control and safeguarding of cash concludes the chapter.

Recognizing and Reporting Sales Revenues and Accounts Receivable

You should be comfortable with the application of the revenue principle to record sales revenue relating to credit card sales and sales on account. Note the differences between strict application of this principle and common practices for recording sales revenue. You will be expected to analyze transactions relating to collections from customers (whether or not they choose to take advantage of the sales discount) and write-offs of customer account balances.

Allowance Method – Recognizing Bad Debt Expense in Conformity with Matching Principle

Measurement and reporting issues arise when the collection of accounts receivable is uncertain. When a company sells to a customer on account, there is a risk that the customer will not pay what is owed. This risk of loss is a cost (or expense) of doing business when a company sells on account. That cost is referred to as bad debt expense. A sale to a customer on account may take place in one accounting period and the company may discover in a subsequent accounting period that the customer is unable to pay the amount owed. As you know, revenues earned must be matched with all of the expenses that were required to generate those revenues. That is, revenues and related expenses must be recorded in the same period.

The allowance method is required by GAAP. When this method is used, bad debts are estimated (based on past experience, industry averages, current conditions, etc.) and then recorded in the same period as the revenues earned. Take the time to understand how this method meets the requirements of the matching principle. You will be introduced to the allowance for doubtful accounts account, a contra-asset account, which represents the company's estimate of the amount that will not be collected from customers.

Direct Write-Off Method – An Unacceptable Approach to Recognizing Bad Debt Expense

For simplicity, some companies use the direct write-off method and record bad debt expense at the time that it becomes obvious that a customer will not pay. You should understand why the method does not conform to generally accepted accounting principles; it violates the matching principle.

Allowance Method – Estimating Bad Debts and Recording the Related Adjusting Entry

As noted above, an estimate must be developed when the allowance method is used. Two different approaches are used to estimate bad debt expense; both are acceptable; you need to be familiar with both methods. When the *percentage of sales method* is used, *bad debt expense* is estimated. This estimate goes directly into the adjusting entry (debit Bad Debt Expense and credit Allowance for Doubtful Accounts). On the other hand, when the *aging of accounts receivable method* is used, the *required balance of the Allowance for Doubtful Accounts* is estimated. That estimate must then be compared to the existing balance in the allowance account in order to determine the amount that should be used in the adjusting entry (debit Bad Debt Expense and credit Allowance for Doubtful Accounts).

The Allowance for Doubtful Accounts is a contra asset account. The allowance account begins the year with a credit balance. During the year, the account decreases (with debits) as accounts are written off. If write-offs during the year exceed the beginning account balance, the allowance account will end up with a debit balance prior to the adjusting entry (meaning that last year's estimate was too low). On the other hand, if write-offs are less than the beginning account balance, the account will have a credit balance prior to the adjusting entry (meaning that last year's estimate was too high). As noted above, when the aging of accounts receivable method is used, the amount used in the adjusting entry depends, in part, on the existing balance in the allowance account. As a result, you must take the time to determine whether that existing balance is a debit or credit; that balance will affect the amount used in the adjusting entry. You may find it helpful to use a T-account to determine the dollar amount to be used in the adjusting entry.

Financial Statement Matters

In addition to being familiar with the reporting of sales revenues, accounts receivable and cash, you will need to know how to compute the gross profit percentage and receivables turnover ratio. You should attempt to understand what these ratios are measuring so that you will be able to interpret them.

Control and Safeguarding of Cash

You should take the time to become familiar with the concept of internal control and understand the importance of separation of duties. You will need to know how to perform an important control procedure, the reconciliation of the company's cash account with its bank statement. You will also be expected to identify, analyze and record the transactions that arise from the reconciliation process.

LEARNING OBJECTIVES

After studying this chapter, you should be able to:

(LO 1) Apply the revenue principle to determine the accepted time to record sales revenue for typical retailers, wholesalers, and manufacturers.

(LO 2) Analyze the impact of credit card sales, sales discounts, and sales returns on the amounts reported as net sales.

(LO 3) Analyze and interpret the gross profit percentage.

(LO 4) Estimate, report, and evaluate the effects of uncollectible accounts receivable (bad debts) on financial statements.

(LO 5) Analyze and interpret the accounts receivable turnover ratio and the effects of accounts receivable on cash flows.

(LO 6) Report, control, and safeguard cash.

READ AND RECALL QUESTIONS

After you read each section of the chapter, answer the related Read and Recall Questions below.

BUSINESS BACKGROUND

How is gross profit calculated?

LEARNING OBJECTIVE
After studying this section of the chapter, you should be able to:
1. Apply the revenue principle to determine the accepted time to record sales revenue for typical retailers, wholesalers, and manufacturers.

ACCOUNTING FOR SALES REVENUE

When should revenues be recorded? What are the four criteria for recording revenue? When do sellers of goods typically record revenue? When do service providers most often record revenue? What is the appropriate amount of revenue to record? What is the cash equivalent sales price? What is disclosed in the notes to the financial statements in this regard?

If goods are shipped F.O.B. shipping point, when does title pass? When does title pass when goods are shipped F.O.B. destination? (Hint: See footnote at bottom of page in the text.)

After studying this section of the chapter, you should be able to:

2. Analyze the impact of credit card sales, sales discounts, and sales returns on the amounts reported as net sales.

CREDIT CARD SALES TO CONSUMERS

What are five reasons for the acceptance of credit cards by merchandisers? What is a credit card discount?

SALES DISCOUNTS TO BUSINESSES

What is a credit sale on open account? What does "n/30" mean? Why do some companies grant sales discounts to customers (or purchasers)? What do the standard credit terms of 2/10, n/30 mean? What are two benefits of offering sales discounts?

If a credit sale of $1,000 is made with the terms 2/10, n/30, how much cash will be received if the customer pays within the discount period? What is the amount of Net Sales that would be reported on the income statement?

FINANCIAL ANALYSIS
TO TAKE THE DISCOUNT, THAT IS THE QUESTION

What is the annual interest rate that is inherent in the terms 2/10, n/30? How is it calculated? When does it make sense to borrow in order to take advantage of cash discounts

SALES RETURNS AND ALLOWANCES

What account is often used to accumulate sales returns? How is this account reported on the income statement?

REPORTING NET SALES

Assuming that customers have returned merchandise and the company separately records credit card discounts and sales discounts in contra revenue accounts, how should the amount of net sales be computed? Are the amounts for each of the contra-revenue amounts typically disclosed in the financial statements?

LEARNING OBJECTIVE
After studying this section of the chapter, you should be able to:
3. Analyze and interpret the gross profit percentage.

KEY RATIO ANALYSIS: GROSS PROFIT PERCENTAGE

How is the gross profit percentage computed? What does it measure? All other things equal, how does a higher gross profit percentage affect net income?

How are companies pursuing a product-differentiation strategy able to charge premium prices and produce higher gross profit percentages? What do companies following a low cost strategy rely on to reduce costs and increase the gross profit percentage?

What must you understand in order to assess a company's ability to sustain new gross margins (or gross profits)? Why?

MEASURING AND REPORTING RECEIVABLES
CLASSIFYING RECEIVABLES

How is an accounts receivable created? What is a note receivable? What do the terms, *principal* and *interest*, mean?

When should a receivable be classified as a *trade receivable*? When should it be classified as a *nontrade receivable*? When should a receivable be classified as *current*? When should it be classified as *noncurrent*?

INTERNATIONAL PERSPECTIVE
FOREIGN CURRENCY RECEIVABLES

When a company (such as Timberland) sells to an international customer who has agreed to pay in its local currency rather than in U.S. Dollars, what must the company do before adding the related amount due to its Accounts Receivable account?

LEARNING OBJECTIVE
After studying this section of the chapter, you should be able to:
4. Estimate, report, and evaluate the effects of uncollectible accounts receivable (bad debts) on financial statements.

ACCOUNTING FOR BAD DEBTS

To be in conformity with the matching principle, when should bad debt expense be recorded? What method of measuring bad debt expense satisfies the matching principle?

Recording Bad Debt Expense Estimates

What is bad debt expense? How is bad debt expense recorded? How is bad debt expense reported on the income statement? How does the entry to record bad debt expense affect income and stockholders' equity?

Why isn't Accounts Receivable credited in the adjusting entry that is used to record bad debt expense? What type of account is the Allowance for Doubtful Accounts? How is it reported on the balance sheet? How does the adjusting entry to record bad debt expense affect the net book value of Accounts Receivable and total assets?

Writing Off Specific Accounts

When should a specific customer's account receivable be written off? What entry is recorded when a customer's account is written off? How does the write-off of a customer's account receivable affect the company's balance sheet? How does it affect the income statement? How does the entry impact the net book value of Accounts Receivable? How does it affect total assets?

Summary of the Accounting Process

What are the two steps in the process of accounting for bad debts? What does Accounts Receivable (gross) include? What does the balance in the Allowance for Doubtful Accounts represent?

REPORTING ACCOUNTS RECEIVABLE AND BAD DEBTS

What information about receivables may be found on the balance sheet? How can this information be used to determine the amount of Accounts Receivable (gross)?

ESTIMATING BAD DEBTS

What are the two methods that can be used to estimate the dollar that is used in the adjusting entry to record bad debt expense at the end of the accounting period?

Percentage of Credit Sales Method

What does the percentage of credit sales method use as a base for its estimate of bad debt expense? How can the average percentage of credit sales calculated? How is bad debt expense calculated using this method?

Aging of Accounts Receivable Method

What does the aging of accounts receivable method rely on? When a company uses this method, what information is required to determine the amount of estimated uncollectible accounts? What does the total of the amounts estimated to be uncollectible represent?

How is the approach inherent in the aging of accounts receivable method different from that in the percentage of credit sales method? When the aging method is used, why do you need to consider the balance in the allowance account in order to determine the amount of bad debt expense to be used in the adjusting entry?

CONTROL OVER ACCOUNTS RECEIVABLE

What three practices can help minimize bad debts?

LEARNING OBJECTIVE
After studying this section of the chapter, you should be able to:
5. Analyze and interpret the accounts receivable turnover ratio and the effects of accounts receivable on cash flows.

KEY RATIO ANALYSIS: RECEIVABLES TURNOVER

How is the receivables turnover ratio computed? What does it measure? What does a higher receivables turnover ratio indicate? What might cause the ratio to be low? Why do analysts watch this ratio?

How is the average collection period or average days sales in receivables determined? What does it measure?

FOCUS ON CASH FLOWS–ACCOUNTS RECEIVABLE

What does the change in Accounts Receivable from the beginning to the end of the period represent? When the indirect method is used to prepare the cash flow statement, why does the change in accounts receivable during the year have to be considered when adjustments are made to reconcile net income to net cash provided by operating activities?

Should an increase in accounts receivable be added to or subtracted from net income when the indirect method is used? How should a decrease in accounts receivable be handled?

LEARNING OBJECTIVE
After studying this section of the chapter, you should be able to:
6. Report, control, and safeguard cash.

REPORTING AND SAFEGUARDING CASH
CASH AND CASH EQUIVALENTS DEFINED

What are cash equivalents? What types of financial instruments are considered cash equivalents?

CASH MANAGEMENT

In addition to protecting the company's cash from theft, fraud or loss through carelessness, what other steps should be taken to ensure effective cash management? (Hint: There are three.)

INTERNAL CONTROL OF CASH

What does the term, *internal controls*, encompass? Why should a significant number of internal control procedures focus on cash? Which three duties should be separated (that is, be assigned to separate individuals) to achieve effective internal control of cash?

What four prescribed policies and procedures should exist to achieve effective internal control over cash?

How does a separation of duties deter theft?

QUESTION OF ETHICS
ETHICS AND THE NEED FOR INTERNAL CONTROL

Why should companies implement formal codes of ethics?

RECONCILIATION OF THE CASH ACCOUNTS AND THE BANK STATEMENTS

What information is listed on a bank statement?

What does the code, NSF, mean on the bank statement? What entry should be made when the bank returns a check marked NSF?

What does the code, SC, mean on the bank statement? What entry should be made to record this item? What does the code, INT, mean on the bank statement? What entry should be made to record this item?

Need for Reconciliation

What is a bank reconciliation? When should this process be completed? Will the ending cash balance shown on the bank statement usually agree with the ending cash balance on the books of the company? Why or why not?

What are *outstanding checks?* How are they identified? What are *deposits in transit?* How are they determined?

What four steps should be performed to prepare a bank reconciliation?

When a bank reconciliation is prepared, what items are added to the cash balance per books? What items are subtracted from the cash balance per books? What items are added to the cash balance per the bank statement? What items are subtracted from the cash balance per bank statement? (Hint: See Exhibit 6.7.)

Why are journal entries recorded for each of the additions and deductions to the ending cash balance per the company's books? Why don't the additions and deductions to the ending cash balance per bank statement need journal entries?

CHAPTER SUPPLEMENT A (Determine whether you are responsible for this supplement.)

Recording Discounts and Returns

Assuming that a contra-account is used to keep track of credit card discounts, what entry should be made when the credit card company charges a 3% fee for its services and credit card sales total $3,000?

Assuming that a contra-revenue account is used to keep track of sales discounts, what entry is recorded when the company makes a $1,000 sale with the terms 2/10, n/30? What entry should be made when the customer then pays within the discount period?

Assuming that a contra-revenue account is used to keep track of sales returns and allowances, what entry should be recorded when a customer returns $500 of the products that were purchased?

CHAPTER TAKE-AWAYS

1. *Apply the revenue principle to determine the accepted time to record sales revenue for typical retailers, wholesalers, and manufacturers..*

   Revenue recognition policies are widely recognized as one of the most important determinants of the fair presentation of financial statements. For most merchandisers and manufacturers, the required revenue recognition point is the time of shipment or delivery of goods. For service companies, it is the time that services are provided.

2. *Analyze the impact of credit card sales, sales discounts, and sales returns on the amounts reported as net sales.*

   Both credit card discounts and cash discounts can be recorded either as contra-revenues or as expenses. When recorded as contra-revenues, they reduce net sales. Sales returns and allowances, which should always be treated as a contra-revenue, also reduce net sales.

3. *Analyze and interpret the gross profit percentage.*

   Gross profit percentage measures the ability to charge premium prices and produce goods and services at lower cost. Managers, analysts, and creditors use this ratio to assess the effectiveness of the company's product development, marketing, and production strategy.

4. *Estimate, report, and evaluate the effects of uncollectible accounts receivable (bad debts) on financial statements.*

   When receivables are material, companies must employ the allowance method to account for uncollectibles. The steps in the process are
   1. The end-of-period adjusting entry to record bad debt expense estimates.
   2. Writing off specific accounts determined to be uncollectible during the period.
   The adjusting entry reduces net income as well as net accounts receivable. The write-off affects neither.

5. **Analyze and interpret the accounts receivable turnover ratio and the effects of accounts receivable on cash flows.**

Accounts receivable turnover ratio—Measures the effectiveness of credit granting and collection activities. It reflects how many times average trade receivables were recorded and collected during the period. Analysts and creditors watch this ratio because a sudden decline in it may mean that a company is extending payment deadlines in an attempt to prop up lagging sales or even is recording sales that later will be returned by customers.

Effects on cash flows—When a net decrease in accounts receivable for the period occurs, cash collected from customers is always more than revenue, and cash flows from operations increases. When a net increase in accounts receivable occurs, cash collected from customers is always less than revenue. Thus, cash flows from operations declines.

6. **Report, control, and safeguard cash.**

Cash is the most liquid of all assets, flowing continually into and out of a business. As a result, a number of critical control procedures, including the reconciliation of bank accounts, should be applied. Also, management of cash may be critically important to decision makers who must have cash available to meet current needs yet must avoid excess amounts of idle cash that produce no revenue.

KEY RATIOS

Gross profit percentage measures the excess of sales prices over the costs to purchase or produce the goods or services sold as a percentage. It is computed as follows:

Gross Profit Percentage = Gross Profit ÷ Net Sales

Receivables turnover ratio measures the effectiveness of credit-granting and collection activities. It is computed as follows:

Receivables Turnover = Net Sales ÷ Average Net Trade Accounts Receivable

Since the amount of net credit sales is normally not reported separately, most analysts use net sales in this equation. Average net trade accounts receivables is determined as follows:

Average Accounts Receivable =
(Accounts Receivable, net of Allowance for Doubtful Accounts, beginning of the year +
Accounts Receivable, net of Allowance for Doubtful Accounts, end of year) ÷ 2

FINDING FINANCIAL INFORMATION

Balance Sheet
Under current assets Accounts receivable (net of allowance for doubtful accounts)

Income Statement
Revenues Net sales (Sales revenue less discounts and sales returns and allowances) **Expenses** Selling expenses (include bad debt expense)

Statement of Cash Flows
Under operating activities (indirect method) Net income + Decreases in accounts receivable (net) − Increases in accounts receivable (net)

Notes
Under summary of significant accounting policies Revenue recognition policy **Under a separate note on Form 10-K** Bad debt expense and write-offs of bad debts

SELF-TEST QUESTIONS AND EXERCISES

MATCHING

Match each of the key terms listed below with the appropriate textbook definition:

____	Accounts Receivable	____	Cash Equivalents
____	Aging of Accounts Receivable Method	____	Credit Card Discount
____	Allowance for Doubtful Accounts	____	Internal Controls
____	Allowance Method	____	Notes Receivable
____	Bad Debt Expense	____	Percentage of Credit Sales Method
____	Bank Reconciliation	____	Sales (or Cash) Discount
____	Bank Statement	____	Sales Returns and Allowances
____	Cash		

A. Bases bad debt expense on the historical percentage of credit sales that result in bad debts.
B. Processes by which the company's board of directors, management, and other personnel provide reasonable assurance regarding the reliability of the company's financial reporting, the effectiveness and efficiency of its operations, and its compliance with applicable laws and regulations.
C. Cash discount offered to encourage prompt payment of an account receivable.
D. Fee charged by the credit card company for its services.
E. Reduction of sales revenue for return of or allowances for unsatisfactory goods.
F. Written promises that require another party to pay the business under specified conditions (amount, time, interest).
G. Contra-asset account containing the estimated uncollectible accounts receivable.
H. Open accounts owed to the business by trade customers.
I. Estimates uncollectible accounts based on the age of each account receivable.
J. Short-term investments with original maturities of three months or less that are readily convertible to cash and whose value is unlikely to change.
K. Bases bad debt expense on an estimate of uncollectible accounts.
L. Process of verifying the accuracy of both the bank statement and the cash accounts of the business.
M. Expense associated with estimated uncollectible accounts receivable.
N. Monthly report from a bank that shows deposits recorded, checks cleared, other debits and credits, and a running bank balance.
O. Money and any instrument that banks will accept for deposit and immediately credit to the company's account, such as a check, money order, or bank draft.

TRUE-FALSE QUESTIONS

For each of the following, enter a T or F in the blank to indicate whether the statement is true or false.

___1. (LO 1) Many companies recognize revenue at shipment regardless of whether title passes at shipment or delivery because it is easier to keep track of shipments.

___2. (LO 2) When the customer pays with a credit card, the retailer receives cash when the customer pays the credit card issuer.

___3. (LO 2) Credit card companies are not expected to absorb losses from fraudulent credit card sales.

___4. (LO 2) Credit card discounts represent the fees charged by the credit card companies for services provided.

___5. (LO 2) Sales discounts are offered to customers as an incentive for prompt payment of their account balances.

___6. (LO 2) Sales revenue should always be recorded at the listed or printed catalog price.

___7. (LO 2) Sales discounts and credit card discounts are often reported as reductions of sales revenue, but may also be reported as expenses on the income statement.

___8. (LO 3) A small change in gross profit percentage can result in a large change in net income.

___9. (LO 3) Comparisons of firms using alternative treatments to report sales discounts and credit card discounts on the income statement can be distorted by the different methods used to report these items.

___10. (LO 4) Bad debt expense should be recorded in the period in which the corresponding sales are made, rather than in the period in which a particular account is actually judged to be uncollectible.

___11. (LO 4) The entry to write-off a customer account balance does not affect the income statement.

___12. (LO 4) A company using the percentage of credit sales method typically estimates its bad debt expense by multiplying credit sales in the current year by its historical percentage of credit sales that resulted in bad debts.

___13. (LO 5) When the aging of accounts receivable method is used, the estimate that is computed becomes the amount that is used in the adjusting entry and, as such, is added to the allowance for doubtful accounts account.

___14. (LO 5) A decrease in the receivables turnover ratio might mean that a company's credit and cash collection procedures have become less effective.

___15. (LO 5) Analysts have a negative opinion of bad debts expense because it implies that a company's credit policy is too lenient or its collection efforts are not aggressive enough.

___16. (LO 6) Cash and cash equivalents can be combined as one amount for reporting purposes.

___17. (LO 6) Internal controls are the policies and procedures that the business has implemented to properly account for and safeguard all of its assets and ensure the accuracy of its financial records.

___18. (LO 6) The segregation of duties deters theft.

___19. (LO 6) All cash receipts should be deposited in a bank on a daily basis.

___20. (Chapter Supplement A) Sales returns and allowances should be recorded in a contra-revenue account that normally has a credit balance.

MULTIPLE CHOICE QUESTIONS

Choose the best answer or response by placing the identifying letter in the space provided.

___1. (LO 1) A company's primary source of cash is

    a. proceeds from short-term lines of credit.
    b. customers as they purchase goods or services and make payments on account.
    c. proceeds from the issuance of new shares of the company's stock.
    d. proceeds from borrowings on long-term debt contracts.
    e. both b and c.

___2. (LO 1) The revenue principles requires that revenues be recognized when

    a. an exchange has taken place.
    b. the earnings process is nearly complete.
    c. collection from the customer is probable.
    d. all of the above.
    e. any of the above.

___3. (LO 1) Title passes from the seller to the purchaser upon shipment of the goods if

    a. a properly executed purchase order was issued.
    b. the customer paid for the goods in advance of the shipment.
    c. collection is reasonably assured.
    d. the goods are shipped FOB shipping point
    e. the goods are shipped FOB destination point.

___4. (LO 2) A credit card discount is

    a. the amount off the list price of an item that the merchant allows a credit card customer.
    b. the amount off the pump price that gas stations offer to customers to induce them to pay with cash rather than with credit cards.
    c. the amount the issuing bank charges a retailer as a handling fee for each credit card sale submitted for payment.
    d. an amount paid by the issuing bank to retailers to encourage the use of their credit cards.
    e. the amount saved by a credit card holder who pays credit card bills in full by their due date.

___5. (LO 2) Sales discounts, also called cash discounts, are often specifically granted to customers in order to

    a. give favorable terms to high-volume buyers.
    b. motivate customers to buy slow-moving merchandise.
    c. encourage early payment of invoices.
    d. increase the company's chances to collect the receivable and, as a result, minimize bad debts.
    e. increase the company's gross profit percentage.

___6. (LO 2) A sales transaction which includes a trade discount is normally recorded

    a. at the gross amount, and the trade discount is recorded in an offsetting contra account.
    b. at the gross amount, and the trade discount is recorded in an expense account.
    c. at the net amount, after the trade discount has been deducted.
    d. either a or b.
    e. either b or c.

___7. (LO 2) The primary difference between accounts receivable and notes receivable is that

    a. accounts receivable are classified as current; notes receivable are classified as long-term.
    b. accounts receivable are classified as trade receivables, whereas notes receivable are classified as nontrade.
    c. a note receivable is a promise in writing, whereas an accounts receivable is created when there is a credit sale on an open account.
    d. all of the above.
    e. none of the above

___8. (LO 4) The primary reason for establishing an allowance account (rather than writing off uncollectible accounts to bad debt expense) is that the allowance method

    a. conforms to the matching principle.
    b. ensures that overdue accounts receivable are not overlooked.
    c. results in a more accurate reporting of revenues on the income statement.
    d. simplifies the bookkeeping effort.
    e. increases the net realizable value of the company's accounts receivable.

___9. (LO 5) The receivables turnover ratio is determined by dividing

    a. Gross sales by accounts receivable.
    b. Net sales by accounts receivable.
    c. Net sales by average accounts receivable.
    d. Net sales by average net accounts receivable.
    e. None of the above.

___10. (LO 6) Upon purchase, a U. S. Treasury bill that matures in two months should be classified as

    a. cash.
    b. a cash equivalent.
    c. a short-term investment.
    d. a long-term investment.
    e. any of the above depending on the company's investment philosophy.

___11. (LO 6) The most important reason to reconcile the company's cash account immediately upon receipt of its monthly bank statement is

    a. the need to know how much cash is available to pay bills.
    b. to ensure that errors made by the bank are corrected by the company.
    c. to ensure that the cash account is being properly accounted for and safeguarded.
    d. to ensure that collusion has not resulted in theft.
    e. the requirement to do so under generally accepted accounting principles.

___12. (LO 6) A credit memo in a bank statement might represent

    a. a bank service charge.
    b. a note receivable collected by the bank for the depositor.
    c. a memo returning a NSF check.
    d. a cash withdrawal at an automated teller machine (ATM).
    e. any of the above.

Answer the next six questions by selecting one of the following:
    a. added to the cash balance per books.
    b. deducted from the cash balance per books.
    c. added to the cash balance per bank statement.
    d. deducted from the cash balance per bank statement.

___13. (LO 6) When a bank reconciliation is being prepared, the amount of outstanding checks should be

___14. (LO 6) When a bank reconciliation is being prepared, a check marked NSF returned with the bank statement should be

___15. (LO 6) When a bank reconciliation is being prepared, bank service charges should be

___16. (LO 6) When a bank reconciliation is being prepared, deposits in transit should be

___17. (LO 6) When a bank reconciliation is being prepared, interest income reflected on the bank statement should be

___18. (LO 6) When a bank reconciliation is being prepared, proceeds of customer notes collected by the bank should be

EXERCISES

Record your answer to each exercise in the space provided. Show your work.

Exercise 1 (LO 2 and 4)

StarTrac Company entered into the following transactions during the year ended December 31, 20A. The company sells merchandise (unit sales price $1,000) on account to its customers with invoice terms of 2/10, n/30. Transactions during the year included the following:

1. Sold merchandise for cash, $13,000.
2. Sold merchandise to Drafke; invoice price, $5,000.
3. Sold merchandise to Schroeder; invoice price, $3,000.
4. Two days after he purchased the merchandise in (b), Drafke returned two of the units and received account credit.
5. Sold merchandise to Patel; invoice price, $16,000.
6. Drafke paid his account in full within ten days of the invoice date.
7. Patel paid her account in full twelve days after the date of invoice (e).
8. Ten days after paying his account balance in full, Drafke returned two additional units (because the units were defective) and received a cash refund.
9. StarTrac wrote-off Schroeder's account balance after deciding the amount would never be collected.
10. Six months later, a check in the amount of $300 was received from Schroeder.
11. Estimated bad debt expense for the year was $4,000.

Part A

Complete the following table by indicating the effect of each of the transactions listed above.

Trans-action	Sales Revenue	Sales Discounts (taken)	Sales Returns and Allowances	Bad Debt Expense
1				
2				
3				
4				
5				
6				
7				
8				
9				
10				
11				
Totals				

Exercise 1, continued
Part B

Assuming that StarTrac uses sales discounts and sales returns and allowances contra-revenue accounts, show the calculation of net sales on the income statement for the year ended December 31, 20A.

Exercise 2

You were introduced to Pixar in chapter 3 of this Study Guide. The selected financial information set forth below was taken from the statements of operations (income statements) and balance sheets included in the Forms 10-K that were filed by Pixar with the SEC for fiscal 2001 (year ending December 29, 2001), fiscal 2000 (year ending December 30, 2001) and fiscal 1999 (year ending January 1, 2000). All dollar amounts shown below are in thousands.

	Fiscal 2001	**Fiscal 2000**	**Fiscal 1999**
Year ended			
Total revenues	$ 70,223,000	$172,267,000	
Cost of revenues			
(that is, cost of goods sold)	12,318,000	37,004,000	
Net income (see below)	36,006,000	78,027,000	
As of the end of the year			
Trade net receivables,			
net of allowance	1,516,000	1,136,000	$ 714,000
Total assets	523,294,000	479,603,000	374,905,000

The net income amounts reported above are described as net income from continuing operations in Pixar's statements of operations.

Part A (LO 3)

Determine Pixar's gross profit percentage and interpret the results.

Fiscal 2001

Fiscal 2000

Interpretation

Exercise 2, continued
Part B (LO 5)

Determine Pixar's receivable turnovers and average collection periods and interpret the results. (Since Pixar did not report its net credit sales, you will need to use its total revenues to calculated this ratio.)

Fiscal 2001

Fiscal 2000

Interpretation

Exercise 3 (LO 4)

Starseekers, Inc. began the year with $4,800 of accounts receivable and an allowance for doubtful accounts of $546. Starseekers' sales were all on account and amounted to $41,800 during the year ended September 30, 20B. Collections from customers amounted to $40,600 and the company wrote-off customer account balances totaling $500 during the year.

Part A

Using T-accounts, determine how much Starseekers' customers owe the company at year-end and the unadjusted balance in its allowance for doubtful accounts account.

Part B

The company currently uses the percentage of credit sales method for determining its bad debt expense. Historically, bad debts have approximated 3% of credit sales. Prepare the related adjusting entry and, using a T-account, determine the ending balance in the allowance for doubtful accounts account.

Strategy Suggestion for Part B – *Percentage of Sales Method*

Not only is the percentage of credit sales method easier for the company to use, it is easier for you to use. The company simply considers the losses from bad debts and total credit sales to come up with an average loss rate. You simply multiply the average loss rate times this year's credit sales to arrive at an estimate of this year's bad debt expense. That estimate goes directly into the adjusting entry (debit bad debit expense and credit allowance for doubtful accounts).

Exercise 3, Part B, continued

Transaction	Account	Debit	Credit

Part C

Assume instead that the company uses the aging of accounts receivable method. This method resulted in an estimate of uncollectible accounts of $1,105. Prepare the related adjusting entry and, using a T-account, determine the ending balance in the allowance for doubtful accounts account.

Strategy Suggestion for Part C – *Aging of Accounts Receivable Method*

The aging of accounts receivable method is harder for the company to use, and it's more work for you. The company must age all of its accounts receivable and then determine probable loss rates for each of the aging categories before it can estimate its uncollectible accounts. Each category total on the aging schedule is multiplied by its respective loss rate. Then, the category totals are added together to arrive at the estimate of uncollectible accounts. (Recall that the allowance for doubtful accounts account (referred to below as the allowance account) is the company's estimate of its uncollectible accounts.) After the adjusting entry is posted, the allowance account balance should equal the estimate that arose from the aging process.

Recall how you determined the amount to be used in the adjusting entry for supplies (in chapter 4). You would compare the amount of supplies on hand to the existing balance in the supplies account; the difference was the amount of supplies used. That difference became the dollar amount used in the adjusting entry (debit supplies expense and credit supplies.)

A similar approach is used here. When you are using the aging of accounts receivable method, you should compare the estimate of uncollectible accounts (which comes from the aging schedule) to the existing balance in the allowance account. The existing balance in the allowance account may be a debit or credit; as such, you should use a T-account to ensure that you properly determine the amount that will be used in the adjusting entry.

Transaction	Account	Debit	Credit

Exercise 4 (LO 6)

Kochano Company's bank statement had an ending balance of $10,300 as of January 31, 20B; the general ledger showed a cash balance of $24,000. During the reconciliation process, the following were noted:

- A comparison of checks written before and during January with the paid checks included with the bank statement showed outstanding checks at the end of January of $33,600.
- A comparison of deposits made with those listed on the bank statement showed that deposits of $33,295 were in transit on January 31st. The comparison also revealed an error made in recording a deposit of a check received from a customer on account. The $1,500 deposit was correctly listed on the bank statement, but was recorded on the company's books at $5,100.
- A monthly service charge of $40 and interest of $135 were listed on the statement.

Exercise 4, continued

- A credit memo in the amount of $4,400 for the collection of a note appeared on the bank statement; the principal amount of the note was $4,000, previously unrecorded interest on the note was $425, and the bank had charged a $25 service fee for collecting the note.
- A customer check in the amount of $14,900 was returned to the company in the January bank statement; the check had been stamped "NSF."

Part A

Using the format illustrated in the textbook, prepare a bank reconciliation for January.

***Strategy Suggestion for Part A** – Preparing a Bank Reconciliation*

Think of the adjustments (that is, the additions and deductions) to the cash balance per books as the items that the company didn't know about until the bank statement was received. Except for book errors (which must be individually analyzed), add or deduct each item based on what the bank did when it processed the item. A journal entry is required for each item reflected as an adjustment to the cash balance per books.

Think of the adjustments to the cash balance per bank statement as items that the bank doesn't know about yet. Except for bank errors (which must be individually analyzed), add or deduct each item based on what the bank will do when it processes the item. No entries are required for the items reflected as adjustments to the cash balance per bank statement.

Kochano Company
Bank Reconciliation
for the month ended January 31, 20B

Ending cash balance per books	$24,000	Ending balance per bank statement	$10,300
Additions:		Additions:	
Deductions:		Deductions:	
Ending correct cash balance	$	Ending correct cash balance	$

Financial Accounting

Exercise 4, continued
Part B

Prepare any required journal entries as a result of the reconciliation.

Date	Account	Debit	Credit

Part C

What amount of cash should be reported on the balance sheet prepared at the end of January? Using a T-account, determine the ending balance in the cash account.

Exercise 5 (LOs 2 and 4 and Chapter Supplement A)

Prepare journal entries for the following transactions:

(a) Sold two items with a list price of $5,000 each to H. Hunter for cash of $9,500.

Transaction	Account	Debit	Credit
(a)			

(b) Sold goods to J. Lange for $2,000 and billed that amount subject to terms 2/10, n/30.

Transaction	Account	Debit	Credit
(b)			

Exercise 5, continued

(c) Sold goods to D. Moore for $6,000 and billed that amount subject to terms 2/10, n/30.

Transaction	Account	Debit	Credit
(c)			

(d) Sold goods to J. Roberts who charged the $5,000 purchase on her credit card; the credit card company charges a 2% fee.

Transaction	Account	Debit	Credit
(d)			

(e) Accepted a return of one item from H. Hunter.

Transaction	Account	Debit	Credit
(e)			

(f) Collected from J. Lange within the discount period.

Transaction	Account	Debit	Credit
(f)			

(g) Collected from D. Moore after the discount period had expired.

Transaction	Account	Debit	Credit
(g)			

(h) Wrote-off a customer's account balance of $35,000.

Transaction	Account	Debit	Credit
(h)			

SOLUTIONS TO SELF-TEST QUESTIONS AND EXERCISES

MATCHING

H	Accounts Receivable	J	Cash Equivalents
I	Aging of Accounts Receivable Method	D	Credit Card Discount
G	Allowance for Doubtful Accounts	B	Internal Controls
K	Allowance Method	F	Notes Receivable
M	Bad Debt Expense	A	Percentage of Credit Sales Method
L	Bank Reconciliation	C	Sales (or Cash) Discount
N	Bank Statement	E	Sales Returns and Allowances
O	Cash		

TRUE-FALSE QUESTIONS

1. T
2. F – The retailer deposits the credit card receipt directly into its bank account on the day of the sale.
3. F – The credit card company absorbs any losses from fraudulent credit card sales as long as the retailer follows the credit card company's verification procedure.
4. T
5. T
6. F – The listed or printed catalog price less the trade discount is the sales price; sales revenue should always be recorded net of trade discounts.
7. T
8. T
9. T
10. T
11. T
12. T
13. F – When the aging of accounts receivable method is used, the estimate that is computed actually represents the desired ending balance in the allowance for doubtful accounts account. The amount used in the adjusting entry is the difference between the desired ending balance and the unadjusted balance that exists in that account.
14. T
15. F – A business that extends credit expects a certain amount of bad debts. Analysts have the same expectation. In fact, an extremely low rate of bad debts might even indicate that the company's credit policy is too tight or restrictive. If this is the case, the company may turn away good customers and experience a loss in sales volume.
16. T
17. T
18. T
19. T
20. F – If the sales returns and allowances experiences by a company are insignificant in amount, the company might choose to simply record them as decreases to the sales revenue account. On the other hand, for monitoring purposes, companies will often record sales returns and allowances in a separate contra-revenue account. That contra account would normally have a debit balance.

MULTIPLE CHOICE QUESTIONS

1. b	5. c	9. d	13. d	17. a
2. d	6. c	10. b	14. b	18. a
3. d	7. c	11. c	15. b	
4. c	8. a	12. b	16. c	

EXERCISES

Exercise 1
Part A

Trans-action	Sales Revenue	Sales Discounts (taken)	Sales Returns and Allowances	Bad Debt Expense
1	+ 13,000	No effect	No effect	No effect
2	+ 5,000	No effect	No effect	No effect
3	+ 3,000	No effect	No effect	No effect
4	No effect	No effect	+ 2,000 (2 @ 1,000)	No effect
5	+ 16,000	No effect	No effect	No effect
6	No effect	+ 60 [(5,000 − 2,000) x .02]	No effect	No effect
7	No effect	No effect	No effect	No effect
8	No effect	− 20 [(2,000 x .02] x 1/2	+ 2,000 (2 @ 1,000)	No effect
9	No effect	No effect	No effect	No effect
10	No effect	No effect	No effect	No effect
11	No effect	No effect	No effect	+ 4,000
Totals	**+ 37,000**	**+ 40**	**+ 4,000**	**+ 4,000**

Part B

Net Sales		$37,000
Less: Sales discounts	40	
Sales returns and allowances	4,000	4,040
Net Sales		$32,960

Exercise 2
Part A

Net sales − Cost of good sold = Gross profit
Gross profit ÷ Net sales = Gross profit percentage
Fiscal 2001
$70,223,000 − $12,318,000 = $57,905,000
$57,905,000 ÷ $70,223,000 = 82.5%
Fiscal 2000
$172,267,000 − $37,004,000 = $135,263,000
$135,263,000 ÷ 172,267,000 = 78.5%

Exercise 2, continued
Interpretation
Pixar's gross profit percentage increased from 78.5% in 2000 to 82.5% in 2001. Given the nature of its business, Pixar probably may be pursuing a product-differentiation strategy and using research and development and product promotion activities to convince customers of the superiority or distinctiveness of its products. This strategy would allow Pixar to negotiate premium prices, producing higher gross profit percentages. Further information about the change may be obtained from Pixar's Annual Report. Comparisons of its gross profit percentage with those of its major competitors and industry averages would provide additional information.

Part B

Receivable Turnover = Net credit sales ÷ Average net trade receivable
Fiscal 2001
$70,223,000 ÷ [($1,136,000 + $1,516,000) ÷ 2] = $70,223,000 ÷ $1,326,000 = 53.0
Fiscal 2000
$172,267,000 ÷ [($714,000 + $1,136,000) ÷ 2] = $172,267,000 ÷ $925,000 = 186.2

Average Age of Receivables = Days in year (365) ÷ Receivable turnover ratio
Fiscal 2001
365 ÷ 53.0 (from above) = 6.9 days
Fiscal 2000
365 ÷ 186.2 (from above) = 0.2 days

Interpretation
The receivables turnover ratio reflects how many times average trade receivables were recorded and collected during the year. Pixar's higher ratio in 2000 indicates faster collection of receivables. The average collection period indicates how long, on the average, it takes a Pixar customer to pay its account balance. Pixar's lower average collection period in 2001 indicates that Pixar's customers are taking approximately 6.7 days more to pay their account balances than they were during 2000. Even so, even in 2001, it should be noted that Pixar's customers are paying their account balances very quickly (in just under 7 days). Further information about such changes may be obtained from Pixar's company's Annual Report. In addition, comparisons of Pixar's receivables turnover with those of its major competitors and the industry average would provide additional information.

Exercise 3
Part A

Accounts Receivable				
Beginning	4,800			
Sales	41,800	Collections	40,600	
		Write-offs	500	
Ending	5,500			

Allowance for Doubtful Accounts			
		Beginning	546
Write-offs	500		
		Unadjusted	46

Exercise 3, continued
Part B

Transaction	Account	Debit	Credit
	Bad debt expense	1,254	
	Allowance for doubtful accounts		1,254
	Calculated as $41,800 x 3%		

Allowance for Doubtful Accounts	
Unadjusted	46
Adjustment	1,254
Adjusted	1,300

Part C

Transaction	Account	Debit	Credit
	Bad debt expense	1,059	
	Allowance for doubtful accounts		1,059
	Calculated as $1,105 - $46		

Allowance for Doubtful Accounts	
Unadjusted	46
Adjustment	1,059
Adjusted	1,105

Exercise 4
Part A

Kochano Company
Bank Reconciliation
For the month ended January 31, 20B

Ending cash balance per books	$24,000	Ending balance per bank statement	$10,300
Additions:			
Collection of note proceeds (A)	4,400	Additions:	
Interest (B)	135	Deposits in transit	33,295
	28,535		43,595
Deductions:		Deductions:	
Bank service charge (C)	40	Outstanding checks	33,600
NSF checks (D)	14,900		
Error in recording deposit (E)			
($5,100 - $1,500)	3,600		
Ending correct cash balance	$ 9,995	Ending correct cash balance	$ 9,995

Part B

Date	Account	Debit	Credit
1/31/20B (A)	Cash	4,400	
	Bank service charge expense	25	
	Note receivable		4,000
	Interest income		425
	To record note collected by bank		

Exercise 4, Part B, continued

1/31/20B (B)	Cash	135	
	Interest income		135
	To record interest income paid by bank		
1/31/20B (C)	Bank service charge expense	40	
	Cash		40
	To record service fees charged by bank		
1/31/20B (D)	Accounts receivable	14,900	
	Cash		14,900
	To record NSF checks		
1/31/20B (E)	Accounts receivable	3,600	
	Cash		3,600
	To correct error made in recording a payment received from a customer		

Part C

Cash in the amount of $9,995 (the ending correct cash balance on the bank reconciliation) should be reported on the balance sheet at January 31, 20B.

```
                    Cash
Per G/L    24,000   1/31 (C)        40
1/31 (A)    4,400   1/31 (D)    14,900
1/31 (B)      135   1/31 (E)     3,600
Corrected   9,995
```

Exercise 5

Transaction	Account	Debit	Credit
(a)	Cash	9,500	
	Sales		9,500
(b)	Accounts receivable	2,000	
	Sales		2,000
(c)	Accounts receivable	6,000	
	Sales		6,000
(d)	Cash ($5,000 x 98%)	4,900	
	Credit card discounts ($5,000 x 2%)	100	
	Sales		5,000
(e)	Sales returns and allowances	4,750	
	Cash ($9,500 x ½)		4,750

Exercise 5, continued

Transaction	Account	Debit	Credit
(f)	Cash ($2,000 x .98)	1,960	
	Sales discounts ($2,000 x 2%)	40	
	Accounts receivable		2,000
(g)	Cash	6,000	
	Accounts receivable		6,000
(h)	Allowance for doubtful accounts	35,000	
	Accounts receivable		35,000

AN IDEA FOR YOUR STUDY TEAM

Assume that your company uses the percentage of credit sales method. During the last five years, write-offs approximated 1% of credit sales. Credit sales during the current year amounted to $3,000,000 and the unadjusted balance in the allowance for doubtful accounts account is a credit balance of $10,000. What adjusting entry would you make to record bad debt expense for the current year? What is the adjusted balance in the allowance for doubtful accounts account?

Get together with the other members of your study team and compare your answers. Then, discuss and consider the following. Assume that, early in the current year, a new Credit and Collections Manager was hired. This strategy certainly seemed to be successful; in fact, most of the company's accounts receivable had been collected by year-end. The $30,000 balance in accounts receivable at year-end represents credit sales made to customers during the final month of the year. What are the implications of this scenario? (Hint: Start by determining the net book value of the company's accounts receivable at year-end. Then, discuss any other implications that come to mind.) What advice would you give to management?

ORGANIZATION OF THE CHAPTER

Nature of Inventory and Cost of Goods Sold	Inventory Costing Methods	Valuation at Lower of Cost or Market	Evaluating Inventory Management	Control of Inventory
• Items included in Inventory • Flow of Inventory Costs • Nature of Cost of Goods Sold	• Specific Identification Method • Cost Flow Assumptions (FIFO, LIFO, Weighted Average) • Financial Statement Effects of Inventory Methods • Managers' Choice of Inventory Methods • Inventory Methods and Financial Statement Analysis		• Measuring Efficiency in Inventory Management • Inventory turnover ratio • Inventory and Cash Flows	• Errors in Measuring Ending Inventory • Perpetual and Periodic Inventory Systems

CHAPTER FOCUS SUGGESTIONS

Overview

Chapter 7 continues the in-depth discussion of various items reported on the financial statements. Initially, emphasis is placed on income statement transactions that involve cost of goods sold. A variety of reporting issues relating to cost of goods sold and inventory are addressed, as is the computation and interpretation of the inventory turnover ratio. In addition to covering the four inventory costing methods, the decision related to the choice of an inventory costing method is overviewed. Measurement issues that arise when damaged, obsolete and deteriorated items exist in inventory are addressed in light of the lower of cost or market rule. Coverage of the two inventory systems commonly used to keep track of inventory quantities and amounts in different circumstances concludes the chapter.

The Cost and Matching Principles

The chapter begins by defining inventory, which is reported as a current asset on the balance sheet in accordance with the cost principle. You will be expected to be able to describe the various types of inventory items that are included on the balance sheets of both merchandisers and manufacturers.

After discussing the nature of cost of goods sold, the flow of inventory costs from inventory to cost of goods sold is described. In conformity with the matching principle, the total cost of the goods sold during the period must be determined and then matched with the sales revenue earned from selling those goods. In this regard, the goods available for sale must be allocated to cost of goods sold and ending inventory (using one of the inventory costing methods described below).

Inventory Costing Methods

You will need to become familiar with each of the four inventory-costing methods: first-in, first-out (FIFO), last-in, first-out (LIFO), average cost and specific identification. All four methods are in conformity with GAAP, but produce different results. You will need to be able to determine both the amount of inventory on hand and the cost of goods sold using the FIFO, LIFO, average cost and specific identification methods.

Given a certain set of assumptions (for example, rising unit prices) you should be able to determine how the choice of an inventory costing method affects the financial statements (that is, the amount of ending inventory reported on the balance sheet and the amounts of cost of goods sold and gross profit reported on the income statement) and the amount of income taxes that are paid (or postponed) by the company. The comparison of financial information of different companies is complicated when the companies use different inventory costing methods. As a result, so that you will be able to make meaningful comparisons, you will also be expected to be able to use the cost of goods sold equation to convert inventory and cost of goods sold and income before taxes from LIFO to FIFO basis amounts.

Financial Statement Matters

You should be familiar with the reporting of inventory and cost of goods sold as well as the calculation of the inventory turnover ratio. You should attempt to understand what this ratio is measuring so that you will be able to interpret it.

Valuation at Lower of Cost or Market

The lower of cost or market (LCM) rule requires that ending inventory be reported on the balance sheet at the lower of actual cost (determined using one of the four inventory costing methods) or replacement cost. The application of this rule can significantly impact the financial statements of companies facing declining unit costs. When the LCM must be applied, ending inventory decreases and causes cost of goods sold to increase and net income to decrease.

Errors in Inventory

Using the relationships of the various items in the cost of goods sold equation, you will be expected to be able to explain how errors in ending inventory affect the financial statements. In this regard, note that this year's ending inventory becomes next year's beginning inventory. As a result, inventory errors always affect two years' worth of income statements and are self-correcting.

Perpetual and Periodic Inventory Systems

You should also become familiar with the two systems used to keep track of inventory. When deciding which system to use, managers must weigh benefits of the availability of this information for inventory management purposes against the higher recordkeeping costs. When a perpetual inventory system is used, detailed inventory records are maintained and updated as transactions affecting inventory occur. As such, management always (or perpetually) knows how much inventory is on hand and its cost of goods sold.

When a periodic inventory system is used, detailed inventory records are not maintained. Instead, the company counts its inventory to determine how much is on hand and the cost of the goods that have been sold. Information necessary for inventory management is lacking (that is, it is available only periodically), but recordkeeping costs are minimal.

LEARNING OBJECTIVES

After studying this chapter, you should be able to:

(LO 1) Apply the cost principle to identify the amounts that should be included in inventory and the matching principle to determine cost of goods sold for typical retailers, wholesalers, and manufacturers.

(LO 2) Report inventory and cost of goods sold using the four inventory costing methods.

(LO 3) Decide when the use of different inventory costing methods is beneficial to a company.

(LO 4) Compare companies that use different inventory costing methods.

(LO 5) Report inventory at the lower of cost or market (LCM).

(LO 6) Evaluate inventory management using the inventory turnover ratio and the effects of inventory on cash flows.

(LO 7) Analyze the effects of inventory errors on financial statements and methods of keeping track of inventory.

READ AND RECALL QUESTIONS

After you read each section of the chapter, answer the related Read and Recall Questions below.

BUSINESS BACKGROUND

What are the two primary goals of inventory management? What three roles does the accounting system play in the inventory management process?

LEARNING OBJECTIVE
After studying this section of the chapter, you should be able to:
1. Apply the cost principle to identify the amounts that should be included in inventory and the matching principle to determine cost of goods sold for typical retailers, wholesalers, and manufacturers.

NATURE OF INVENTORY AND COST OF GOODS SOLD
ITEMS INCLUDED IN INVENTORY

What is inventory? Why is inventory reported as a current asset on a classified balance sheet? Goods in inventory are initially recorded at cost; what is cost? What is included in inventory cost?

What type of inventory do merchandisers hold? What three types of inventory do manufacturers hold?

FINANCIAL ANALYSIS
APPLYING THE MATERIALITY CONSTRAINT IN PRACTICE

How are incidental costs such as inspection and preparation costs reported when they are not material in amount? For practical reasons, how do many companies determine a unit cost for raw materials or merchandise?

Flows of Inventory Costs

What account is increased when a wholesaler or retailer purchases merchandise? What account is increased and what account is decreased when the goods are sold?

What are raw materials (or direct materials)? What account is increased when raw materials are purchased? What account is increased and what account is decreased when raw materials are used in the manufacturing process?

What is direct labor? What are factory overhead costs?

Financial Accounting

What account are direct labor and factory overhead costs added to when these costs are incurred in the manufacturing process? What account is increased and what account is decreased when the manufactured goods are completed and ready for sale? What account is increased and what account is decreased when finished goods are sold?

FINANCIAL ANALYSIS
MODERN MANUFACTURING TECHNIQUES AND INVENTORY COSTS

Why would companies (such as Harley-Davidson) want to minimize its raw materials and purchased parts inventories? How does the company minimize these inventories?

NATURE OF COST OF GOODS SOLD

How is the amount of goods available for sale computed? What is the cost of goods sold equation?

LEARNING OBJECTIVE
After studying this section of the chapter, you should be able to:
2. Report inventory and cost of goods sold using the four inventory costing methods.

INVENTORY COSTING METHODS

What is the total dollar amount of goods available for sale assigned to? What are the four generally accepted inventory costing methods?

SPECIFIC IDENTIFICATION METHOD

What does the company need to keep track of when it uses the specific identification method? How does the company track this information? How can net income be manipulated when this method is used?

COST FLOW ASSUMPTIONS

Why are the various inventory costing methods considered alternative allocation methods? Does a company's physical flow of goods affect its choice of inventory costing methods? Why or why not?

First-In, First-Out Method

What does FIFO stand for? What does the FIFO method assume? What unit costs does FIFO allocate to cost of goods sold? What unit costs are allocated to ending inventory?

Last-In, First-Out Method

What does LIFO stand for? What does the LIFO method assume? What unit costs does LIFO allocate to cost of goods sold? What unit costs are allocated to ending inventory?

Average Method

What per unit amount needs to be computed when the average inventory costing method is used? How is this per unit amount computed? How is ending inventory determined when this method is used? How is cost of goods sold determined?

FINANCIAL STATEMENT EFFECTS OF INVENTORY METHODS

Which cost method gives income and inventory amounts that are between the other two methods? When unit costs are rising, which inventory costing method (ignoring the specific identification method) produces the lower income and lower inventory valuation? When units costs are declining, which inventory valuation method produces higher income and higher inventory valuation?

Which method causes the newer (or the latest) unit costs to be reflected in cost of goods sold on the income statement? Which method causes the older (or the earliest) unit costs to be reflected in cost of goods sold on the income statement?

On the balance sheet, which inventory costing method bases the ending inventory amount on the oldest units? Which inventory costing method bases the ending inventory amount on the newest units?

LEARNING OBJECTIVE
After studying this section of the chapter, you should be able to:
3. Decide when the use of different inventory costing methods is beneficial to a company.

MANAGERS' CHOICE OF INVENTORY METHODS

What two factors do managers consider when choosing inventory costing methods? How is a conflict between the two motives normally resolved? Why is the choice of inventory costing methods a special case? What is the LIFO conformity rule?

Increasing Cost Inventories, Decreasing Cost Inventories

For inventories with increasing costs, which method is used on the tax return? Why? For inventories with decreasing costs, which method is often used for both the tax return and financial statements? Why?

Consistency in Use of Inventory Methods

Does the physical flow of goods dictate which inventory costing method must be used? Are companies required to use the same inventory costing method for all inventory items? Is justification needed for the selection of one or more of the acceptable methods? What do accounting rules require with regards to accounting methods?

LEARNING OBJECTIVE
After studying this section of the chapter, you should be able to:
4. Compare companies that use different inventory costing methods.

INVENTORY COSTING METHODS AND FINANCIAL STATEMENT ANALYSIS

What information must be disclosed if a U.S. public company uses LIFO? What is the cost of goods sold equation? What is the LIFO Reserve?

Converting the Income Statement to FIFO

Does the choice of a cost flow assumption affect ending inventory and cost of goods sold? Does if affect the recording of purchases? What is the LIFO Reserve? How can the cost of goods sold equation be used to determine the effects of the difference in cost flow assumptions on cost of goods sold?

Converting the Balance Sheet to FIFO

How can the inventory amounts on the balance sheet be converted from LIFO to FIFO?

LIFO AND INTERNATIONAL COMPARISONS

What can create comparability problems when one attempts to compare companies across international borders? Why?

LEARNING OBJECTIVE
After studying this section of the chapter, you should be able to:
5. Report inventory at the lower of cost or market (LCM).

VALUATION AT LOWER OF COST OR MARKET

When the goods remaining in ending inventory can be replaced with identical goods at a lower cost, what unit cost should be used for inventory valuation? When the goods remaining in ending inventory are damaged, obsolete, or deteriorated, what unit cost should be used for inventory valuation? What is the lower of cost or market (LCM) rule?

What constraint justifies the departure from the cost principle when the lower cost or market rule is followed? What is a holding loss? What is replacement cost? What is a holding loss?

What is a write-down? How does an inventory write-down affect the amounts of cost of goods sold and net income reported in the year of the write-down? How does the inventory write-down affect the amounts of cost of goods sold and net income reported in the following year?

What is net realizable value? When net realizable value drops below cost, what are the effects on the current year's cost of goods sold and net income? What are the effects on the following year's cost of goods sold and net income?

Evaluating Inventory Management
Measuring Efficiency in Inventory Management

How is the inventory turnover ratio computed? What does it measure? What does a higher inventory turnover ratio mean in terms of how quickly inventory moves through the production process to the customer? Why does a higher inventory turnover ratio benefit the company? What are the causes of a low inventory turnover ratio?

Why do analysts and creditors watch the inventory turnover ratio? How is the average number of days to sell inventory computed? What does this number indicate?

FINANCIAL ANALYSIS
LIFO AND INVENTORY TURNOVER RATIO

Why can the inventory turnover ratio be deceptive for certain companies?

CONTROL OF INVENTORY
ERRORS IN MEASURING ENDING INVENTORY

Does the measurement of ending inventory quantities and costs affect the balance sheet, the income statement, or both? Why? Does the measurement of ending inventory affect net income for the current period, the next period, or both? Why?

Assume that ending inventory is overstated as a result of a clerical error and the error is not discovered. How does this error affect the current year's cost of goods sold and income before taxes? How does this error affect the following year's beginning inventory, cost of goods sold and income before taxes?

PERPETUAL AND PERIODIC INVENTORY SYSTEMS
Perpetual Inventory Systems

What is a perpetual inventory system? What records are maintained when a perpetual inventory system is used? How is ending inventory determined when a perpetual inventory system is used? What account is used to accumulate purchases when a perpetual inventory system is used? What account is used to accumulate purchases when a periodic inventory system is used?

Periodic Inventory Systems

What is a periodic inventory system? How is ending inventory determined when a periodic inventory system is used? How is cost of goods sold calculated? In the past, what was the primary reason for using a periodic inventory system? What is the primary disadvantage of a periodic inventory system? Where is cost of good sold measured when a perpetual inventory system is used? Where is cost of goods sold measured when a periodic inventory system is used?

CHAPTER SUPPLEMENT A (*Determine whether you are responsible for this supplement.*)

FINANCIAL STATEMENT EFFECTS OF LIFO LIQUIDATIONS

What causes a LIFO liquidation? How do many firms avoid LIFO liquidations and extra tax payments? What information must be disclosed in the financial statements if a LIFO liquidation has taken place?

FINANCIAL ANALYSIS
INVENTORY MANAGEMENT AND LIFO LIQUIDATIONS

How do many firms avoid LIFO liquidations and the accompanying increase in tax expense? What costs increase as a result? What normally occurs when a company switches to a just-in-time inventory system? What incentive does tax law provide for U.S. companies?

CHAPTER SUPPLEMENT B (*Determine whether you are responsible for this supplement.*)

ADDITIONAL ISSUES IN MEAUSRING PURCHASES

Why would goods that are purchased be returned to the vendor? What account accumulates purchase returns when a perpetual inventory system is used? What is a purchase discount? What account accumulates purchase discounts when a perpetual inventory system is used?

CHAPTER SUPPLEMENT C (*Determine whether you are responsible for this supplement.*)

COMPARISON OF PERPETUAL AND PERIODIC INVENTORY SYSTEMS

What account is debited for the purchase of inventory when perpetual records are maintained? What account is debited when periodic records are maintained?

When periodic records are maintained, a sale to a customer on account requires a single journal entry; why must a second entry be recorded if the company instead maintains perpetual records?

How is cost of goods sold determined at the end of the accounting period if the company maintains perpetual records? How is it recorded if the company maintains periodic records?

Which inventory costing method is normally used to keep track of the costs of individual items or lots when a perpetual inventory system is in use? Why is this method normally used? Why aren't perpetual records kept on a LIFO basis?

CHAPTER TAKE-AWAYS

1. *Apply the cost principle to identify the amounts that should be included in inventory and the matching principle to determine cost of goods sold for typical retailers, wholesalers, and manufacturers.*

   Inventory should include all items owned that are held for resale. Costs flow into inventory when goods are purchased or manufactured. They flow out (as an expense) when they are sold or disposed of. In conformity with the matching principle, the total cost of the goods sold during the period must be matched with the sales revenue earned during the period.

2. *Report inventory and cost of goods sold using the four inventory costing methods.*

   The chapter discussed four different inventory costing methods used to allocate costs between the units remaining in inventory and to the units sold, and their applications in different economic circumstances. The methods discussed were FIFO, LIFO, average cost, and specific identification. Each of the inventory costing methods conforms with GAAP. Public companies using LIFO must provide note disclosures that allow conversion of inventory and cost of goods sold to FIFO amounts. Remember that the cost flow assumption need not match the physical flow of inventory.

3. *Decide when the use of different inventory costing methods is beneficial to a company.*

   The selection of an inventory costing method is important because it will affect reported income, income tax expense (and hence cash flow), and the inventory valuation reported on the balance sheet. In a period of rising prices, FIFO normally results in a higher income, and higher taxes, than LIFO; in a period of falling prices, the opposite occurs. The choice of methods is normally made to minimize taxes.

4. *Compare companies using different inventory methods.*

   These comparisons can be made by converting the LIFO company's statements to FIFO. Public companies using LIFO must disclose the differences between LIFO and FIFO values for beginning and ending inventory. These amounts are often called the LIFO reserve. The beginning LIFO reserve minus the ending LIFO reserve equals the difference in cost of goods sold under FIFO. Pretax income is affected by the same amount in the opposite direction. This amount times the tax rate is the tax effect.

5. *Report inventory at the lower-of-cost-or-market (LCM).*

   Ending inventory should be measured based on the lower of actual cost or replacement cost (LCM basis). This practice can have a major effect on the statements of companies facing declining costs. Damaged, obsolete, and out-of-season inventory should also be written down to their current estimated net realizable value, if below cost. The LCM adjustment increases cost of goods sold, decreases income, and decreases reported inventory in the year of the write-down.

6. *Evaluate inventory management using the inventory turnover ratio and the effects of inventory on cash flows.*

The inventory turnover ratio measures the efficiency of inventory management. It reflects how many times average inventory was produced and sold during the period. Analysts and creditors watch this ratio because a sudden decline may mean that a company is facing an unexpected drop in demand for its products or is becoming sloppy in its production management. When a net decrease in inventory for the period occurs, sales are more than purchases; thus, the decrease must be added in computing cash flows from operations. When a net increase in inventory for the period occurs, sales are less than purchases; thus, the increase must be subtracted in computing cash flows from operations.

7. *Analyze the effects of inventory errors on financial statements and methods for keeping track of inventory.*

An error in the measurement of ending inventory affects cost of goods sold on the current period's income statement and ending inventory on the balance sheet. Because this year's ending inventory becomes next year's beginning inventory, it also affects cost of goods sold in the following period, by the same amount, but in the opposite direction. These relationships can be seen through the cost of goods sold equation (BI + P – EI = CGS). A company can keep track of the ending inventory and cost of goods sold for the period using: (1) the perpetual inventory system, which is based on the maintenance of detailed and continuous inventory records, and (2) the periodic inventory system, which is based on a physical count of ending inventory and use of the inventory equation to determine cost of goods sold.

KEY RATIOS

Inventory turnover ratio measures the efficiency of inventory management. It reflects how many times average inventory was produced and sold during the period. It is computed as follows:

Inventory Turnover = Cost of goods sold ÷ Average inventory

Average inventory is determined as follows:

(Inventory, beginning of the year + Inventory, end of year) ÷ 2

FINDING FINANCIAL INFORMATION

Balance Sheet	Income Statement

Under Current Assets
  Inventories
	Expenses
	  Cost of goods sold

Statement of Cash Flows	Notes

Under Operating Activities (Indirect Method)
Net income
  – Decreases in inventory
  + Increases in inventory
  + Increases in accounts payable
  – Decreases in accounts payable
	Under Summary of Significant Accounting Policies
	  Description of management's choice of inventory accounting policy (FIFO, LIFO, LCM, etc)
	In a Separate Note
	  If not listed on balance sheet, components of inventory (merchandise, raw materials, work in progress, finished goods)
	  If using LIFO, LIFO reserve (excess of FIFO over LIFO)

SELF-TEST QUESTIONS AND EXERCISES

MATCHING

Match each of the key terms listed below with the appropriate textbook definition:

____ Average Cost Method	____ Lower of Cost or Market (LCM)
____ Cost of Goods Sold Equation	____ Merchandise Inventory
____ Direct Labor	____ Net Realizable Value
____ Factory Overhead	____ Periodic Inventory System
____ Finished Goods Inventory	____ Perpetual Inventory System
____ First-In, First-Out Method (FIFO)	____ Purchase Discount
____ Goods Available for Sale	____ Purchase Returns and Allowances
____ Inventory	____ Raw Materials Inventory
____ Last-In, First-Out Method (LIFO)	____ Replacement Cost
____ LIFO Liquidation	____ Specific Identification Method
____ LIFO Reserve	____ Work in Progress Inventory

A. Assumes that the oldest units are the first units sold.

B. Cash discount received for prompt payment of an account payable.

C. Assumes that the most recently acquired units are sold first.

D. The sum of beginning inventory and purchases (or transfers to finished goods) for the period.

E. A contra-asset for the excess of FIFO over LIFO inventory.

F. BI + P – EI = CGS

G. Goods in the process of being manufactured.

H. Items acquired for the purpose of processing into finished goods.

I. Manufacturing costs that are not raw material or direct labor costs.

J. The earnings of employees who work directly on the products being manufactured.

K. Tangible property held for sale in the normal course of business or used in producing goods or services for sale.

L. Manufactured goods that are completed and ready for sale.

M. A detailed inventory record maintained recording each purchase and sale during the accounting period.

N. The expected sales price less selling costs (e.g., repair and disposal costs).

O. The current purchase price for identical goods.

P. The average unit cost of the goods available for sale for both cost of goods sold and ending inventory.

Q. A sale of a lower-cost inventory item from beginning LIFO inventory.

R. Ending inventory and cost of goods sold determined at the end of the accounting period based on a physical inventory count.

S. Valuation method departing from cost principle that recognizes a loss when replacement cost or net realizable value drops below cost.

T. Goods held for resale in the ordinary course of business.

U. A reduction in the cost of purchases associated with unsatisfactory goods.

V. Identifies the cost of the specific item that was sold.

TRUE-FALSE QUESTIONS

For each of the following, enter a T or F in the blank to indicate whether the statement is true or false.

____1. (LO 1) The primary goals of inventory management are to have sufficient quantities of goods on hand to meet customer needs while minimizing the costs of carrying those goods.

____2. (LO 1) Work in progress inventory for a merchandiser consists of items not yet displayed for sale.

____3. (LO 1) Goods manufactured by a business, completed and ready for sale, are classified as finished goods inventory.

____4. (LO 1) The company should stop accumulating purchase costs when raw materials are ready for use.

____5. (LO 1) If the costs are incidental and not material in amount, the materiality constraint allows a merchandiser to expense transportation charges for shipments to the warehouse instead of inventorying these costs.

____6. (LO 1) Factory overhead includes raw materials, direct labor and all other manufacturing costs.

____7. (LO 2) FIFO allocates the oldest unit costs to cost of goods sold and the most recent unit costs to ending inventory.

____8. (LO 2) LIFO allocates the most recent unit costs to cost of goods sold and the oldest unit costs to the ending inventory.

____9. (LO 2) The average unit cost is computed by dividing the cost of goods sold by the number of units available for sale.

____10. (LO 2) Manipulation of results is impossible when the specific identification method is used.

____11. (LO 3) The inventory costing method that gives the highest ending inventory amount also gives the highest gross margin and income amounts and vice versa.

____12. (LO 3) When unit costs and inventory quantities are rising, FIFO produces a lower inventory valuation than LIFO.

____13. (LO 3) A company's choice of an inventory costing method must at least approximate the physical flow of its inventory (that is, the actual physical flow of a company's inventory determines which method it must use).

____14. (LO 3) The LIFO conformity rule leads many companies to adopt LIFO for both tax and financial reporting purposes.

____15. (LO 3) In theory, the tax savings provided by LIFO are not permanent.

____16. (LO 4) The LIFO Reserve provides the needed information to convert the balances in inventory and cost of goods sold from LIFO to FIFO.

____17. (LO 5) A holding loss is recognized when the purchase price of an item exceeds the current purchase price for an identical item.

____18. (LO 5) The lower of cost or market rule requires that damaged, deteriorated or obsolete items be assigned a unit cost that represents their current estimated net realizable value.

____19. (LO 6) Higher inventory turnover indicates that inventory is turned into cash more quickly.

____20. (LO 7) The cost of goods sold equation states that beginning inventory plus purchases plus ending inventory equals cost of goods sold.

___21. (LO 7) An error in ending inventory affects not only the net income for that period but also the net income for the next accounting period.

___22. (LO 7) The primary disadvantage of a periodic inventory system is the lack of information.

___23. (LO 7) Perpetual inventory records are rarely kept on a LIFO basis.

___24. (LO 7) When a periodic inventory system is used, managers who wish to prepare monthly or quarterly financial statements for internal use estimate the cost of goods sold and ending inventory.

___25. (Chapter Supplement A) A LIFO liquidation takes place when a LIFO company purchases or manufactures more inventory than it sells.

___26. (Chapter Supplement B) Purchase returns and allowances and purchase discounts are accounted for as deductions from the cost of purchases.

MULTIPLE CHOICE QUESTIONS

Choose the best answer or response by placing the identifying letter in the space provided.

___1. (LO 1) In a manufacturing company, raw materials are

    a. items purchased as spare parts for their products.
    b. items intended for resale.
    c. items that will be used to manufacture the company's products.
    d. completed products that have not yet been sold.
    e. items ordered but not yet received.

___2. (LO 1) A merchandiser's inventory consists of

    a. raw materials and finished goods.
    b. raw materials, work in process and finished goods.
    c. finished goods.
    d. merchandise inventory intended for resale.
    e. raw materials.

___3. (LO 2) The inventory costing method least likely to be used by a candy store is

    a. LIFO
    b. FIFO
    c. LCM
    d. specific identification
    e. average

___4. (LO 3) If a company uses LIFO for tax purposes, then for financial reporting purposes

    a. they are free to choose any inventory method they wish.
    b. they must disclose this fact.
    c. they must also use LIFO.
    d. they must use either LIFO or FIFO.
    e. they cannot use LIFO.

___5. (LO 4) A LIFO liquidation occurs when a company

    a. converts from LIFO to FIFO.
    b. sells off all of its inventory.
    c. sells in one period more inventory than is purchased or manufactured.
    d. goes out of business.
    e. using LIFO experiences a decrease instead of an increase in merchandise cost.

___6. (LO 5) The lower of cost or market rule (LCM) is applied

    a. when inventory costs less than it can be sold for.
    b. when the market value of a long-lived asset is less than its cost.
    c. when inventory has been held for more than one year.
    d. when the replacement cost or net realizable value of inventory drops below cost.
    e. all of the above.

___7. (LO 6) Inventory turnover is computed by dividing

    a. Gross sales by inventory.
    b. Net sales by inventory.
    c. Net sales by average inventory.
    d. Cost of goods sold by average inventory.
    e. None of the above.

___8. (LO 7) A company overstated its ending inventory at the end of year one. Ignoring taxes, if the error went undetected, retained earnings would be _____ by the same amount at the end of year one and _____ at the end of year two.

    a. overstated; understated by the same amount.
    b. overstated; overstated by the same amount.
    c. understated; overstated by the same amount
    d. overstated; unaffected
    e. understated; understated by the same amount

___9. (LO 7) In order to calculate cost of goods sold in a periodic inventory system, it is necessary to

    a. subtract gross profit from sales.
    b. add up sales receipts for the period.
    c. refer to the balance of the cost of goods sold account.
    d. physically count the merchandise inventory that is on hand.
    e. all of the above.

___10. (LO 7) A perpetual inventory system differs from a periodic system in that

    a. up-to-date inventory records are maintained.
    b. a uniform base stock of inventory is always kept on hand.
    c. the books of account are closed more often.
    d. a perpetual system regularly takes physical counts of inventory on hand.
    e. a periodic system breaks the year into measurable accounting periods.

EXERCISES

Record your answers to each part of these exercises in the space provided. Show your work.

Exercise 1

Claremont Sweet Shoppe orders and sells toffees by the pound. On July 1st, Claremont had 500 pounds of toffee on hand which was purchased at $1.00 per pound. Claremont made a number of purchases of toffee during July:

Date of Purchase	Pounds	Cost per Pound	Total Cost
July 5	1,000	$1.10	$1,100
July 9	1,200	1.15	1,380
July 20	1,200	1.20	1,440
July 30	1,500	1.25	1,875

During July, the company sold 3,800 pounds of toffee at $1.45 per pound.

Part A (LO 1)

Compute the number of pounds of toffee on hand on July 31st, and the cost of goods available for sale for the month of July.

Exercise 1, continued
Part B (LO 2)

Assume that the company uses the average inventory method. Compute its ending inventory on July 31st, the cost of goods sold during July, and the company's gross profit during July.

Part C (LO 2)

Assume that the company uses FIFO. Compute its ending inventory on July 31st, the cost of goods sold during July, and the company's gross profit during July.

Strategy Suggestion for Part C
Recall that the cost of ending inventory using FIFO is composed of the latest purchases.

Part D (LO 2)

Assume that the company uses LIFO. Compute its ending inventory on July 31st, the cost of goods sold during July, and the company's gross profit during July.

Strategy Suggestion for Part D
Recall that the cost of ending inventory using LIFO is composed of the earliest purchases.

©The McGraw-Hill Companies, Inc., 2004

198   *Financial Accounting*

Exercise 1, continued
Part E (LO 4)

Compute the amount of the company's LIFO Reserve at the end of July. Using an effective income tax rate of 40%, determine the amount of tax savings that the company would realize for the month of July if it adopts LIFO rather than FIFO.

Exercise 2

Nassau Navigational Supplies, Inc. had $104,000, $92,000, and $78,000 of inventory, and accounts payable of $43,000, $38,000, and $29,000 on December 31, 20A, 20B and 20C, respectively. Nassau purchased $815,000 of inventory during 20B and $699,000 of inventory during 20C. Nassau reported net income of $319,000 for 20B and $327,000 for 20C.

Part A (LO 1)

Compute Nassau's cost of goods sold for the years ended December 31, 20B and 20C.

Part B (LO 6)

Compute Nassau's inventory turnover ratio for 20B and 20C. What does this ratio measure? Comment on the change, if any, in the ratio between 20B and 20C.

Exercise 2, continued
Part C (LO 6)

Using only the information provided above, compute Nassau's net cash flows from operating activities for the year ended December 31, 20B and 20C.

Part D (LO 7)

Assume that Nassau made a computational error that understated its ending inventory by $5,000 at December 31, 20B. Compute the corrected amounts of cost of goods sold and net income for 20B and 20C. Determine the effect on retained earnings at December 31, 20C.

Strategy Suggestion for Part D

Recall that the ending inventory at December 31, 20B becomes the beginning inventory at January 1, 20C. As a result, inventory errors always affect two income statements (the income statement for the year in which the error was made and the income statement for the following year). Also recall that inventory errors are self-correcting. (You will prove this statement when you determine the effect on retained earnings at December 31, 20C.)

Financial Accounting

Exercise 3 (LO 5)

Amanda Corporation is preparing its financial statements for the year ending December 31, 20B. Ending inventory information about the three major items stocked for regular sale follows:

Item	Quantity on Hand	Unit Cost When Acquired (FIFO)	Replacement Cost (Market) at Year-End
AA	100	$ 30	$ 26
BB	150	80	80
CC	200	100	104

Compute the valuation that should be used for the 20B ending inventory using the LCM rule applied on an item-by-item basis.

Strategy Suggestion for Exercise 3

Set up a table with the following column headings: Item, Quantity, Total Cost, Total Market, and LCM Valuation.

SOLUTIONS TO SELF-TEST QUESTIONS AND EXERCISES

MATCHING

P	Average Method	S	Lower of Cost or Market (LCM)
F	Cost of Goods Sold Equation	T	Merchandise Inventory
J	Direct Labor	N	Net Realizable Value
I	Factory Overhead	R	Periodic Inventory System
L	Finished Goods Inventory	M	Perpetual Inventory System
A	First-In, First-Out Method (FIFO)	B	Purchase Discount
D	Goods Available for Sale	U	Purchase Returns and Allowances
K	Inventory	H	Raw Materials Inventory
C	Last-In, First-Out Method (LIFO)	O	Replacement Cost
Q	LIFO Liquidation	V	Specific Identification Method
E	LIFO Reserve	G	Work in Progress Inventory

TRUE-FALSE QUESTIONS

1.   T
2.   F – All goods held for resale in the ordinary course of business by a merchandiser, whether displayed for sale or not, are classified as merchandise inventory. Goods in the process of being manufactured are classified as work in progress inventory for a manufacturer.
3.   T
4.   T
5.   T
6.   F – All manufacturing costs *other than* raw materials and direct labor costs are classified as factory overhead costs.
7.   T
8.   T
9.   F – The average unit cost is computed by dividing the cost of goods *available for sale* by the number of units available for sale.
10.   F – The specific identification method may be manipulated when the units are identical; a manager could affect the cost of goods sold and the ending inventory by picking and choosing from among the several available units costs, even though the goods are identical in other respects.
11.   T
12.   F – When unit costs and inventory quantities are rising, FIFO produces a *higher* inventory valuation than LIFO. FIFO uses the most recent unit costs, LIFO uses the oldest unit costs to value ending inventory.
13.   F – The inventory costing method does not need to approximate the physical flow of its inventory.
14.   T
15.   T
16.   T
17.   T
18.   F – The lower of cost or market rule requires that a damaged, deteriorated or obsolete item be assigned a unit cost that represents its current estimated net realizable value *only* if the net realizable value of the item is below its cost.
19.   T
20.   F – The cost of goods sold equation states that beginning inventory plus purchases *less* ending inventory equals cost of goods sold.
21.   T
22.   T
23.   T
24.   T
25.   F – A LIFO liquidation takes place when a LIFO company sells more inventory than it purchases or manufacturers.
26.   T

MULTIPLE CHOICE QUESTIONS

| 1. c | 3. d | 5. c | 7. d | 9. d |
| 2. d | 4. c | 6. d | 8. d | 10. a |

EXERCISES

Exercise 1
Part A

Pounds of toffee on hand on July 31st:

Beginning inventory		500
Purchases:		
July 5	1,000	
July 9	1,200	
July 20	1,200	
July 30	1,500	4,900
Available for sale		5,400
Less pounds sold		3,800
Ending inventory		1,600

Cost of goods available for sale for the month of July:

Beginning inventory (500 @ $1.00)		$ 500
Purchases:		
July 5 (1,000 @ $1.10)	$1,100	
July 9 (1,200 @ $1.15)	1,380	
July 20 (1,200 @ $1.20)	1,440	
July 30 (1,500 @ $1.25)	1,875	5,795
Goods available for sale		$6,295

Part B *(Average Cost)*

Goods available for sale ÷ Number of units available for sale = Average unit cost
$6,295 ÷ 5,400 pounds = $1.1657 per pound (could round to $1.17)
Ending inventory = 1,600 pounds @ $1.1657 per pound = $1,865
Cost of goods sold = 3,800 pounds @ $1.1657 per pound = $4,430

Alternatively, cost of goods sold can be determined as follows:

Sales (3,800 @ $1.45)		$5,510
Goods available for sale (Part A)	6,295	
Less ending inventory (computed above)	1,865	
Cost of goods sold (agrees to Part C)		4,430
Gross profit		$1,080

Part C *(FIFO)*

Sales (3,800 @ $1.45)		$5,510
Goods available for sale (Part A)	6,295	
Less ending inventory:		
from July 30 purchase (1,500 @ $1.25)	$1,875	
from July 20 purchase (100 @ $1.20)	120	1,995
Cost of goods sold		4,300
Gross profit		$1,210

Exercise 1, continued
Part D *(LIFO)*

Sales (3,800 @ $1.45)			$5,510
Goods available for sale (Part A)		6,295	
Less ending inventory:			
from beginning inventory (500 @	$ 500		
$1.00)			
from July 5 purchase (1,000 @ $1.10)	1,100		
from July 9 purchase (100 @ $1.15)	115	1,715	
Cost of goods sold			4,580
Gross profit			$ 930

Part E

Ending inventory at FIFO (from above)	$1,995
Ending inventory at LIFO (from above)	1,715
LIFO Reserve	$ 280
Gross profit (FIFO) (from above)	$1,210
Gross profit (LIFO) (from above)	930
Difference in pretax income	280
Effective tax rate	x .40
Difference in taxes	$ 112

Exercise 2
Part A

	20B	20C
Beginning inventory	$104,000	$ 92,000
Purchases	815,000	699,000
Goods available for sale	919,000	791,000
Less ending inventory	92,000	78,000
Cost of goods sold	$827,000	$713,000

Part B

Cost of goods sold ÷ Average inventory = Inventory turnover

20B:
$827,000 (from above) ÷ [($104,000 + $92,000) ÷ 2] = $827,000 ÷ $98,000 = 8.44
20C:
$713,000 (from above) ÷ [($92,000 + $78,000) ÷ 2] = $713,000 ÷ $85,000 = 8.39

Inventory turnover measures the liquidity (nearness to cash) of the inventory. The lower inventory ratio in 20C indicates that inventory is being turned into cash less quickly. This ratio also measures the efficiency of using inventory. The lower ratio means less efficiency.

Exercise 2, continued
Part C

	20B	20C
Cash flows from operating activities:		
Net income	$319,000	$327,000
Plus decrease in inventory	12,000	14,000
Less increase in accounts payable	(5,000)	(9,000)
Net cash flows from operating activities	$326,000	$332,000

Part D

	Year ended December 31			
	20B		20C	
	As Reported	Corrected	As Reported	Corrected
Cost of goods sold	$827,000	$822,000	$713,000	$718,000
Net income	319,000	324,000	327,000	322,000

The error made in the inventory at the end of 20B understated 20B net income by $5,000 and overstated 20C net income by $5,000. Unless repeated, inventory errors are self-correcting over a two-year period. As a result, retained earnings at the end of 20C will be correctly reported.

Exercise 3

Valuation of the 20B ending inventory using the LCM rule applied on an item-by-item basis:

Item	Quantity	Total Cost	Total Market	LCM Valuation
AA	100	$ 3,000 (1)	$ 2,600 (2)	$ 2,600
BB	150	12,000 (3)	12,000 (3)	12,000
CC	200	20,000 (4)	20,800 (5)	20,000
				$34,600

Calculations:
(1) 100 units @ $30 per unit = $3,000
(2) 100 units @ $26 per unit = $2,600
(3) 150 units @ $80 per unit = $12,000
(4) 200 units @ $100 per unit = $20,000
(5) 200 units @ $104 per unit = $20,800

AN IDEA FOR YOUR STUDY TEAM

List the actions that management can take to impact a company's gross profit (either as a dollar amount or as a ratio).

Then, get together with the other members of your study team, compare your lists, and discuss the following questions. Is the gross profit ratio subject to manipulation? What can users of financial statements do to assure themselves as to the reliability of inventory information?

CHAPTER 8
REPORTING AND INTERPRETING
PROPERTY, PLANT, AND EQUIPMENT;
NATURAL RESOURCES; AND INTANGIBLES

ORGANIZATION OF THE CHAPTER

Acquisition and Maintenance of Plant and Equipment	Use, Impairment, and Disposal of Plant and Equipment	Natural Resources and Intangible Assets
• Classifying Long-Lived Assets • Fixed Asset Turnover Ratio • Measuring and Recording Acquisition Cost • Repairs, Maintenance, and Additions	• Depreciation Concepts • Alternative Depreciation Methods • How Managers Choose • Measuring Asset Impairment • Disposal of Property, Plant and Equipment	• Acquisition and Depletion of Natural Resources • Acquisition and Amortization of Intangible Assets

CHAPTER FOCUS SUGGESTIONS

Overview

Accounting and reporting issues related to long-lived assets, the resources that determine the productive capacity of a business, are the focal points of this chapter. Long-lived assets include both tangible assets (such as property, plant, and equipment, and natural resources) and intangible assets (such as patents, copyrights, franchises, licenses and trademarks).

Acquisition Costs and Subsequent Expenditures

In general, the acquisition cost of a long-lived asset includes all reasonable and necessary expenditures made to acquire the asset, place it in its operational setting and prepare it for its intended use. You will need to know how to measure and record the acquisition cost.

Most long-lived assets require substantial expenditures during their lives. Ordinary repair and maintenance costs relating to property, plant, and equipment are classified as revenue expenditures and immediately expensed. Extraordinary repairs and additions are classified as capital expenditures and added to the related asset accounts. In this regard, make sure that you are able to distinguish between revenue and capital expenditures and properly record these additional expenditures.

Depreciation, Amortization and Accretion

Recall the discussion of a deferral from chapter 4. *A deferral results when cash is paid to a vendor, supplier or other entity before the related expense is incurred. The amount is initially recorded in an asset account when the company acquires the asset because a benefit will be realized in the future. As time passes, adjusting entries are used to reduce the asset that is being used up (as the benefit is realized) and record the expense (which matches it with the related revenues generated).*

A long-lived asset represents a future benefit paid for in advance that will be used to generate revenues during the life of the long-lived asset (in essence, it is a deferral). Accordingly, in conformity with the matching principle, the expense associated with the use of the long-lived asset must be matched with, or allocated to the same period as, the revenues that are generated. The allocation process is called depreciation for property, plant, and equipment, depletion for natural resources, and amortization for intangibles. In addition to being able to determine and record depreciation expense using the straight-line, units-of-production and declining balance methods, you will need to know how to compute and record depletion and amortization expense.

Impairments and Disposals

When the estimated future cash flows of a long-lived asset falls below its book value, the book value should be written down to the fair value of the asset. You will need to know how to write down impaired long-lived assets. When long-lived assets are disposed of, the cost of the asset and the related accumulated depreciation, depletion, or amortization must be removed from the related accounts. You should know how to compute the gain or loss that will result when the disposal price is different from the book value of the asset.

Financial Statement Analysis Matters

Finally, you will also need to know how to compute the fixed asset turnover ratio. You should attempt to understand what this ratio is measuring so that you will be able to interpret this ratio.

LEARNING OBJECTIVES

After studying this chapter, you should be able to:

(LO 1) Define, classify, and explain the nature of long-lived productive assets and interpret the fixed asset turnover ratio.
(LO 2) Apply the cost principle to measure the acquisition and maintenance of property, plant, and equipment.
(LO 3) Apply various cost allocation methods as assets are held and used over time.
(LO 4) Explain the effect of asset impairment on the financial statements.
(LO 5) Analyze the disposal of property, plant, and equipment.
(LO 6) Apply measurement and reporting concepts for natural resources and intangible assets.
(LO 7) Explain the impact on cash flows of acquiring, using, and disposing of long-lived assets.

READ AND RECALL QUESTIONS

After you read each section of the chapter, answer the related Read and Recall Questions below.

> **LEARNING OBJECTIVE**
> *After studying this section of the chapter, you should be able to:*
> 1. Define, classify, and explain the nature of long-lived productive assets and interpret the fixed asset turnover ratio.

ACQUISITION AND MAINTENANCE OF PLANT AND EQUIPMENT
CLASSIFYING LONG-LIVED ASSETS

What are long-lived assets? How are these assets reported on the balance sheet? What are the two types of long-lived assets? What are the characteristics of each type?

KEY RATIO ANALYSIS: FIXED ASSET TURNOVER

How is the fixed asset turnover ratio computed? What is measured by the fixed asset turnover ratio? What does a high fixed asset turnover ratio normally suggest? What might a lower or declining rate indicate?

> **LEARNING OBJECTIVE**
> *After studying this section of the chapter, you should be able to:*
> 2. Apply the cost principle to measure the acquisition and maintenance of property, plant, and equipment.

MEASURING AND RECORDING ACQUISITION COST

What does "capitalized" mean? What are four types of costs that should be capitalized when a long-lived asset is acquired? What two types of costs sometimes associated with the acquisition of a long-lived asset should not be capitalized?

What is the definition of acquisition cost? How is acquisition cost determined?

For Equity (or Other Noncash Considerations)

When noncash consideration is included in the purchase of a long-lived asset, how is the cash equivalent price measured?

By Construction

What types of costs are capitalized when a company constructs an asset for its own use? What is capitalized interest? What is the amount of capitalized interest based on?

REPAIRS, MAINTENANCE, AND ADDITIONS

What are revenue expenditures? How are revenue expenditures recorded? What are ordinary repairs and maintenance?

What are capital expenditures? How are capital expenditures recorded?

Why do many managers prefer to capitalize expenditures for financial reporting purposes? Why do most managers prefer to classify the expenditure as a deductible expense for tax purposes?

LEARNING OBJECTIVE
After studying this section of the chapter, you should be able to:
3. Apply various cost allocation methods as assets are held and used over time.

USE, IMPAIRMENT, AND DISPOSAL OF PROPERTY, PLANT AND EQUIPMENT
DEPRECIATION CONCEPTS

What does the matching principle require with regards to long-lived assets? What is the purpose of depreciation? When an asset is depreciated, does the remaining balance sheet amount represent the asset's current market value? Why or why not?

Which account accumulates the amount of depreciation expense reported since the acquisition date of an asset? How is book (or carrying) value determined?

FINANCIAL ANALYSIS
BOOK VALUE AS AN APPROXIMATION OF REMAINING LIFE

What can be approximated when book value is compared to original cost?

What three amounts are required in order to compute depreciation expense? Which of the amounts are estimates? What is useful life? What is residual value? How is residual value estimated?

FINANCIAL ANALYSIS
DIFFERENCES IN ESTIMATED USEFUL LIVES WITHIN A SINGLE INDUSTRY

Why would companies in a single industry, such as the airline industry, use different estimated useful lives for the same assets, such as aircraft? What factors affect the estimate of a useful life?

ALTERNATIVE DEPRECIATION METHODS

What are the three most common depreciation methods? Once a depreciation method is selected, what is required?

Straight-Line Method

How is an asset's depreciable cost allocated to each accounting period over its estimated useful life when the straight line method is used? What is the formula for computing straight-line depreciation?

Units-of-Production Method

What is the formula for computing units-of-production depreciation? Why is depreciation expense considered to be a variable expense when the units-of-production method is used? What other estimate enters into the calculation of depreciation expense when this method is used?

Declining-Balance Method

What is meant by *accelerated* depreciation? How is the declining-balance rate determined? What is the formula for computing double-declining balance depreciation? How and when does residual value affect the calculation of depreciation expense when this method is used?

FINANCIAL ANALYSIS
IMPACT OF ALTERNATIVE DEPRECIATION METHODS

If one company uses accelerated depreciation and another the straight-line method, which company would you expect to report lower depreciation expense and, as such, higher net income?

HOW MANAGERS CHOOSE
Financial Reporting

Which depreciation method is easy to use and explain? Which depreciation method reports lower depreciation expense and, as a result, higher net income compared to other methods during the early years of the life of an asset? Why might mangers instead select an accelerated method?

Tax Reporting

Why do companies (such as Delta Air Lines) maintain two sets of accounting records? Is it legal and ethical to do so? Why or why not? What is the *least and the latest* rule? What depreciation method do most companies use for tax purposes? Why isn't this method acceptable under GAAP? What principle is violated by this method?

LEARNING OBJECTIVE
After studying this section of the chapter, you should be able to:
4. Explain the effect of asset impairment on the financial statements.

IMPAIRED ASSETS

What is *impairment*? When is an asset considered to be impaired? What must be determined to compute an impairment loss? If the net book value of flight equipment is $8,320 million and future cash flows are estimated to be $8,000 million, what journal entry is required? How would this entry impact the accounting equation?

Account	Debit	Credit

_____ Assets _____ = _____ Liabilities _____ + _____ Stockholders' Equity _____

LEARNING OBJECTIVE
After studying this section of the chapter, you should be able to:
5. Analyze the disposal of property, plant, and equipment.

DISPOSAL OF PROPERTY, PLANT AND EQUIPMENT

Why might a business voluntarily decide not to hold a long-lived asset for its entire life? On the other hand, what could cause a business to involuntarily dispose of such an asset?

What two journal entries are usually required to record the disposal of a long-lived asset? Why might a gain or loss occur upon the disposal of a long-lived asset? How is the amount of the gain or loss on disposal determined?

FINANCIAL ANALYSIS
TAKING A DIFFERENT STRATEGY TO SUCCESS

Why does Singapore Airlines report significantly higher depreciation expense when compared to the rest of the airline industry? What happens when Singapore Airlines sells its aircraft? What does the management of Singapore Airlines accomplish with this strategy for managing the company's long-lived productivity?

LEARNING OBJECTIVE
After studying this section of the chapter, you should be able to:
6. Apply measurement and reporting concepts for natural resources and intangible assets.

NATURAL RESOURCES AND INTANGIBLE ASSETS
Acquisition and Cost Allocation

What are natural resources? Why are natural resources called *wasting assets*?

What does the matching principle require with regards to natural resources? What is depletion? What method is often used to compute depletion? How is depletion expense recorded?

ACQUISITION AND AMORTIZATION OF INTANGIBLE ASSETS

What is an intangible asset? When are intangible assets recorded at historical cost? If an intangible asset is developed internally, how is the cost of development recorded?

If a separate intangible has a definite life, what method is usually used to amortize the intangible asset? How does residual value affect amortization expense? How are amortization expense and intangible assets reported in the financial statements? How is amortization expense recorded?

Are intangible assets with indefinite lives amortized? What two step process is used with regards to these assets? How is an impairment loss recorded for these assets?

Goodwill

What is goodwill? What factors give rise to goodwill? What is *internally generated* goodwill? Is internally generated goodwill reported in the financial statements? When is the only time that goodwill is reported as an asset? Does goodwill have a definite or indefinite life? What process must take place on an annual basis with regards to goodwill? How is the amount of goodwill determined when one company purchases another?

Trademarks

What is a trademark? Are trademarks typically reported on the balance sheet? Why or why not? How should the costs of developing a trademark be recorded?

Copyrights

What is a copyright? What period of time is covered by a copyright? When and how are copyrights recorded?

Patents

What is a patent? How is cost measured when a patent is purchased? What costs can be recorded as an intangible asset when a patent is developed internally?

Technology

What types of technology intangible assets are reported by companies? What costs are capitalized for these assets? How are the capitalized costs amortized?

Franchises

What is a franchise? How is the life of a franchise agreement determined?

License and Operating Rights

What are operating rights?

Research and Development Costs

Can internal research and development costs be capitalized as intangible assets? Why or why not? How are such costs handled?

LEARNING OBJECTIVE

After studying this section of the chapter, you should be able to:
7. Explain the impact on cash flows of acquiring, using, and disposing of long-lived assets.

FOCUS ON CASH FLOWS
PRODUCTIVE ASSETS AND DEPRECIATION

Why is depreciation expense commonly referred to as a *noncash* expense? When the indirect method is used, should depreciation expense be added back to or deducted from net income to compute cash flows from operations?

Are transactions involving the purchase and sale of intangible assets classified as operating, investing, or financing activities on the statement of cash flows? When an intangible asset is sold, is the gain on the sale added to or deducted from net income when the indirect method is used to compute cash flows from operations?

Chapter Take-Aways

1. ***Define, classify, and explain the nature of long-lived productive assets and interpret the fixed asset turnover ratio.***

Noncurrent assets are those that a business retains for long periods of time for use in the course of normal operations rather than for sale. They may be divided into tangible assets (land, buildings, equipment, natural resources) and intangible assets (including goodwill, patents, and franchises).

The cost allocation method utilized affects the amount of net property, plant, and equipment that is used in the computation of the fixed asset turnover ratio. Accelerated methods reduce book value and increase the turnover ratio.

2. ***Apply the cost principle to measure the acquisition and maintenance of property, plant, and equipment.***

Acquisition cost of property, plant, and equipment is the cash-equivalent purchase price plus all reasonable and necessary expenditures made to acquire and prepare the asset for its intended use. These assets may be acquired using cash, debt, stock, or through self-construction. Expenditures made after the asset is in use are either capital expenditures or revenue expenditures:

Capital expenditures provide benefits for one or more accounting periods beyond the current period. Amounts are debited to the appropriate asset accounts and depreciated, depleted, or amortized over their useful lives.

Revenue expenditures provide benefits during the current accounting period only. Amounts are debited to appropriate current expense accounts when the expenses are incurred.

3. *Apply various cost allocation methods as assets are held and used over time.*

Cost allocation methods: in conformity with the matching principle, cost (less any estimated residual value) is allocated to periodic expense over the periods benefited. Because of depreciation, the net book value of an asset declines over time and net income is reduced by the amount of the expense. Common depreciation methods include straight-line (a constant amount over time), units-of-production (a variable amount over time), and double-declining-balance (a decreasing amount over time).

- Depreciation—buildings and equipment.
- Depletion—natural resources.
- Amortization— intangibles.

4. *Explain the effect of asset impairment on the financial statements.*

When events or changes in circumstances reduce the estimated future cash flows of long-lived assets below their book value, the book value should be written down (by recording a loss) to the fair value of the asset.

5. *Analyze the disposal of property, plant, and equipment.*

When assets are disposed of through sale or abandonment,

- Record additional depreciation since the last adjustment was made,
- Remove the cost of the old asset and its related accumulated depreciation, depletion, or amortization,
- Recognize the cash proceeds,
- Recognize any gains or losses when the asset's net book value is not equal to the cash received.

6. *Apply measurement and reporting concepts for natural resources and intangible assets.*

The cost principle should be applied in recording the acquisition of natural resources and intangible assets. Natural resources should be depleted (usually by the units-of-production method) usually with the amount of the depletion expense capitalized to an inventory account. Intangibles with definite useful lives are amortized using the straight-line method. Intangibles with indefinite useful lives, including goodwill, are not amortized, but are reviewed at least annually for impairment. Report intangibles at net book value on the balance sheet.

7. *Explain the impact on cash flows of acquiring, using, and disposing of long-lived assets.*

Depreciation expense is a noncash expense that has no effect on cash. It is added back to net income on the statement of cash flows to determine cash from operations. Acquiring and disposing of long-lived assets are investing activities.

Key Ratio

The fixed asset turnover ratio measures how efficiently a company utilizes its investment in property, plant, and equipment over time. Its ratio can be compared to competitors' ratios. It is computed as follows:

Fixed Asset Turnover = Sales Revenues ÷ Average Net Fixed Assets

Average net fixed assets is determined as follows:

(Net Fixed Assets, beginning of the year + Net Fixed Assets, end of year) ÷ 2

Finding Financial Information

Balance Sheet
Under Noncurrent Assets Property, Plant, and Equipment (net of accumulated depreciation) Natural resources (net of accumulated depletion) Intangibles (net of accumulated amortization, if any)

Income Statement
Under Operating Expenses Depreciation, depletion, and amortization expense or included in Selling, general and administrative expenses and Cost of goods sold (with amount of depreciation expense disclosed in a note)

Statement of Cash Flows
Under Operating Activities (Indirect Method) Net income + Depreciation and amortization expense − Gains on sales of assets + Losses on sales of assets **Under investing activities:** + Sales of assets for cash − Purchases of assets for cash

Notes
Under Summary of Significant Accounting Policies Description of management's choice for depreciation and amortization methods, including useful lives and the amount of annual depreciation expense, if not listed on the income statement. **Under a Separate Footnote** If not specified on the balance sheet, a listing of the major classifications of long-lived assets at cost and the balance in accumulated depreciation, depletion, and amortization.

SELF-TEST QUESTIONS AND EXERCISES

MATCHING

Match each of the key terms listed below with the appropriate textbook definition:

_____ Acquisition Cost
_____ Amortization
_____ Book Value (or Carrying Value)
_____ Capital Expenditures
_____ Capitalized Interest
_____ Copyright
_____ Declining-Balance (DB) Depreciation
_____ Depletion
_____ Depreciation
_____ Estimated Useful Life
_____ Extraordinary Repairs
_____ Franchise
_____ Goodwill (Cost in Excess of Net Assets Acquired)

_____ Intangible Assets
_____ Licenses and Operating Rights
_____ Long-Lived Assets
_____ Natural Resources
_____ Ordinary Repairs and Maintenance
_____ Patent
_____ Residual (or Salvage) Value
_____ Revenue Expenditures
_____ Straight-Line (SL) Depreciation
_____ Tangible Assets (or Fixed Assets)
_____ Technology
_____ Trademark
_____ Units-of-Production Depreciation

Financial Accounting

A. Assets that have physical substance.
B. Expenditures that provide future benefits and are recorded as increases in asset accounts, not as expenses.
C. Systematic and rational allocation of the acquisition cost of an intangible asset over its useful life.
D. An exclusive legal right to use a special name, image, or slogan.
E. Interest expenditures included in the cost of a self-constructed asset.
F. Expenditures for the normal operating upkeep of long-lived assets.
G. Obtained through agreements with governmental units or agencies, permit owners to use public property in performing its services.
H. Includes costs for computer software and Web development.
I. Method that allocates the cost of an asset over its useful life based on its periodic output related to its total estimated output.
J. Assets occurring in nature, such as mineral deposits, timber tracts, oil, and gas.
K. Acquisition cost of the asset less accumulated depreciation, depletion, or amortization.
L. Expenditures for major, high-cost, long-term repairs that increase the economic usefulness of the asset.
M. Expenditures that provide benefits during the current accounting period only and are recorded as expenses.
N. For accounting purposes, the excess of the purchase price of a business over the market value of the business's assets and liabilities.
O. Assets that have special rights but not physical substance.
P. Net cash equivalent amount paid or to be paid for the asset.
Q. Systematic and rational allocation of the cost of property, plant, and equipment (but not land) over their useful lives.
R. Tangible and intangible resources owned by a business and used in its operations over several years.
S. A contractual right to sell certain products or services, use certain trademarks, or perform activities in a geographical region.
T. Estimated amount to be recovered, less disposal costs, at the end of the company's estimated useful life of an asset.
U. Systematic and rational allocation of the cost of a natural resource over the period of exploitation.
V. Exclusive right to publish, use, and sell a literary, musical, or artistic work.
W. The method that allocates the cost of an asset over its useful life based on a multiple of (often two times) the straight-line rate.
X. Expected service life of an asset to the present owner.
Y. Method that allocates the cost of an asset in equal periodic amounts over its useful life.
Z. Granted by the federal government for an invention; gives the owner the right to use, manufacture, and sell the subject of the patent.

TRUE-FALSE QUESTIONS

For each of the following, enter a T or F in the blank to indicate whether the statement is true or false.

___1. (LO 1) Fixed asset turnover is computed by dividing average fixed assets (net) by sales or operating revenues.

___2. (LO 2) The cost of a long-lived asset includes all reasonable and necessary costs to acquire the asset, place it in its long-lived setting, and prepare it for its intended use.

___3. (LO 2) If the market value of the noncash consideration that is included in the purchase of a long-lived asset cannot be determined, the cash-equivalent cost of the asset should be limited to the cash paid.

___4. (LO 2) Interest on self-constructed assets should only be capitalized when funds are borrowed directly to support the construction.

___5. (LO 2) Revenue expenditures are expenditures that provide benefits during the current accounting period only.

___6. (LO 2) If material, repair and maintenance expenditures should be added to the asset account.

___7. (LO 2) The decision as to whether an expenditure is a capital expenditure or a revenue expenditure can be based on the materiality of the amount involved.

___8. (LO 3) Depreciation expense is an estimate.

___9. (LO 3) Amortization, depletion and depreciation are cost allocation processes.

___10. (LO 3) The useful life estimated for a piece of equipment should be based on the number of years that the equipment would be expected to last under normal use by an average user of the equipment.

___11. (LO 3) More companies use the declining balance accelerated depreciation method for financial reporting purposes than all other methods combined.

___12. (LO 3) The declining balance rate is found by computing the straight-line rate, ignoring residual value, and then multiplying that rate by a selected acceleration rate which may not exceed 200%.

___13. (LO 3) The declining balance method is used by companies in industries that expect fairly rapid obsolescence of equipment.

___14. (LO 3) The consistency principle requires that accounting information reported in the financial statements should be comparable across accounting periods, and, as such, changes in estimates of useful life and residual value are not allowed under GAAP.

___15. (LO 3) The depreciation conformity rule requires companies to use the same depreciation method for financial reporting and tax return purposes.

___16. (LO 5) A loss on disposal occurs when the book value of the long-lived asset is less than the resources received.

___17. (LO 6) The acquisition cost of natural resources (or wasting assets) must be reported as a revenue expenditure because these assets are depleted.

___18. (LO 5) A company wishing to improve its cash flow should use the straight-line method rather than an accelerated method of depreciation for financial reporting purposes.

MULTIPLE CHOICE QUESTIONS

Choose the best answer or response by placing the identifying letter in the space provided.

___1. (LO 1) _____ assets have physical substance, whereas _____ assets have no physical substance, but rather grant rights to their owner.

    a. Natural resource; long-lived
    b. Tangible; intangible
    c. Operating; non-operating
    d. Intangible; tangible
    e. Tangible; natural resource

___2. (LO 2) The acquisition cost of a long-lived asset may include

    a. the market value of any noncash consideration given.
    b. incidental costs, such as title fees, sales commissions, legal fees, etc.
    c. renovation and repair costs incurred prior to use.
    d. capitalized interest.
    e. all of the above.

___3. (LO 2) If a company completely rebuilds a motor on a piece of equipment during its useful life, and the rebuilt motor extends the useful life of the equipment and increases the residual value, this expenditure would be classified as a

    a. capital expenditure and capitalized as a separate asset.
    b. capital expenditure and capitalized as part of the cost of the equipment.
    c. revenue expenditure and capitalized as part of the cost of the equipment.
    d. revenue expenditure and expensed in the period in which it was spent.
    e. capital expenditure and expensed in the period in which it was spent.

___4. (LO 3) The primary purpose of depreciation is to

    a. allocate the cost of an asset over its useful life in conformity with the matching principle.
    b. determine the market value of an asset at any point of its life.
    c. delay as long as possible the payment of taxes by charging expense against income.
    d. approximate the total cost of using an asset.
    e. decrease the value of an asset in conformity with the conservatism principle.

___5. (LO 3) Residual value is

    a. the difference at any point in time between net book value and market value.
    b. the excess of cost over accumulated depreciation.
    c. the part of the acquisition cost of an asset expected to be recovered when the asset is disposed of at the end of its usefulness to the current owner.
    d. the part of an asset not yet depreciated at any point in time.
    e. the scrap value of the asset.

___6. (LO 3) Accelerated depreciation methods include the sum-of-the-years' digits method and the

    a. straight-line method.
    b. declining-balance method.
    c. units-of-production method.
    d. depletion method.
    e. annuity method.

___7. (LO 3) For tax purposes, Delta Air Lines probably uses the _____ to compute depreciation.

    a. Modified Accelerated Cost Recovery System
    b. straight-line method
    c. sum-of-the-years' digits
    d. 200% declining balance
    e. units of service

___8. (LO 4) Impairment of long-lived tangible and intangible assets

    a. occurs when events or changed circumstances cause the estimated future cash flows (future benefits) of the assets to exceed their book value.

    b. results in a gain when the assets' fair value exceeds its book value.

    c. requires a write down when the asset's estimated future cash flows (future benefits) are less than its book value.

    d. All of the above.

___9. (LO 5) Disposals of long-lived assets:

    a. may be voluntary or involuntary.

    b. Seldom occur on the last day of the accounting period.

    c. Usually results in two journal entries: (1) an adjusting entry to update the depreciation expense and accumulated depreciation accounts, and (2) an entry to record the disposal.

    d. All of the above.

___10. (LO 6) All of the following are intangible assets except

    a. a copyright.

    b. a fast food restaurant franchise.

    c. goodwill.

    d. an offshore oil well.

    e. a leasehold on a large office building.

___11. (LO 6) Depletion is the term used to describe the periodic cost allocation process over the life of

    a. an intangible asset.

    b. land.

    c. a building.

    d. supplies.

    e. a natural resource.

___12. (LO 7) Assuming the indirect method is used, acquiring, selling, and depreciating long-lived assets result in the following adjustments to net income to determine cash flows from operating activities:

    a. depreciation expense should be added.

    b. gains on sale of long-term assets should be added.

    c. losses on sales of long-term assets should be subtracted.

    d. losses due to asset impairment write-down should be subtracted.

    e. All of the above.

EXERCISES

Record your answers to each part of these exercises in the space provided. Show your work.

Exercise 1 (LO 1)

Pixie Industries reported property and equipment, net, of $4,655,000 and $1,552,000 on its balance sheets at December 31, 20B and 20A, respectively. Revenues earned from software, animation, film and patent licensing amounted to $38,227,000 and $12,113,000 for 20B and 20A, respectively.

Part A

Compute Pixie's fixed asset turnover ratio for the year ended December 31, 20B.

Part B

Assume that Pixie's fixed asset turnover rate increased from 20A to 20B. How might an analyst interpret an increasing ratio? Alternatively, assume that Pixie's fixed asset turnover rate decreased. Does a declining ratio always indicate a negative trend?

Exercise 2 (LO 2)

On January 1, 20A, Coopers Industries bought a parcel of land for use in its operations by paying the seller $100,000 in cash, signing a five year, 12% note payable in the amount of $100,000, and issuing 3,000 shares of Coopers Industries $1 par value common stock ($100 per share market value). In connection with the purchase of the land, Coopers incurred legal fees of $19,000, a real estate agent sales commission of $25,000, surveying fees of $1,000, and an appraisal fee of $5,000.

Part A

Compute the total acquisition cost of the parcel of land.

Exercise 2, continued
Part B

Prepare the journal entry to record the purchase of the parcel of the land.

Date	Account	Debit	Credit
1/1/20A			

Exercise 3

On January 1, 20A, Trueblood, Inc. purchased a piece of machinery for use in operations. The total acquisition cost was $33,000. The machine has an estimated useful life of three years and a residual value of $3,000. Assume that units produced by the machine will total 16,000 during 20A, 23,000 during 20B and 21,000 during 20C.

Part A (LO 3)

Use this information to complete the following table.

Method	Depreciation Expense 20A	Depreciation Expense 20B	Depreciation Expense 20C	Book Value at End of Year 20A	Book Value at End of Year 20B	Book Value at End of Year 20C
Straight-line						
Units of production						
Double declining balance						

Part B (LO 3)

On January 1, 20B, the machine was rebuilt at a cost of $7,000. After it was rebuilt, the total estimated life of the machine was increased to five years (from the original estimate of three years) and the residual value to $6,000 (from $3,000). Assume that the company chose the straight-line method for depreciation. Compute the annual depreciation expense after the change in estimates.

Exercise 3, continued
Part C (LO 4)

Prepare the adjusting entry to record the depreciation expense for the year ended December 31, 20B.

Date	Account	Debit	Credit
12/31/20B			

Part D (LO 5)

On December 31, 20E, the machine was sold for $7,500. Compute the book value on that date.

Part E (LO 5)

Prepare the journal entry to record the sale.

Date	Account	Debit	Credit
12/31/20E			

Exercise 4 (LO 6)

On January 1, 20A, Morris Minerals paid $300,000 for a mineral deposit in Morris, Illinois, and then spent $45,000 to develop the deposit for exploitation. It was estimated that 690,000 total cubic yards could be extracted economically. During 20A, 69,000 yards were extracted. Compute the amount of depletion expense for the year ended December 31, 20A.

Exercise 5 (LO 6)

On January 1, 20C, Drafke Companies paid $15,000 to Beltran Industries for a patent. Beltran had registered the patent with the U. S. Patent Office two years earlier on January 1, 20A.

Part A

Calculate the amount of annual amortization expense.

Part B

Prepare the journal entries to record the purchase of the patent on January 1, 20C and the amortization expense for the year ended December 31, 20C.

Date	Account	Debit	Credit
1/1/20C			
12/31/20C			

SOLUTIONS TO SELF-TEST QUESTIONS AND EXERCISES

MATCHING

P	Acquisition Cost	O	Intangible Assets
C	Amortization	G	Licenses and Operating Rights
K	Book Value (or Carrying Value)	R	Long-Lived Assets
B	Capital Expenditures	J	Natural Resources
E	Capitalized Interest	F	Ordinary Repairs and Maintenance
V	Copyright	Z	Patent
W	Declining-Balance (DB) Depreciation	T	Residual (or Salvage) Value
U	Depletion	M	Revenue Expenditures
Q	Depreciation	Y	Straight-Line (SL) Depreciation
X	Estimated Useful Life	A	Tangible Assets (or Fixed Assets)
L	Extraordinary Repairs	H	Technology
S	Franchise	D	Trademark
N	Goodwill (Cost in Excess of Net Assets Acquired)	I	Units-of-Production Depreciation

TRUE-FALSE QUESTIONS

1. F – Fixed asset turnover is computed by dividing sales (or operating revenues) by average fixed assets (net).
2. T
3. F – If the market value of the noncash consideration given cannot be determined, the current market value of the asset purchased should be used for measurement purposes.
4. F – Interest on self-constructed assets should be capitalized *even* in cases where funds were not borrowed directly to support the construction.
5. T
6. F – Ordinary repairs and maintenance are recorded as an expense in the period in which incurred; extraordinary repairs are added to the related asset account.
7. T
8. T
9. T
10. F – Estimated useful life represents the useful economic life to the present owner rather than the total economic life to all potential users.
11. F – More companies use straight-line depreciation for financial reporting purposes than all other methods combined.
12. T
13. T
14. F – The consistency principles places a significant *constraint* on changing depreciation estimates unless the effect is to improve the measurement of depreciation expense and net income; however, GAAP does permit changes in estimates of useful life and residual value when it is clear that either estimate should be revised to a material degree.
15. F – Some of the depreciation methods used for financial reporting purposes are not acceptable for federal income tax reporting and vice versa; most corporations use the Modified Accelerated Cost Recovery System (not permitted under GAAP) for calculating depreciation expense for tax purposes.
16. F – A loss on disposal occurs when the book value of the long-lived asset is *greater than* the resources received.
17. F – When a natural resource is acquired or developed, it is recorded in conformity with the cost principle, and, as the natural resource is used up, its acquisition cost is apportioned among the various periods in which the resulting revenues are earned. That is, the cost is recorded in a separate noncurrent asset account and then depletion expense is recorded over the economic life of the natural resource.
18. F – The depreciation expense recorded for financial reporting purposes is a noncash expense, which does not directly affect cash flows.

MULTIPLE CHOICE QUESTIONS

1.	b	3.	b	5.	c	7.	a	9.	d	11.	e
2.	e	4.	a	6.	b	8.	c	10.	d	12.	a

EXERCISES

Exercise 1
Part A

Sales (or operating revenues) ÷ Average fixed assets (net) = Fixed asset turnover ratio

$38,227,000 ÷ [($4,655,000 + $1,552,000) ÷ 2] = $38,227,000 ÷ $3,103,500 = 12.3

Part B

The fixed asset turnover ratio measures how efficiently the company utilizes its investment in property, plant, and equipment over time. For each dollar invested in average fixed assets, the company generated $12.30 of sales. An increasing fixed asset turnover rate suggests improvements in efficiency, and vice versa. On the other hand, a declining rate may indicate that the company is expanding in anticipation of higher sales in the future.

Exercise 2
Part A

Purchase price:		
Cash		$100,000
Noncash consideration:		
Note payable	$100,000	
Common stock (3,000 shares @ $100/share)	300,000	400,000
Incidental costs paid by purchaser:		
Legal fees	$ 19,000	
Commission	25,000	
Surveying fees	1,000	
Appraisal fee	5,000	50,000
Total acquisition cost		$550,000

Part B

Date	Account	Debit	Credit
1/1/20A	Land	550,000	
	Cash ($100,000 + $50,000)		150,000
	Note payable		100,000
	Common stock		3,000
	(3,000 shares @ $1/share.)		
	Contributed capital in excess of par (3,000 shares @ $99/share)		297,000

Exercise 3
Part A

	Depreciation Expense			Book Value at End of Year		
Method	**20A**	**20B**	**20C**	**20A**	**20B**	**20C**
Straight-line	$10,000 (1)	$10,000 (1)	$10,000 (1)	$23,000	$13,000	$3,000
Units of production	8,000 (2)	11,500 (3)	10,500 (4)	25,000	13,500	3,000
Double declining balance	22,000 (5)	7,333 (6)	667 (7)	11,000	3,667	3,000

Calculations:

(1) ($33,000 - $3,000) ÷ 3 = $10,000

(2) 16,000 ÷ (16,000 + 23,000 + 21,000) x ($33,000 - $3,000) = $8,000

(3) 23,000 ÷ (16,000 + 23,000 + 21,000) x ($33,000 - $3,000) = $11,500

(4) 21,000 ÷ (16,000 + 23,000 + 21,000) x ($33,000 - $3,000) = $10,500

(5) ($33,000 - $0) x 2/3 = $22,000

(6) ($33,000 - $22,000) x 2/3 = $7,333

(7) ($33,000 - $22,000 - $7,333) x 2/3 = $2,445; however, recording this amount of depreciation expense in 20C would cause the book value to drop below the residual value, so record only $667 ($3,667 - $3,000) of depreciation expense.

Part B

Acquisition cost	$ 33,000
Less accumulated depreciation at December 31, 20A	(10,000)
Add extraordinary repair (considered to be an addition)	7,000
Book value at January 1, 20B	30,000
Less residual value	(6,000)
Undepreciated balance	24,000
Divided by remaining useful life (5 years - 1 year)	4
Revised amount of annual depreciation	$ 6,000

Part C

Date	Account	Debit	Credit
12/31/20B	Depreciation expense	6,000	
	Accumulated depreciation		6,000

Part D

Acquisition cost		$33,000
Add extraordinary repair:		7,000
Balance in machinery account		40,000
Accumulated depreciation:		
20A	$10,000	
20B through 20E ($6,000 x 4)	24,000	34,000
Book value at December 31, 20E		$ 6,000

©The McGraw-Hill Companies, Inc., 2004

Exercise 3, continued
Part E

Date	Account	Debit	Credit
12/31/20E	Cash	7,500	
	Accumulated depreciation	34,000	
	Machinery		40,000
	Gain on sale ($7,500 - $6,000)		1,500

Exercise 4

Depletion expense for 20A = ($300,000 + $45,000) x 69,000 ÷ $690,000 = $34,500

Exercise 5
Part A

Annual amortization expense = [$15,000 ÷ (17 - 2)]

Part B

Date	Account	Debit	Credit
1/1/20C	Patent	15,000	
	Cash		15,000
12/31/20C	Amortization expense [$15,000 ÷ (17 - 2)]	1,000	
	Patent		1,000

AN IDEA FOR YOUR STUDY TEAM

You may recall that residual value is the estimated amount to be recovered less any estimated costs of dismantling, disposal, and sale. The useful life represents the estimated useful economic life to the present owner of the long-lived asset. Assume that you were the accounting manager for a manufacturer. List the factors that would you consider when you estimate the residual value and useful life of a major piece of machinery recently installed in the factory.

If a manager wanted to recognize a modest gain upon the ultimate disposal of the machinery at the end of its life, would you tend to understate or overstate the estimate of residual value? Would you tend to understate or overstate the useful life?

Get together with the other members of your study team and compare your answers. Then, discuss the following. Would it be appropriate to intentionally misstate the estimated residual value and useful life in order to recognize a modest gain? Each opinion should be supported by references to the appropriate accounting principle(s) or constraint(s).

ORGANIZATION OF THE CHAPTER

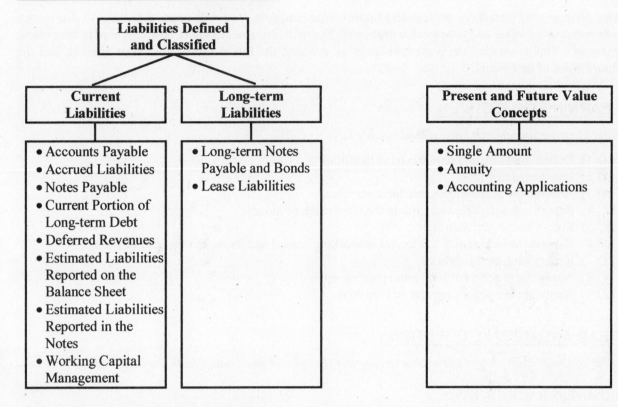

```
                    ┌─────────────────────┐
                    │  Liabilities Defined │
                    │    and Classified    │
                    └─────────────────────┘
```

Current Liabilities	Long-term Liabilities	Present and Future Value Concepts
• Accounts Payable • Accrued Liabilities • Notes Payable • Current Portion of Long-term Debt • Deferred Revenues • Estimated Liabilities Reported on the Balance Sheet • Estimated Liabilities Reported in the Notes • Working Capital Management	• Long-term Notes Payable and Bonds • Lease Liabilities	• Single Amount • Annuity • Accounting Applications

CHAPTER FOCUS SUGGESTIONS

Overview

The last three chapters addressed the reporting and interpretation of assets. The next three chapters address the other side of the balance sheet. A variety of business and accounting issues arise when managers need to obtain funds to finance the acquisition of assets and the operations of the business. Measurement and reporting issues relating to liabilities are covered in chapters 9 and 10 and issues relating to owners' equity are addressed in chapter 11.

Measurement and Reporting Issues

Chapter 9 focuses on the liabilities that are common to most companies: accounts payable; accrued liabilities relating to income taxes and payroll; notes payable; long-term debt; deferred revenues; and contingent liabilities. You should be familiar with the characteristics and measurement of each type of liability, and able to classify each as current or noncurrent.

Financial Statement Analysis Matters

You will need to know how to compute the current ratio, the amount of working capital and the payable turnover ratio. You should attempt to understand what these ratios are measuring so that you will be able to interpret them.

Present and Future Value Concepts

This chapter also introduces present and future value concepts. You will need to be able to distinguish between present value and future value problems. You will also need to know how to compute the present value of a single amount, the present value of an annuity, the future value of a single amount, and the future value of an annuity.

LEARNING OBJECTIVES

After studying this chapter, you should be able to:

(LO 1) Define, measure and report current liabilities.
(LO 2) Use the current ratio.
(LO 3) Analyze the accounts payable turnover ratio.
(LO 4) Report notes payable and explain the time value of money.
(LO 5) Report contingent liabilities.
(LO 6) Explain the importance of changes in working capital and its impact on cash flows.
(LO 7) Report long-term liabilities.
(LO 8) Apply the concepts of future and present values.
(LO 9) Apply present value concepts to liabilities.

READ AND RECALL QUESTIONS

After you read each section of the chapter, answer the related Read and Recall Questions below.

BUSINESS BACKGROUND

How do businesses finance the acquisition of their assets? Why is debt capital more risky than equity? Given the risk associated with debt, why do most companies include borrowed funds in their capital structure?

LEARNING OBJECTIVE
After studying this section of the chapter, you should be able to:
1. Define, measure and report current liabilities.

LIABILITIES DEFINED AND CLASSIFIED

What are liabilities? How do liabilities arise? How is a liability measured when it is first recorded? What are current liabilities? What are noncurrent liabilities? What is liquidity?

KEY RATIO ANALYSIS: CURRENT RATIO

How is the current ratio computed? What does it measure? What is normally suggested by a high current ratio? How could a company with a high current ratio have liquidity problems? How can the current ratio be manipulated?

CURRENT LIABILITIES
ACCOUNTS PAYABLE

How are trade accounts payable created? Why isn't it advisable to delay payment to suppliers for as long as possible to conserve cash?

KEY RATIO ANALYSIS: ACCOUNTS PAYABLE RATIO

How is the payable turnover ratio computed? What does it measure? How is the average age of payables determined?

Usually, what would be suggested by a low accounts payable ratio? Under which circumstances might this ratio not reflect reality? How can this ratio be manipulated?

ACCRUED LIABILITIES

What are accrued liabilities?

Income Taxes Payable

What types of income taxes do corporations pay?

Accrued Payroll

Are salaries typically owed to employees at the end of each accounting period? In addition to salaries that have been earned but unpaid, what other payroll liabilities might need to be accrued?

What adjusting entry would be required at the end of the accounting period if there is $125,000 of accrued vacation time? How would this entry impact the accounting equation?

Account	Debit	Credit

_____ Assets _____ = _____ Liabilities _____ + _____ Stockholders' Equity _____

What entry would be required when the $125,000 of accrued vacation time is taken by employees? How would this entry impact the accounting equation?

Account	Debit	Credit

_____ Assets _____ = _____ Liabilities _____ + _____ Stockholders' Equity _____

Payroll Taxes

Assume that General Mills accumulated the following information in its payroll records: Salaries and wages earned - $1,800,000; Income taxes withheld - $275,000; and FICA taxes (employee's share) - $105,000. (Remember: Both the employer and the employee pay FICA taxes.) What entry would be required to record the payroll? How would this entry impact the accounting equation?

Account	Debit	Credit

_____ Assets _____ = _____ Liabilities _____ + _____ Stockholders' Equity _____

LEARNING OBJECTIVE
After studying this section of the chapter, you should be able to:
4. Report notes payable and explain the time value of money.

NOTES PAYABLE

What are the characteristics of notes payable? What is the "time value of money?" What is the formula to calculate interest? In conformity with the matching principle, when should interest expense be recorded?

Assume that General Mills borrows $100,000 on a one-year, 12% note payable with interest payable on March 31, 2004, and October 31, 2004. The principal is payable at the maturity date, October 31, 2004. What entry would be required to record the borrowing? How would this entry impact the accounting equation?

Account	Debit	Credit

_____ Assets _____ = _____ Liabilities _____ + _____ Stockholders' Equity _____

How much interest is owed on the note payable at December 31, 2003, the end of the year? What adjusting entry is required in this regard at December 31, 2003? How would this entry impact the accounting equation?

Account	Debit	Credit

_____ Assets _____ = _____ Liabilities _____ + _____ Stockholders' Equity _____

How much interest will be paid on the note payable on March 31, 2004? What entry would be made to record this payment? How would this entry impact the accounting equation?

Account	Debit	Credit

_____ Assets _____ = _____ Liabilities _____ + _____ Stockholders' Equity _____

CURRENT PORTION OF LONG-TERM DEBT

What is the current portion of long-term debt?

FINANCIAL ANALYSIS
REFINANCED DEBT: CURRENT OR NONCURRENT?

If a company intends to refinance debt and has the ability to do so, should currently maturing debt that will be refinanced be classified as a current or long-term liability?

DEFERRED REVENUE

What are deferred revenues? What does the revenue principle require? How are deferred revenues reported on the financial statements?

ESTIMATED LIABILITES REPORTED ON THE BALANCE SHEET

Why are some recorded liabilities based on estimates? What are some examples of liabilities that are based on estimates?

LEARNING OBJECTIVE
After studying this section of the chapter, you should be able to:
5. Report contingent liabilities.

ESTIMATED LIABILITIES REPORTED IN THE NOTES

What is a contingent liability? What two factors must be considered to decide if a given transaction or event results in an actual or contingent liability? What are the three types of "probabilities of occurrence?" How is each type defined?

What are the general guidelines for (1) recording a liability, (2) not recording but disclosing a liability, and (3) not reporting or disclosing a liability?

LEARNING OBJECTIVE
After studying this section of the chapter, you should be able to:
6. Explain the importance of working capital and its impact on cash flows.

WORKING CAPITAL MANAGEMENT

Why is the management of working capital such an important activity?

FOCUS ON CASH FLOWS
Working Capital And Cash Flows

When the indirect method is used to determine the cash flow from operations, should increases in current assets be added to or subtracted from net income? Should decreases in current assets be added to or subtracted from net income? Should increases in current liabilities be added to or subtracted from net income? Should decreases in current liabilities be added to or subtracted from net income?

LEARNING OBJECTIVE
After studying this section of the chapter, you should be able to:
7. Report long-term liabilities.

LONG-TERM LIABILITIES

What are long-term liabilities? What do some companies do to reduce risk for creditors? What is secured debt? What is unsecured debt?

LONG-TERM NOTES PAYABLE AND BONDS

What is a private placement? What is this type of debt often called? What are bonds? How are bonds similar to notes?

LEASE LIABILITIES

What is an operating lease? What is a capital lease? What criteria would distinguish a lease as a capital lease? How many of the criteria must be met for such a classification?

```
LEARNING OBJECTIVE
After studying this section of the chapter, you should be able to:
8. Apply the concepts of future and present values.
```

PRESENT AND FUTURE VALUE CONCEPTS

What is a "present value problem?" What is a "future value problem?" How does an annuity differ from a single payment?

FUTURE AND PRESENT VALUE OF A SINGLE AMOUNT
Future Value of a Single Amount

To solve a future value problem, what three items need to be known? Assuming an interest rate of 10%, the future value of $1,000 in three years is $1,331. What does this mean?

Present Value of a Single Amount

Assuming an interest rate of 10%, the present value of $1,000 received three years from now is $751.30. What does this mean?

FUTURE AND PRESENT VALUES OF AN ANNUITY

What are the three characteristics of an annuity?

Future Value of an Annuity

Assuming an interest rate of 10%, the future value of a deposit of $1,000 each year for three years is $3,310. What does this mean?

Present Value of an Annuity

Assuming an interest rate of 10%, the present value of three annual payments of $1,000 is $2,487 (rounded). What does this mean?

A QUESTION OF ETHICS
TRUTH IN ADVERTISING

How do many consumers misinterpret seasonal promotions with special financing incentives that are offered by many car companies? (For example, a car dealer may offer 4% interest on car loans when banks are charging 10%.)

LEARNING OBJECTIVE
After studying this section of the chapter, you should be able to:
9. Apply present value concepts to liabilities.

ACCOUNTING APPLICATIONS OF FUTURE AND PRESENT VALUES
Case A

Assume that on January 31, 2003, General Mills purchases a truck and signs a note agreeing to pay $200,000 for a truck in two years, and the market rate of interest is 12%. Is this a present value or future value problem? Is a single payment or an annuity involved?

What is the present value of $200,000 at 12% for two years? What entry should be used to record the acquisition of the delivery truck? How would this entry impact the accounting equation?

Account	Debit	Credit

_____ Assets _____ = _____ Liabilities _____ + _____ Stockholders' Equity _____

How much interest expense should be recorded in the first year? What adjusting entry is required? How would each of these entries impact the accounting equation?

Account	Debit	Credit

_____ Assets _____ = _____ Liabilities _____ + _____ Stockholders' Equity _____

How much interest expense should be recorded in the second year? What adjusting entry is required? How would each of these entries impact the accounting equation?

Account	Debit	Credit

_____ Assets _____ = _____ Liabilities _____ + _____ Stockholders' Equity _____

What entry would be made on December, 31, 2004, to record payment of the debt? How would this entry impact the accounting equation?

Account	Debit	Credit

_____ Assets _____ = _____ Liabilities _____ + _____ Stockholders' Equity _____

Case B

Assume that General Mills purchases new printing equipment and signs a note agreeing to pay three equal annual installments of $163,686, and that each installment includes principal plus interest on the unpaid balance of 11%. Is this a present value or future value problem? Is a single payment or an annuity involved?

What is the present value of three annual payments of $163,686 at 11%? What entry should be used to record the acquisition of the printing equipment? How would this entry impact the accounting equation?

Account	Debit	Credit

_____ Assets = _____ Liabilities + _____ Stockholders' Equity

How much interest expense should be recorded at the end of the first year? What entry should be made at the end of the first year to record the payment on this note?

Account	Debit	Credit

_____ Assets = _____ Liabilities + _____ Stockholders' Equity

How much interest expense should be recorded at the end of the second year? What entry should be made at the end of the second year to record the payment on this note?

Account	Debit	Credit

_____ Assets = _____ Liabilities + _____ Stockholders' Equity

How much interest expense should be recorded at the end of the third year? What entry should be made at the end of the third year to record the payment on this note?

Account	Debit	Credit

_____ Assets = _____ Liabilities + _____ Stockholders' Equity

INCOME TAXES AND RETIREMENT BENEFITS
DEFERRED TAXES

Why do deferred taxes exist? What are temporary differences? Why do deferred tax amounts always reverse themselves? What happens when a deferred tax liability reverses?

ACCRUED RETIRMENT BENEFITS

What is the employer's obligation in a defined contribution program? What is the employer's obligation in a defined benefit program?

If an employer continues to pay for health care costs after their employees retire, when must the cost of those future benefits be recorded?

Federal Income Tax Concepts

What type(s) of business organizations are not required to pay Federal income taxes? Which type(s) is (are) required to pay Federal income taxes?

CALCULATION OF TAXES PAYABLE

How is a large (that is, one with taxable income in excess of $10 million) corporation's tax obligation determined? How does the calculation differ from that used for smaller corporations?

REVENUE AND EXPENSE RECOGNITION FOR INCOME TAX PURPOSES

What are five common examples of differences between GAAP and the rules that govern the preparation of the federal income tax returns?

TAX EVASION AND TAX MINIMIZATION

What is tax evasion? Are tax minimization efforts considered to be tax evasion?

CHAPTER TAKE-AWAYS

1. Define, measure, and report liabilities.

Strictly speaking, accountants define liabilities as probable future sacrifices of economic benefits that arise from past transactions. They are classified on the balance sheet as either current or long-term. Current liabilities are short-term obligations that will be paid within the current operating cycle of the business or within one year of the balance sheet date, whichever is longer. Long-term liabilities are all obligations not classified as current.

2. Use the current ratio.

The current ratio is a comparison of current assets and current liabilities. Analysts use this ratio to assess the liquidity of a company.

3. Analyze the accounts payable turnover ratio.

This ratio is computed by dividing cost of goods sold by accounts payable. It shows how quickly management is paying its trade creditors and is considered to be a measure of liquidity.

4. Report notes payable and explain the time value of money.

A note payable specifies the amount borrowed, when it must be repaid and the interest rate associated with the debt. Accountants must report the debt and the interest as it accrues. The time value of money refers to the fact that interest accrues on borrowed money with the passage of time.

5. Report contingent liabilities.

A contingent liability is a potential liability that has arisen as the result of a past event. Such liabilities are disclosed in a note if the obligation is reasonably possible.

6. Explain the importance of working capital and its impact on cash flows.

Working capital is used to fund the operating activities of a business. Changes in working capital accounts affect the statement of cash flows. Cash flows from operating activities are increased by decreases in current assets (other than cash) or increases in current liabilities. Cash flows from operating activities are decreased by increases in current assets (other than cash) or decreases in current liabilities.

7. Report long-term liabilities.

Usually, long-term liabilities will be paid more than one year in the future. Accounting for long-term debt is based on the same concepts used in accounting for short-term debt.

8. Apply the concepts of present and future values.

These concepts are based on the time value of money. Simply stated, a dollar to be received in the future is worth less than a dollar available today (present value). Alternatively, a dollar invested today will grow to a larger amount in the future (future value). These concepts are applied either to a single payment or multiple payments called *annuities*. Either tables or calculators can be used to determine present and future values.

9. Apply present value concepts to liabilities.

Accountants use present value concepts to determine the reported amounts of liabilities. A liability involves the payment of some amount at a future date. The reported liability is not the amount of the future payment. Instead, the liability is reported at the amount of the present value of the future payment.

KEY RATIOS

Current ratio measures the ability of a company to pay its current obligations. It is computed as follows:

Current Ratio = Current assets ÷ Current liabilities

Accounts payable turnover is a measure of how quickly a company pays its creditors. It is computed as follows:

Accounts Payable Turnover = Cost of Goods Sold ÷ Average Accounts Payable

Average accounts payable is determined as follows:

Average Accounts Payable =
(Accounts Payable, beginning of the year + Accounts Payable, end of year) ÷ 2

FINDING FINANCIAL INFORMATION

Balance Sheet	Income Statement
Under Current Liabilities Liabilities listed by account title, such as: Accounts payable Accrued liabilities Notes payable Current portion of long-term debt *Under Noncurrent Liabilities* Liabilities listed by account title, such as: Long-term debt Deferred taxes Bonds	Liabilities are shown only on the balance sheet, never on the income statement. Transactions affecting liabilities often affect an income statement account. For example, accrued salary compensation affects an income statement account (compensation expense) and a balance sheet account (salaries payable).

Statement of Cash Flows	Notes
Under Operating Activities (Indirect Method) Net income + Increases in most current liabilities − Decreases in most current liabilities **Under financing activities** + Increase in long-term liabilities − Decreases in long-term liabilities	**Under Summary of significant accounting policies** Description of pertinent information concerning accounting treatment of liabilities. Normally, there is minimal information. **Under a separate note** If not listed on the balance sheet, a listing of the major classifications of liabilities with information about maturities and interest rates. Information about contingent liabilities is reported in the notes.

SELF-TEST QUESTIONS AND EXERCISES

MATCHING

Match each of the key terms listed below with the appropriate textbook definition:

____	Accrued Liabilities	____	Liabilities
____	Annuity	____	Liquidity
____	Capital Lease	____	Long-Term Liabilities
____	Contingent Liability	____	Operating Lease
____	Current Liabilities	____	Present Value
____	Deferred Revenues and Deferred Expenses	____	Temporary Differences
____	Deferred Tax Items	____	Time Value of Money
____	Future Value	____	Working Capital

A. Potential liability that has arisen as the result of a past event; not an effective liability until some future event occurs.

B. The dollar difference between total current assets and total current liabilities.

C. Short-term obligations that will be paid in cash (or other current assets) or satisfied by providing service within the coming year.

D. All of the entity's obligations that are not classified as current liabilities.

E. Expenses that have been incurred but have not been paid at the end of the accounting period.

F. The sum to which an amount will increase as the result of compound interest.

G. Timing differences that cause deferred income taxes and will reverse, or turn around, in the future.

H. A series of periodic cash receipts or payments that are equal in amount each interest period.

I. The current value of an amount to be received in the future; a future amount discounted for compound interest.

J. Previously recorded assets, liabilities, revenues, and expenses that need to be adjusted at the end of the period to reflect earned revenues or incurred expenses.

K. Probable debts or obligations of the entity that result from past transactions, which will be paid with assets or services.

L. Timing differences caused by reporting revenues and expenses according to GAAP on a company's income statement and according to the Internal Revenue Code on the tax return.

M. Interest that is associated with the use of money over time.

N. Meets at least one of the four criteria established by GAAP and results in the recording of an asset and liability.

O. The ability to pay current obligations.

P. Does not meet any of the four criteria established by GAAP and does not cause the recording of an asset and liability.

TRUE-FALSE QUESTIONS

For each of the following, enter a T or F in the blank to indicate whether the statement is true or false.

___1.   (LO 1) Current liabilities are likely to be satisfied with current assets.

___2.   (LO 2) A company with a high current ratio does not have liquidity problems.

___3.   (LO 3) Trade accounts payable are generally incurred as a result of the purchase of goods and services in the normal course of business.

___4.   (LO 4) A retailer should defer revenue from sales of furniture on a 90-day financing agreement.

___5.   (LO 3) When all or part of a company's long-term debt is due within the next year, it is reported as a noncurrent liability on the balance sheet and disclosed in the footnotes to the financial statements.

___6.   (LO 4) Working capital is computed by subtracting liabilities from assets.

___7.   (LO 5) A contingent liability that is material in amount and has at least a remote possibility of occurrence must be disclosed in a footnote to the financial statements.

___8.   (LO 7) Companies generally use long-term debt to finance long-lived assets, matching the life of the asset to the term of the debt.

___9.   (LO 9) In a present value problem, the value in the future of a known cash flow today needs to be determined.

___10. (LO 8) Since compound interest problems involve more complex interest calculations, the simple interest formula cannot be used to compute interest expense.

MULTIPLE CHOICE QUESTIONS

Choose the best answer or response by placing the identifying letter in the space provided.

___1.   (LO 2) The current ratio is computed by

   a.   subtracting current assets from current liabilities.
   b.   subtracting current liabilities from current assets.
   c.   dividing current assets by current liabilities.
   d.   dividing current liabilities by current assets.
   e.   dividing current liabilities by noncurrent liabilities.

___2.   (LO 3) Deferred revenues represent a liability because

   a.   no cash has changed hands.
   b.   collection is uncertain.
   c.   goods or services have been paid for, but not yet provided to the customer.
   d.   the company is transferring them to another period for tax reasons.
   e.   the customer may someday return items purchased for a refund.

___3.   (LO 4) Interest expense is computed by multiplying

   a.   the face value of the note by the annual percentage rate
   b.   the face value of the note by the annual interest rate by the number of days outstanding.
   c.   the face value of the note by the annual interest rate by the time period for the loan (expressed as a portion of the year that the loan has been outstanding).
   d.   the face value of the note by the annual interest rate divided by 365.
   e.   the face value of the note by the annual interest rate divided by 360.

___4. (LO 5) In order to be recorded as a liability on the balance sheet, an item must be

    a. reasonably possible and subject to estimate.
    b. probable.
    c. remote, but subject to estimate.
    d. probable, and subject to estimate.
    e. all of the above.

___5. (LO 5) A contingent liability

    a. is dependent on another company in order to occur.
    b. will result from a future event.
    c. cannot be estimated.
    d. is only remotely possible.
    e. is a potential liability that has arisen because of a past event or transaction.

___6. (LO 5) A contingent liability that cannot be reasonably estimated

    a. may be recorded as a balance sheet item or disclosed in a footnote to the financial statements, at the discretion of management.
    b. may be disclosed in a footnote to the financial statements at the discretion of the management.
    c. need not be disclosed in the footnotes to the financial statements.
    d. must be reported as a liability on the balance sheet.
    e. requires disclosure in a footnote to the financial statements if it is at least reasonably possible.

___7. (LO 6) Working capital is computed by

    a. subtracting current assets from current liabilities.
    b. subtracting current liabilities from current assets.
    c. dividing current assets by current liabilities.
    d. dividing current liabilities by current assets.
    e. dividing current liabilities by noncurrent liabilities.

___8. (LO 8) An annuity is

    a. a series of annual payments of the same amount.
    b. any group of payments, equally spaced.
    c. any payments to a beneficiary from a fund set aside for that purpose.
    d. a series of consecutive equal payments, equally spaced, with the same implicit interest rate each period.
    e. annual payments of equal amounts at a fixed interest rate.

___9. (LO 8) The present value of a known future amount

    a. will always be more than the future amount.
    b. will be equal to the future amount.
    c. will always be less than the future amount.
    d. may be greater than or less than the future amount, depending on the interest rate used.
    e. may be greater than or less than the future amount, depending on the amount of time between.

___10. (LO 8) An example of a future value problem for a single amount is

    a. a defined benefit pension plan.
    b. a savings account to be established to fund $100,000 college tuition in 6 years.
    c. a mortgage.
    d. a Individual Retirement Account.
    e. an inheritance that will be invested in a mutual fund.

EXERCISES

Record your answers to each part of these exercises in the space provided. Show your work.

Exercise 1 (LO 1)

At the end of December 20A, there were two days' wages unpaid and unrecorded because the weekly payroll will not be paid until January 3, 20B. Wages for the last two days of December amounted to $2,000. In addition, at December 31, 20A, vacation time not yet taken or recorded amounted to $12,000. Prepare the adjusting entries that are required at December 31, 20A. (Ignore any accrued payroll tax liabilities at this time.)

Transaction	Account	Debit	Credit
12/31/20A			
12/31/20A			

Exercise 2 (LO 1)

On December 15, 20A, Newco, Inc. paid $6,000 in rent to Property Managers, Inc. for the two month period which began on that date. Property Managers credited the rent in full to Rent Revenue. Prepare the adjusting entry that is required at December 31, 20A for Property Managers, Inc.

Transaction	Account	Debit	Credit
12/31/20A			

Exercise 3

You were introduced to Pixar in chapter 3 of this Study Guide. The selected financial information set forth below was taken from the statements of operations (income statements) and balance sheets included in the Forms 10-K that were filed by Pixar with the SEC for fiscal 2001 (year ending December 29, 2001), fiscal 2000 (year ending December 30, 2000) and fiscal 1999 (year ending January 1, 2000).

	Fiscal 2001	Fiscal 2000	Fiscal 1999
As of the end of the year			
Current assets	$310,948,000	$311,680,000	$250,110,000
Accounts payable	4,842,000	1,622,000	458,000
Current liabilities	17,608,000	43,883,000	30,462,000
Year ended			
Cost of revenues	12,318,000	37,004,000	31,705,000

Exercise 3, continued
Part A (LO 2)

Compute Pixar's current ratio as of end of fiscal 2001 and 2000.

2001   *2000*

Part B (LO 6)

Compute Pixar's working capital as of end of fiscal 2001 and 2000.

2001   *2000*

Part C (LO 3)

Compute Pixar's accounts payable turnover during fiscal 2001 and 2000.

2001   *2000*

Part D (LO 2, 3, and 6)

Comment on Pixar's liquidity.

Exercise 4 (LO 4)

On December 31, 20A, Newco borrowed $100,000 from First National Bank, and signed a 12% note payable due in two years. Interest on the note is due at maturity.

Part A

Prepare the journal entry to record the borrowing transaction.

Transaction	Account	Debit	Credit
12/31/20A			

Part B

How should the note be reported on Newco's balance sheet at December 31, 20A? How should it be reported on the balance sheet at December 31, 20B?

Exercise 4, continued

Part C

Prepare the adjusting entry that is required at December 31, 20B.

Transaction	Account	Debit	Credit
12/31/20B			

Part D

Prepare the entry to record the payment of the note on December 31, 20C.

Transaction	Account	Debit	Credit
12/31/20C			

Exercise 5 (LO 8 and 9)

Safety Net, Inc. entered into the following transactions on January 1, 20A. Assume an interest rate of 6%.

- Established Fund A by making a deposit of $150,000.
- Established Fund B by agreeing to make four annual deposits of $10,000 at the end of each year.
- Established Fund C by depositing a single amount that will increase to $250,000 by the end of 20E.
- Established Fund D by depositing a single amount that will provide six equal annual year-end payments of $5,000 to a retired employee beginning on December 31, 20A.

Part A

Compute the balance of Fund A at the end of 20C (year 3).

Part B

Compute the balance of Fund B at the end of 20D (year 4).

Part C

Compute the single amount that must be deposited in Fund C on January 1, 20A.

Exercise 5, continued
Part D

Compute the single amount that must be deposited in Fund D on January 1, 20A.

SOLUTIONS TO SELF-TEST QUESTIONS AND EXERCISES

MATCHING

E	Accrued Liabilities	K	Liabilities
H	Annuity	O	Liquidity
N	Capital Lease	D	Long-Term Liabilities
A	Contingent Liability	P	Operating Lease
C	Current Liabilities	I	Present Value
J	Deferred Revenues and Deferred Expenses	G	Temporary Differences
L	Deferred Tax Items	M	Time Value of Money
F	Future Value	B	Working Capital

TRUE-FALSE QUESTIONS

1. T
2. F – Normally, a high current ratio suggests good liquidity; however, a company with a high current ratio might still have liquidity problems if significant funds are tied up in assets that will not be easily converted into cash (such as slow-moving inventory).
3. T
4. F – This revenue would not be deferred, since the goods have presumably been delivered, and payment reasonably assured.
5. F – long-term debt, or a portion thereof, which is due within the next year, must be reported on the balance sheet as a *current* liability.
6. F – Working capital is computed by subtracting current liabilities from current assets.
7. F – A contingent liability with only a remote possibility of occurrence does not need to be disclosed in the footnotes to the financial statements.
8. T
9. F – The simple interest formula is used for all interest calculations, simple or compound. The rate and time are adjusted in compound interest calculations for compounding more frequently than annually.
10. F – A present value problem requires the calculation of the value *today* of a known future cash flow.

MULTIPLE CHOICE QUESTIONS

1.	c	3.	c	5.	e	7.	b	9.	c
2.	c	4.	d	6.	e	8.	d	10.	e

EXERCISES

Exercise 1

Transaction	Account	Debit	Credit
12/31/20A	Wage expense	2,000	
	Wages payable		2,000
12/31/20A	Wage expense	12,000	
	Accrued vacation liability		12,000

Exercise 2

Transaction	Account	Debit	Credit
12/31/20A	Rent revenue ($6,000 x (1.5 ÷ 2))	4,500	
	Deferred revenue (or unearned revenue)		4,500

Exercise 3
Part A

Current assets ÷ Current liabilities = Current ratio
End of fiscal 2001
$310,948,000 ÷ $17,608,000 = 17.66 to 1
End of fiscal 2000
$311,680,000 ÷ $43,883,000 = 7.10 to 1

Part B

Current assets – Current liabilities = Working capital
End of fiscal 2001
$310,948,000 – $17,608,000 = $293,340,000
End of fiscal 2000
$311,680,000 – $43,883,000 = $267,797,000

Part C

Accounts Payable Turnover = Cost of Goods Sold ÷ Average Accounts Payable
2001
$12,318,000 ÷ [($1,622,000 + $4,842,000) ÷ 2] = $12,318,000 ÷ $3,232,000 = 3.8
2000
$37,004,000 ÷ [($458,000 + $1,622,000) ÷ 2] = $37,004,000 ÷ $1,040,000 = 35.6

Part D

Pixar's current ratio increased from 7.10 to 1 to 17.66 to 1 from the end of fiscal 2000 to 2001. In addition, its working capital increased by $25,543,000 (or $293,340,000 - $267,797,000) during fiscal 2001. Pixar seems to be able to meet its short-term obligations. On the other hand, the accounts payable turnover ratio measures how quickly management is paying trade accounts payable. Pixar's accounts payable turnover ratio decreased from 35.6 to 3.8 during fiscal 2001. Usually, a low ratio would raise questions concerning a company's liquidity. However, while a low accounts payable turnover ratio might be a concern in many circumstances, it is not the case of Pixar because other indications of liquidity are good. Further information may be obtained from the company's Annual Report. Comparisons with those of its major competitors and industry averages would provide additional information.

Exercise 4
Part A

Transaction	Account	Debit	Credit
12/31/20A	Cash	100,000	
	Note payable		100,000

Part B

The note should be classified as a long-term (noncurrent) liability on the balance sheet at December 31, 20A, and as a current liability on the balance sheet at December 31, 20B.

Part C

Transaction	Account	Debit	Credit
12/31/20B	Interest expense ($100,000 x .12 x 360 / 360)	12,000	
	Interest payable		12,000

Part D

Transaction	Account	Debit	Credit
12/31/20C	Note payable	100,000	
	Interest payable	12,000	
	Interest expense ($100,000 x .12 x 360 / 360)	12,000	
	Cash		124,000

Exercise 5
Part A

Refer to Table A-1, Future Value of $1.

For i = 6%, n = 3, the value is 1.1910.
The balance at the end of year 3 will be $150,000 x 1.1910 = $178,650.

Part B

Refer to Table A-3, Future Value of Annuity of $1.

For i = 6%, n = 4, the value is 4.3746.
The balance at the end of year 4 will be $10,000 x 4.3746 = $43,746.

Part C

Refer to Table A-2, Present Value of $1.

For i = 6%, n = 5, the value is 0.7473.
The amount that must be deposited on January 1, 20A, is $250,000 x 0.7473 = $186,825.

Part D

Refer to Table A-4, Present Value of Annuity of $1.

For i = 6%, n = 6, the value is 4.9173
The amount that must be deposited on January 1, 20A, is $5,000 x 4.9173 = $24,586.50.

AN IDEA FOR YOUR STUDY TEAM

Circle the correct choice to complete the following statements about present and future values. Then get together with the other members of your study team, and compare your answers.

1. The higher the interest rate, the (higher) (lower) the present value of a known future amount.
2. The more often interest is compounded, the (higher) (lower) the present value of a known future amount will be.
3. The more often interest is compounded, the (higher) (lower) the future value of a known present cash flow will be.
4. The present value of an annuity of a given amount will always be (greater) (less) than that amount, whereas the present value of a single sum is always (greater) (less) than that sum.
5. As the number of compounding periods increases, present value (increases) (decreases) but future value (increases) (decreases).

ORGANIZATION OF THE CHAPTER

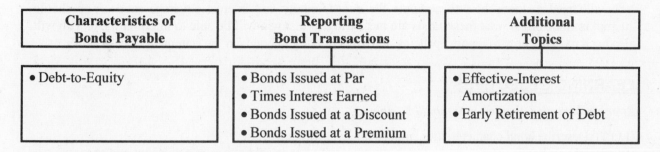

Characteristics of Bonds Payable	Reporting Bond Transactions	Additional Topics
• Debt-to-Equity	• Bonds Issued at Par • Times Interest Earned • Bonds Issued at a Discount • Bonds Issued at a Premium	• Effective-Interest Amortization • Early Retirement of Debt

CHAPTER FOCUS SUGGESTIONS

Overview

This chapter completes the coverage of liabilities. Emphasis is placed on the use of bonds as a primary way of obtaining funds to acquire long-term assets and to expand the company's operations. After the various issues relating to the reporting of bonds and interest expense are addressed, the focus shifts to the other side of the balance sheet with a discussion of reporting issues relating to investments in bonds.

Reporting Bonds Payable and Interest Expense

Many students are not familiar with the terminology that relates to bonds and the impact that interest rates have on selling prices of bonds. Carefully read the section of the chapter that addresses the characteristics of bonds and devote some time to the demands of creditors and interest rates. If you understand how interest rates affect the selling prices of bonds, you will be better equipped to tackle the calculation of interest expense, which is complicated when bonds are sold at an amount other than par.

Bonds may be sold at par, at a premium or at a discount. The determining factor is the relationship between the interest rate stated on the bonds and the market rate of interest. If the stated rate equals the market rate, the bonds will be sold at par. If the stated rate is higher than the market rate, the bonds will be sold at a premium. If the stated rate is less than the market rate, the bonds will be sold at a discount. You will use the present and future value concepts that were introduced in chapter 9 to calculate the selling price of a bond. *(If necessary, take the time to go back and review these concepts before proceeding.)* You will also be expected to analyze and record entries relating to the sale of bonds.

Premiums and discounts on bonds payable represent adjustments to the interest expense relating to the bonds. You will need to know how to amortize premiums and discounts using both the straight-line and effective-interest methods. Take the time to work through the calculations for each of the Harrrah's examples (Learning Objective 2) and trace the amounts to the entries that are illustrated.

Other Issues

You should be familiar with other reporting issues relating to bonds, such as the early retirement of bonds that are called or redeemed and the use of bond sinking funds.

Investments in Bonds to be Held to Maturity

This chapter also covers investments in bonds issued by other companies. These bonds may be purchased at par, at a premium, or at a discount. You should be familiar with the reporting of bonds in a held-to-maturity portfolio and interest earned on such investments.

Financial Statement Analysis Matters

You will need to know how to compute the debt-to-equity and interest coverage ratios. You should attempt to understand what these ratios are measuring so that you will be able to interpret them. You will also need to know how to report financing activities relating to bonds in the statement of cash flows.

LEARNING OBJECTIVES

After studying this chapter, you should be able to:

(LO 1) Describe bond characteristics and use the debt-to-equity ratio.
(LO 2) Report bonds payable and interest expense, with bonds sold at par, at a discount and at a premium.
(LO 3) Analyze the times interest earned ratio.
 (LO 4) Use the effective-interest method of amortization.
(LO 5) Report the early retirement of bonds.
(LO 6) Explain how financing activities are reported in the statement of cash flows (SCF).

READ AND RECALL QUESTIONS

After you read each section of the chapter, answer the related Read and Recall Questions below.

LEARNING OBJECTIVE
After studying this section of the chapter, you should be able to:
1. Describe bond characteristics and use the debt-to-equity ratio.

BUSINESS BACKGROUND

What are bonds? Why would a creditor prefer to lend money by purchasing a bond? Why does the use of bonds allow companies to reduce the cost of borrowing money for long periods of time?

What are three significant advantages of using bonds to raise long-term capital? What are the two primary disadvantages of the issuance of bonds?

CHARACTERISTICS OF BONDS PAYABLE

What is bond principal? What three other terms are used to describe bond principal? What is meant by the par value of a bond?

How are the periodic interest payments on a bond computed? What is the term used to describe the interest rate that is used in this calculation?

What is a bond indenture? What four types of provisions are set forth in a bond indenture? What types of covenants may be set forth in the indenture to protect the creditors?

What is a prospectus? What is a bond certificate? What is included on the face of a bond certificate? What is a bond trustee? What are the duties of a trustee?

What is default risk? What are junk bonds?

KEY RATIO ANALYSIS: DEBT-TO-EQUITY RATIO

How is the debt-to-equity ratio computed? What does it measure?

What does a high debt-to-equity ratio normally suggest? What risk is increased as a result of a high ratio? What other information should an analyst consider when evaluating a company's debt-to-equity ratio?

REPORTING BOND TRANSACTIONS

When a corporation (such as Harrah's) issues its bonds, what two types of cash payment are specified in the bond contract? What are three terms used to describe the interest rate stated in the bond contract?

How does the market determine the price at which bonds sell? What are the two components of the underlying calculation?

Why do creditors demand a certain rate of interest? What is the term used to describe the interest rate demanded by the creditors when bonds are sold? What other two terms are used to describe this rate?

When would a bond sell at par? What is a bond premium? Why do bonds sell at a premium? What is a bond discount? Why do bonds sell at a discount?

When bonds are issued, does the issuer receive cash greater than, equal to or less than par if the bonds are issued at (1) par, (2) a discount, or (3) a premium?

FINANCIAL ANALYSIS
BOND INFORMATION FROM THE BUSINESS PRESS

After issuance, do daily changes in the market price of the bonds affect the financial statement of the company that issued the bonds? Why or why not?

BONDS ISSUED AT PAR

Why would bonds sell at par value?

What entry would be required to record the issuance of bonds if the present value of the future cash flows on the date of issue is $100,000? How would this entry impact the accounting equation?

Account	Debit	Credit

_____ Assets   = _____ Liabilities   + _____ Stockholders' Equity _____

When the effective rate of interest is equal to the stated rate of interest, will the present value of the future cash flows associated with a bond be more than, equal to, or less than the par amount of the bond?

Reporting Interest Expense on Bonds Issued at Par

If 10% bonds that mature in ten years with a par value of $100,000 are issued, what is the amount of the semiannual interest payment on those bonds?

What entry would be used to record the semiannual interest payments relating to the bonds described above? How would this entry impact the accounting equation?

Account	Debit	Credit

_____ Assets   = _____ Liabilities   + _____ Stockholders' Equity _____

What must be done at the end of the accounting period when bond interest payment dates do not coincide with the last day of a company's fiscal year? What two account balances change as a result?

KEY RATIO ANALYSIS: TIMES INTEREST EARNED

How is the times interest earned ratio computed? What does it measure?

What does a high times interest earned ratio normally suggest? Why are analysts particularly interested in the times interest earned ratio? When interpreting this ratio, what does a margin of protection mean? Why is the times interest earned ratio often misleading for new or rapidly growing companies? What other comparison do some analysts prefer?

INTERNATIONAL FINANCIAL MARKETS

What does the abbreviation, LIBOR, stand for? What is it?

BONDS ISSUED AT A DISCOUNT

Why would bonds sell at a discount? How is the cash issue price of the bonds computed? What interest rate should be used in that computation?

If the market rate of interest is 12%, what is the cash issue price of bonds with a par value of $100,000 and a stated interest rate of 10%, payable semiannually, which mature in ten years?

What does a price of 88.5 mean? When a bond is issued at a discount, will the cash received by the issuer be more than, equal to, or less than the par value of the bonds? Why?

What entry would be used to record the issuance of the bonds described above? How would this entry impact the accounting equation?

Account	Debit	Credit

_____ Assets _____ = _____ Liabilities _____ + _____ Stockholders' Equity _____

Refer to your entry above. What account was used to record the difference between the cash received and the par value of the bonds issued? What type of account is it? What is the normal balance of this account?

Reporting Interest Expense on Bonds Issued at a Discount

What does *amortize* mean? When should discount be amortized? Does the amortization of bond discount increase or decrease the amount of interest expense recorded for a period?

How is the amount of discount amortization determined each period using the straight-line method? How much discount would be amortized during each interest period on the bonds described above? What entry would be used to record the semiannual interest payment relating to the bonds described above? How would this entry impact the accounting equation?

Account	Debit	Credit

_____ Assets _____ = _____ Liabilities _____ + _____ Stockholders' Equity _____

Refer to your entry above. What account was used to record this period's amortization of the bond discount? Was this account balance increased or decreased as a result of this entry? Was the amortization of bond discount added to or deducted from the amount of interest paid to the bondholders to compute interest expense for the period?

The balance sheet reports the bonds payable at their book value. How is the book value computed when bonds are sold at a discount? What happens to the amount of unamortized discount (that is, the balance in the discount on bonds payable account) each succeeding interest period? Upon maturity, what is the relationship between the maturity amount of the bonds that were issued at a discount and their book value?

Accounting for Zero Coupon Bonds

What are zero coupon bonds? Why is a bond with a zero coupon interest rate called a deep discount bond? Does the accounting for zero coupon bonds differ from that of any bond sold at a discount? Why or Why not?

BONDS ISSUED AT A PREMIUM

Why would bonds sell at a premium? How is the cash issue price of the bonds computed? What interest rate should be used in that computation?

When a bond is issued at a premium, will the cash received by the issuer be more than, equal to, or less than the par value of the bonds? Why?

If the market rate of interest is 8%, what is the cash issue price of bonds with a par value of $100,000 and a stated interest rate of 10%, payable semiannually, which mature in ten years?

What entry would be used to record the issuance of the bonds described above? How would this entry impact the accounting equation?

Account	Debit	Credit

_____ = _____ + _____
       Assets   Liabilities   Stockholders' Equity

Refer to your entry above. What account was used to record the difference between the cash received and the par value of the bonds issued? What type of account is it? What is the normal balance of this account?

Reporting Interest Expense on Bonds Issued at a Premium

When should the premium be amortized? What event triggers amortization? How is the amount of premium amortization determined each period using the straight-line method?

What entry would be used to record the semiannual interest payment relating to the bonds described above? How would this entry impact the accounting equation?

Account	Debit	Credit

_____ = _____ + _____
       Assets   Liabilities   Stockholders' Equity

Refer to your entry above. What account was used to record this period's amortization of the bond premium? Was this account balance increased or decreased as a result of this entry? Was the amortization of bond premium added to or deducted from the amount of interest paid to the bondholders to compute interest expense for the period?

The balance sheet reports the bonds payable at their book value. How is the book value computed when bonds are sold at a premium? What happens to the amount of unamortized premium (that is, the balance in the premium on bonds payable account) each succeeding interest period? Upon maturity, what is the relationship between the maturity amount of the bonds that were issued at a premium and their book value?

LEARNING OBJECTIVE

After studying this section of the chapter, you should be able to:

4. Use the effective-interest method of amortization.

ADDITIONAL TOPICS
EFFECTIVE-INTEREST AMORTIZATION

What is the only advantage of the straight-line method of amortization of bond discounts and premiums? When does GAAP allow the use of the straight-line method of amortization?

What is meant when an interest rate is referred to as the true interest rate? When a bond is sold, is the actual amount borrowed equal to the cash received from the issuance or is it equal to the market value of the bond?

When the effective-interest method is used, how is interest expense for a bond computed? How is the amount of periodic amortization of the bonds discount or premium determined?

Assume that Harrah's received cash of $88,529 when it issued bonds with a par value of $100,000 on January 1, 2003. Interest is paid to bondholders (the creditors) every six months. The stated rate of interest was 10%; the market rate was 12%. Considering the difference in these two rates, were these bonds issued at par, at a discount or at a premium? Complete the second line (which corresponds to the date of the first interest payment) of the table below without looking at the example in your textbook; then check your answers.

Date	Interest Paid	Interest Expense	Amortization	Book Value
1/1/2003 – issuance	–	–	–	$88,529
6/30/2003– 1st interest payment				

Refer to the table that you completed above (which represents the first two lines of a typical effective-interest bond amortization table). Upon issuance, what amount is placed on the first line in the unpaid balance column (designated by (A) below)? At the date of the first interest period, how did you determine the amount of interest that was paid (designated by (B) below)? How did you determine the amount of interest expense (designated by (C) below)? How did you calculate the amortization (designated by (D) below)? How did you calculated the book value designated by (E) below)?

Date	Interest Paid	Interest Expense	Amortization	Book Value
Issuance	–	–	–	(A)
1st interest period	(B)	(C)	(D)	(E)

(A)

(B)

(C)

(D)

(E)

FINANCIAL ANALYSIS
UNDERSTANDING ALTERNATIVE AMORTIZATION METHODS

How does the materiality constraint affect the choice between the straight-line and effective-interest amortization methods? Which method is preferred conceptually? When may the other method be used?

LEARNING OBJECTIVE
After studying this section of the chapter, you should be able to:
5. Report the early retirement of bonds.

EARLY RETIREMENT OF DEBT

Who can decide to call bonds in for early retirement if the bonds have a call feature? What is a call premium? How is the call premium often stated?

Assume that Harrah's issued bonds in the amount of $1 million at par in 1994 and that the bonds were called in 2003 at 102% of par. What entry would be required to record this transaction? How would this entry impact the accounting equation?

Account	*Debit*	*Credit*

_____ = _____ + _____
Assets   Liabilities   Stockholders' Equity

Refer to your entry above. How would you describe the amount that was debited to the bonds payable account? How did you determine the amount of the loss on the bond call?

If the bond does not have a call feature, what would the issuer do if it wants to retire the debt early? When would this be an attractive approach?

How is the gain or loss on the early retirement of debt reported in the financial statements? Why would analysts use caution when evaluating gains from debt retirement?

LEARNING OBJECTIVE
After studying this section of the chapter, you should be able to:
6. Explain how financing activities are reported in the Statement of Cash Flows (SCF).

FOCUS ON CASH FLOWS

Does an inflow or an outflow of cash result from the sale (issuance) of bonds? How is this cash flow reported on the statement of cash flows (that is, as an operating, investing or financing activity)? Does an inflow or an outflow of cash result when bond principal is repaid? How is this cash flow reported on the statement of cash flows (that is, as an operating, investing or financing activity)?

Does an inflow or an outflow of cash result from the payment of interest on bonds? How is this cash flow reported on the statement of cash flows (that is, as an operating, investing or financing activity)? Why? What other related disclosure must be made in the financial statements?

CHAPTER TAKE-AWAYS

1. *Describe the characteristics of bonds and use the debt-to-equity ratio.*

   Bonds have a number of characteristics designed to meet the needs of both the issuing corporation and the creditor. A complete listing of bond characteristics is shown in Exhibit 10.1.

   Corporations use bonds to raise long-term capital. Bonds offer a number of advantages compared to stock, including the ability to earn a higher return for stockholders, the tax deductibility of interest, and the fact that control of the company is not diluted. Bonds do carry additional risk, however, because interest and principal payments are not discretionary.

   The debt-to-equity ratio compares the amount of capital supplied by creditors to the amount supplied by owners. It is a measure of a company's debt capacity. It is an important ratio because of the high risk associated with debt capital which requires obligatory interest and principal payments.

2. *Report bonds payable and interest expense, for bonds sold at par, at a discount and at a premium.*

   Three types of events must be recorded over the life of a typical bond: (1) the receipt of cash when the bond is first sold, (2) the periodic payment of cash interest, and (3) the repayment of principal upon the maturity of the bond.

   Bonds are sold at a discount whenever the coupon interest rate is less than the market rate of interest. A discount is the dollar amount of the difference between the par value of the bond and its selling price. The discount is recorded as a contra-liability when the bond is sold and is amortized over the life of the bond as an adjustment to interest expense.

   Bonds are sold at a premium whenever the coupon interest rate is more than the market rate of interest.

   A premium is the dollar amount of the difference between the selling price of the bond and its par value.

   The premium is recorded as a liability when the bond is sold and is amortized over the life of the bond as an adjustment to interest expense.

3. *Analyze the times interest earned ratio.*

   This ratio measures a company's ability to meet its interest obligations with resources from its profit-making activities. It is computed by comparing interest expense to earnings (including net income, interest expense, and income tax expense).

4. *Use the effective-interest method of amortization.*

   There are two methods of amortizing bond discounts and premiums, the straight-line method and the effective-interest method. Under the effective-interest method, interest expense is computed by multiplying the current amount of the bond liability by the market rate of interest when the bonds were issued.

5. *Report the early retirement of bonds.*

   A corporation may retire bonds before their maturity date. The difference between the book value and the amount paid to retire the bonds is reported as a gain or loss, depending on the circumstances.

6. **Explain how financing activities are reported on the statement of cash flows.**

Cash flows associated with transactions involving long-term creditors are reported in the Financing Activities section of the statement of cash flows. Interest expense is reported in the Operating Activities section.

KEY RATIOS

Debt-to-equity ratio measures the balance between debt and equity. Debt funds are viewed as being riskier than equity funds. The ratio is computed as follows:

Debt-to-Equity = Total Liabilities ÷ Owners' Equity

Times interest earned ratio measures a company's ability to generate resources from current operations to meet its interest obligations. The ratio is computed as follows:

Times Interest Earned = (Net Income + Interest Expense + Income Tax Expense) ÷ Interest Expense

FINDING FINANCIAL INFORMATION

Balance Sheet	Income Statement
Under Current Liabilities Bonds are normally listed as long-term liabilities. An exception occurs when the bonds are within one year of maturity. Such bonds are reported as current liabilities with the following title: Current portion of long-term debt *Under Noncurrent Liabilities* Bonds are listed under a variety of titles, depending on the characteristics of the bond. Titles include: Bonds payable Debentures Convertible bonds	Bonds are shown only on the balance sheet, never on the income statement. Interest expense associated with bonds is reported on the income statement. Most companies report interest expense in a separate category on the income statement.

Statement of Cash Flows	Notes
Under Financing Activities + Cash inflows from long-term creditors − Cash outflows to long-term creditors *Under Operating Activities* The cash outflow associated with interest expense is reported as an operating activity.	*Under Summary of Significant Accounting Policies* Description of pertinent information concerning accounting treatment of liabilities. Normally, there is minimal information. Some companies report the method used to amortize bond discounts and premiums. *Under a Separate Note* Most companies include a separate note called "Long-Term Debt" that reports information about each major debt issue, including amount and interest rate. The note also provides detail concerning debt covenants.

SELF-TEST QUESTIONS AND EXERCISES

MATCHING

Match each of the key terms listed below with the appropriate textbook definition:

___ Bond Certificate	___ Face Amount
___ Bond Discount	___ Indenture
___ Bond Premium	___ Market Interest Rate
___ Bond Principal	___ Net Interest Cost
___ Callable Bonds	___ Par Value
___ Convertible Bonds	___ Stated Rate
___ Coupon Rate	___ Straight-Line Amortization
___ Debenture	___ Trustee
___ Effective-Interest Method	___ Yield
___ Effective-Interest Rate	

A. Interest cost less any income tax savings associated with interest expense.
B. The stated rate of interest on bonds.
C. The difference between selling price and par when a bond is sold for less than par.
D. Simplified method of amortizing a bond discount or premium that allocates an equal dollar amount to each interest period.
E. An unsecured bond; no assets are specifically pledged to guarantee repayment.
F. The bond document that each bondholder receives.
G. Another name for bond principal or the maturity amount of a bond.
H. Another term for market interest rate or effective interest rate.
I. A bond contract that specifies the legal provisions of a bond issue.
J. Current rate of interest on a debt when incurred; also called *yield* or *effective-interest rate*.
K. The difference between selling price and par when a bond is sold for more than par.
L. The rate of cash interest per period specified in the bond contract.
M. Amortizes a bond discount or premium on the basis of the effective-interest rate; theoretically preferred method.
N. Another name for the market rate of interest on a bond.
O. Another name for principal or the principal amount of a bond.
P. An independent party appointed to represent the bondholders.
Q. Bonds that may be converted to other securities of the issuer (usually common stock).
R. Bonds that may be called for early retirement at the option of the issuer.
S. The amount (a) payable at the maturity of the bond and (b) on which the periodic cash interest payments are computed.

TRUE-FALSE QUESTIONS

For each of the following, enter a T or F in the blank to indicate whether the statement is true or false.

___ 1. (LO 1) One disadvantage of bonds, compared to stock, for financing a company's operations is that dividends on stock are discretionary, whereas bond interest must be paid.

___ 2. (LO 1) Financial leverage is the ratio of debt to equity financing.

___3. (LO 1) A debenture is another word for any bond.

___4. (LO 1) An independent trustee is appointed in a bond issue to control the money raised and the payment of interest and principal.

___5. (LO 1) The par value of a bond is a minimum legal amount below which the bond cannot be issued.

___6. (LO 2) When a company issues bonds, it tries to set the coupon rate on the bond slightly higher than the market rate so that the bond can be issued at a premium and they will receive more money.

___7. (LO 2) A zero coupon bond is one on which no periodic cash interest payments are made.

___8. (LO 2 and 5) Straight-line amortization of discount or premium is simpler, but the effective-interest method is conceptually preferable.

___9. (LO 2) The net liability of a bond at any point in time is the present value of the future cash flows from the bond, discounted at the market interest rate on the date of issue of the bond.

___10. (LO 2) The sum of the cash interest payments less the premium on the bond payable on the date of issue is the total interest expense on the bond.

___11. (LO 3) A high times interest earned ratio suggests that there is an extra margin of protection in case of deterioration in profitability.

___12. (LO 4) Payments of interest expense on bonds are reported as outflows of cash in the financing section of the SCF.

___13. (LO 6) A call premium, stated as a percentage of par value, is often included in the bond indenture in the event that bonds are retired before their maturity date.

___14. (LO 7) A bond sinking fund is always established as part of the bond indenture to provide for the retirement of the bonds at maturity.

___15. (LO 8) Investors classify bonds as held-to-maturity securities, because they have a definite maturity date.

MULTIPLE CHOICE QUESTIONS

Choose the best answer or response by placing the identifying letter in the space provided.

___1. (LO 1) The capital structure of a company is

   a. its property, plant and equipment.
   b. the mixture of debt and equity used to finance its operations.
   c. the composition of its stockholders' equity.
   d. the different types of debt the company has outstanding.
   e. its management plan.

___2. (LO 1) A significant advantage for the holders of bonds, as opposed to other debt, is the

   a. freedom from risk that is provided by an investment in bonds.
   b. liquidity or ability to convert the investment into cash.
   c. low cost of such investments.
   d. high interest rate that is paid.
   e. convertibility of such an instrument.

___3. (LO 2) When a bond is issued at a discount,

   a. the company did not receive as much money as it needed.
   b. the market rate was lower than the coupon rate.
   c. the market rate was higher than the stated rate.
   d. the company was not able to sell the bonds as easily as they'd anticipated.
   e. fewer bonds were sold than were offered.

___4. (LO 2) When bonds are issued at a premium, interest expense

   a. will be equal to cash interest paid each compounding period.
   b. will be less than the cash interest paid each compounding period.
   c. will be equal to the amount of premium amortized each period.
   d. will be more than cash interest paid each compounding period.
   e. will be calculated based on the face value of the bond.

___5. (LO 4) The effective interest method of amortizing discount or premium

   a. yields a consistent amount of interest, but a different interest rate, each period.
   b. is not materially different in most cases from the straight-line method.
   c. yields a consistent interest rate, but a different amount of interest expense, each period.
   d. divides the discount or premium into equal amounts for each year of the bond's life.
   e. calculates interest expense based on the net liability and the coupon interest rate.

___6. (LO 5) Blazing Lasers Co. retired $400,000 face value of bonds when the discount on bonds payable account had a balance of $32,495. They paid $360,000 to retire the bonds. Blazing Lasers would report a _____ on its income statement.

   a. gain of $72,475.
   b. loss of $40,000
   c. gain of $40,000.
   d. loss of $7,505.
   e. a gain of $7,505.

Use the following information to answer the last eight questions. Scuppers Boat Works, Inc. issued 200 bonds to finance expansion into a new line of designs. The bonds had a total principal of $200,000. They would pay interest semiannually at a rate of 9% per annum and will be paid off in five years. On the day the bonds were issued, January 15, 20A, similar securities were yielding a rate of 10% per annum. Scuppers' underwriter, Reedham and Ouip, purchased the entire issue to resell them to individual investors. Scuppers retained the right to buy back the bonds from the bondholders in two years at a price of $102. The bondholders may at any time trade in their bonds for common stock of Scuppers, Inc. at a rate of 50 shares of stock for each bond.

___7. (LO 2) The par value of the bond issue is

   a. $200,000.
   b. $18,000.
   c. $20,000.
   d. $102,000.
   e. $192,275.

©The McGraw-Hill Companies, Inc., 2004

___8. (LO 2) The stated rate of interest on the bonds is __; bondholders will be paid $_____ every _____.

    a. 9%; $18,000; year.
    b. 9%; $18,000; six months.
    c. 9%; $9,000; six months.
    d. 10%; $10,000; six months.
    e. 10%; $20,000; year.

___9. (LO 1) When Scuppers decided to issue the bonds, they would have executed a bond contract, or _____, which spelled out the terms of the bond, and any privileges and covenants.

    a. certificate
    b. debenture
    c. indenture
    d. trustee
    e. commitment

___10. (LO 1) Since Reedham and Ouip has agreed to buy the bonds from Scuppers, Reedham and Ouip would be called a(n)

    a. indenture.
    b. trustee.
    c. investment banker.
    d. firm commitment underwriter.
    e. best efforts underwriter.

___11. (LO 1) The provision allowing retirement of the bonds before maturity makes these _____ bonds.

    a. debenture
    b. subordinated
    c. convertible
    d. redeemable
    e. callable

___12. (LO 5) Should Scuppers decide to redeem the bonds after two years have gone by, each individual bond will be bought back for

    a. $1,020.
    b. $102.
    c. $1,000.
    d. $1,002.
    e. $981.

___13. (LO 1) The privilege of trading the bonds for common stock is called a _____ feature.

    a. capitalized
    b. retirement
    c. callable
    d. redeemable
    e. convertible

___14. (LO 1) The 10% rate for similar securities on the date of issue is known as the

    a. stated rate.
    b. par rate.
    c. market rate.
    d. coupon rate.
    e. contract rate.

EXERCISES

Record your answers to each part of these exercises in the space provided. Show your work.

Exercise 1 (LO 2)

On January 1, 20A, First Canadian, Inc. plans to issue $500,000, five year, 8% bonds that will mature on December 31, 20E. Interest is payable semiannually each June 30 and December 31.

Part A

Assuming that the market (yield) rate is also 8%, prepare the journal entry to record the issuance of the bonds.

Transaction	Account	Debit	Credit
1/1/20A			

Part B

Compute the amount of interest that will be paid on a semiannual interest to the bondholders.

Exercise 1, continued
Part C

Prepare the journal entries to record the payment of interest on June 30, 20A, and December 31, 20A.

Transaction	Account	Debit	Credit
6/30/20A			
12/31/20A			

Exercise 2

On January 1, 20A, First Australian, Inc. plans to issue $500,000, five year, 8% bonds that will mature on December 31, 20E. Interest is payable semiannually each June 30 and December 31.

Part A (LO 2)

Assuming that the market (yield) rate is 6%, compute the issue (sale) price on January 1, 20A.

Part B (LO 2)

Prepare the journal entry to record the issuance of the bonds.

Transaction	Account	Debit	Credit
1/1/20A			

Exercise 2, continued
Part C (LO 2)

Assuming that First Australian uses the straight-line method for amortization purposes, prepare the journal entries to record the payment of interest on June 30, 20A, and December 31, 20A.

Transaction	Account	Debit	Credit
6/30/20A			
12/31/20A			

Part D (LO 2)

Compute the book value of the bonds on December 31, 20A.

Part E (LO 4)

Assuming instead that First Australian uses the effective-interest method for amortization purposes, prepare the journal entries to record the payment of interest on June 30, 20A, and December 31, 20A.

Transaction	Account	Debit	Credit
6/30/20A			
12/31/20A			

Part F (LO 4)

Again, assuming that First Australian uses the effective-interest method, compute the book value of the bonds on December 31, 20A.

Exercise 3

On January 1, 20A, First Finland, Inc. plans to issue $500,000, five year, 8% bonds that will mature on December 31, 20E. Interest is payable semiannually each June 30 and December 31.

Part A (LO 2)

Assuming that the market (yield) rate is 10%, compute the issue (sale) price on January 1, 20A.

Part B (LO 2)

Prepare the journal entry to record the issuance of the bonds.

Transaction	Account	Debit	Credit
1/1/20A			

Part C (LO 2)

Assuming that First Finland uses the straight-line method for amortization purposes, prepare the journal entries to record the payment of interest on June 30, 20A, and December 31, 20A.

Transaction	Account	Debit	Credit
6/30/20A			
12/31/20A			

Part D (LO 2)

Compute the book value of the bonds on December 31, 20A.

Exercise 3, continued
Part E (LO 4)

Assuming instead that First Finland uses the effective-interest method for amortization purposes, prepare the journal entries to record the payment of interest on June 30, 20A, and December 31, 20A.

Transaction	Account	Debit	Credit
6/30/20A			
12/31/20A			

Part F (LO 4)

Again, assuming that First Finland uses the effective-interest method, compute the book value of the bonds on December 31, 20A.

Exercise 4

Summit Companies reported total liabilities of $400,000 and $351,000, and stockholders' equity of $4,000,000 and $3,900,000 at December 31, 20B and 20A, respectively. Interest expense amounted to $82,000 during 20B and $97,000 during 20A, and income before interest and taxes was $256,000 during 20B and $212,000 in 20A.

Part A (LO 1)

Compute Summit's debt-to-equity ratios as of December 31, 20B and 20A, and comment on the change noted, if any.

Part B (LO 3)

Compute Summit's times interest earned ratios for 20B and 20A, and comment on the change noted, if any.

SOLUTIONS TO SELF-TEST QUESTIONS AND EXERCISES

MATCHING

F	Bond Certificate	O	Face Amount
C	Bond Discount	I	Indenture
K	Bond Premium	J	Market Interest Rate
S	Bond Principal	A	Net Interest Cost
R	Callable Bonds	G	Par Value
Q	Convertible Bonds	L	Stated Rate
B	Coupon Rate	D	Straight-Line Amortization
E	Debenture	P	Trustee
M	Effective-Interest Method	H	Yield
N	Effective-Interest Rate		

TRUE-FALSE QUESTIONS

1. T
2. F – Financial leverage is the ability of a company to invest borrowed money at a rate of return higher than their borrowing rate, thus increasing return to stockholders.
3. F – A debenture is an unsecured bond. Some bonds are secured by specific assets, and, as such, are not considered debentures.
4. F – An independent trustee is appointed to monitor the interests of the bondholders.
5. F – The par value is the face value of the bond; the bond might be issued at par, at a premium (above par), or at a discount (below par) depending on the relationship between the coupon rate and the market rate on the date of issuance.
6. F – Companies try to select a coupon rate that will approximate the market rate that is expected to be in effect on the date of issuance.
7. T
8. T
9. T
10. T
11. T
12. F – Cash inflows from the sale of bonds and outflows for the payment of principal on bonds are reported in the financing activities section of the SCF; however, bond interest payments are directly related to earning income and, as such, are reported in the operating activities section of the SCF.
13. T
14. F – A bond sinking fund may or may not be required by the bond contract.
15. F – Bonds are the only security that *can* be classified as held-to-maturity securities, but bonds can only be classified as held-to-maturity if the company has both the ability and the intent to hold them to maturity.

MULTIPLE CHOICE QUESTIONS

1.	b	4.	b	7.	a	10.	d	13.	e
2.	b	5.	c	8.	c	11.	e	14.	c
3.	c	6.	e	9.	c	12.	a		

EXERCISES

Exercise 1
Part A

Transaction	Account	Debit	Credit
1/1/20A	Cash	500,000	
	Bonds payable		500,000

Part B

Semiannual interest payment = $500,000 x .08 x 6/12 = $20,000.

Part C

Transaction	Account	Debit	Credit
6/30/20A	Interest expense	20,000	
	Cash		20,000
12/31/20A	Interest expense	20,000	
	Cash		20,000

Exercise 2
Part A

Present Value of Principal
Refer to Table A-2, For i = 3%, n = 10, the value is 0.7441
Present value of principal is $500,000 x 0.7441 $372,050
Present Value of Interest
Refer to Table A-4, For i = 3%, n = 10, the value is 8.5302
Present value of interest payments are $20,000 x 8.5302   170,604
Present Value of Principal and Interest $542,654

Part B

Transaction	Account	Debit	Credit
1/1/20A	Cash	542,654	
	Bonds payable		500,000
	Premium on bonds payable		42,654

Part C

Transaction	Account	Debit	Credit
6/30/20A	Interest expense ($20,000 - $4,265)	15,735	
	Premium on bonds payable ($42,654 ÷ 10)	4,265	
	Cash		20,000
12/31/20A	Interest expense ($20,000 - $4,265)	15,735	
	Premium on bonds payable ($42,654 ÷ 10)	4,265	
	Cash		20,000

Exercise 2, continued
Part D

Bonds payable			$500,000
Premium on bonds payable		$42,654	
Less amortization during 20A:			
June 30	$(4,265)		
December 31	(4,265)	(8,530)	34,124
Book value at end of 20A			$534,124

Part E

Transaction	Account	Debit	Credit
6/30/20A	Interest expense ($542,654 x .06 x 6 ÷12)	16,280	
	Premium on bonds payable ($20,000 - $16,280)	3,720	
	Cash		20,000
12/31/20A	Interest expense [($542,654 - $3,720) x .06 x 6/12]	16,168	
	Premium on bonds payable ($20,000 - $16,168)	3,832	
	Cash		20,000

Part F

Bonds payable			$500,000
Premium on bonds payable		$42,654	
Less amortization during 20A:			
June 30	$(3,720)		
December 31	(3,832)	(7,552)	35,102
Book value at end of 20A			$535,102

Exercise 3
Part A

Present Value of Principal
Refer to Table A-2, For i = 5%, n = 10, the value is 0.6139
Present value of principal is $500,000 x 0.6139 .... $306,950
Present Value of Interest
Refer to Table A-4, For i = 5%, n = 10, the value is 7.7217
Present value of interest payments is $20,000 x 7.7217 154,434
Present Value of Principal and Interest $461,384

Exercise 3, continued

Part B

Transaction	Account	Debit	Credit
1/1/20A	Cash	461,384	
	Discount on bonds payable	38,616	
	Bond payable		500,000

Part C

Transaction	Account	Debit	Credit
6/30/20A	Interest expense ($20,000 + $3,862)	23,862	
	Discount on bonds payable ($38,616 ÷ 10)		3,862
	Cash		20,000
12/31/20A	Interest expense ($20,000 + $3,862)	23,862	
	Discount on bonds payable ($38,616 ÷ 10)		3,862
	Cash		20,000

Part D

Bonds payable			$500,000
Less discount on bonds payable		$(38,616)	
Less amortization during 20A:			
June 30	$3,862		
December 31	3,862	7,724	(30,892)
Book value at December 31, 20A			$469,108

Part E

Transaction	Account	Debit	Credit
6/30/20A	Interest expense ($461,384 x .10 x 6/12)	23,069	
	Discount on bonds payable ($23,069 - $20,000)		3,069
	Cash		20,000
12/31/20A	Interest expense [($461,384 + $3,069) x .10 x 6/12]	23,223	
	Discount on bonds payable ($23,223 - $20,000)		3,223
	Cash		20,000

Exercise 3, continued
Part F

Bonds payable			$500,000
Less discount on bonds payable		$(38,616)	
Less amortization during 20A:			
June 30	$3,069		
December 31	3,223	6,292	(32,324)
Book value at December 31, 20A			$467,676

Exercise 4
Part A

Total Debt ÷ Total Equity = Debt-to-Equity Ratio
December 31, 20B
$400,000 ÷ $4,000,000 = .10
December 31, 20A
$351,000 ÷ $3,900,000 = .09
Summit's debt-to-equity ratio increased slightly during 20B. Summit is therefore more highly leveraged, and, as a result, has more risk

Part B

(Net income + Interest expense + Income tax expense) ÷ Interest expense = Times interest earned ratio
for the year ended December 31, 20B
$256,000 ÷ $82,000 = 3.1
for the year ended December 31, 20A
$212,000 ÷ $97,000 = 2.2
Summit's interest coverage ratio increased during 20B. Summit is generating more income compared to obligatory payments to creditors. This suggests a lower risk of defaulting on required interest payments.

AN IDEA FOR YOUR STUDY TEAM

Some years ago, the Tennessee Valley Authority (the TVA), a large power company, issued some 50-year maturity bonds, including zero coupon bonds. Although there were some doubts at the time about the company's ability to sell bonds with such a long life, the bonds sold very well. Most were purchased by pension plans. Answer the following questions. Then, get together with the members of your study team, and compare your answers.

1. Why would the TVA issue bonds?

2. Why would a company want to issue bonds with such a long-term maturity?

3. Why might a 50-year bond be difficult to sell?

4. Why do you think these 50-year bonds were so attractive to pension funds? (Refer back to chapter 9, if necessary.)

CHAPTER 11
REPORTING AND INTERPRETING OWNERS' EQUITY

ORGANIZATION OF THE CHAPTER

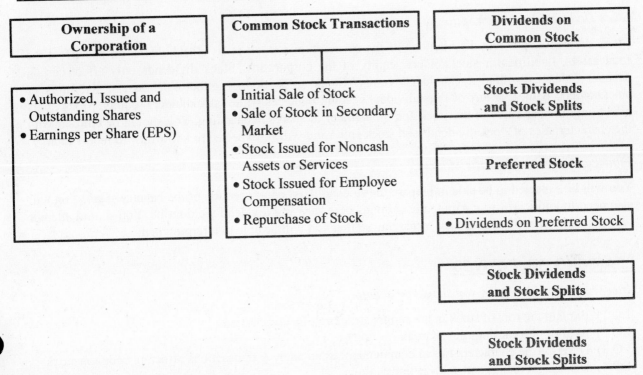

Ownership of a Corporation	Common Stock Transactions	Dividends on Common Stock

- Authorized, Issued and Outstanding Shares
- Earnings per Share (EPS)

- Initial Sale of Stock
- Sale of Stock in Secondary Market
- Stock Issued for Noncash Assets or Services
- Stock Issued for Employee Compensation
- Repurchase of Stock

Stock Dividends and Stock Splits

Preferred Stock

- Dividends on Preferred Stock

Stock Dividends and Stock Splits

Stock Dividends and Stock Splits

CHAPTER FOCUS SUGGESTIONS

Overview

This chapter concludes the coverage of the right side of the balance sheet. As you know, a variety of business and accounting issues arise when managers need to obtain funds to finance the acquisition of assets and the operations of the business. The last two chapters addressed the reporting and interpretation of liabilities (one of the sources of funds). This chapter addresses the issues that relate to owners' equity (the other source of funds). Emphasis is placed on the two basic sources of owners' equity in a corporation: contributed capital and retained earnings.

Types of Stock and Related Transactions

You should be familiar with the process of incorporating a business, and the advantages and disadvantages of this form of business. Corporations issue two types of capital stock: common and preferred. You should be familiar with the characteristics, and advantages and disadvantages of each. You will need to know how to record transactions relating to the issuance (sale) of capital stock to investors and the purchase of treasury stock.

Dividends

Corporate earnings that do not need to be retained in the business for growth and expansion are distributed to stockholders as dividends. Cash dividends reduce total assets and total stockholders' equity. You should understand how current and cumulative dividend preferred stock preferences affect the declaration of dividends on common stock. You will be expected to know how to record dividend transactions.

Stock Dividends and Stock Splits

Stock dividends, pro rata distributions of the corporation's stock to its stockholders, do not affect the total assets, liabilities or stockholders' equity of the corporation. Stock dividends only affect certain account balances within stockholders' equity. Stock splits do not affect total assets, liabilities or stockholders' equity, or any of the individual account balances within stockholders' equity. Stock splits affect only the par value of the stock and the number of shares outstanding. You should be familiar with the characteristics of stock dividends and stock splits and will be expected to know how to report each.

Financial Statement Analysis Matters

You will be expected to be able to prepare the stockholders' equity section of the balance sheet. You will also need to know how to compute the earnings per share and dividend yield ratios. You should attempt to understand what these ratios are measuring so that you will be able to interpret them.

LEARNING OBJECTIVES

After studying this chapter, you should be able to:

(LO 1) Explain the role of stock in the capital structure of a corporation.
(LO 2) Analyze the earnings per share ratio.
(LO 3) Describe the characteristics of common stock and analyze transactions affecting common stock.
(LO 4) Discuss dividends and analyze transactions.
(LO 5) Analyze the dividend yield ratio.
(LO 6) Discuss the purpose of stock dividends, stock splits, and report transactions.
(LO 7) Describe the characteristics of preferred stock and analyze transactions affecting preferred stock.
(LO 8) Discuss the impact of capital stock transactions on cash flows.

READ AND RECALL QUESTIONS

After you read each section of the chapter, answer the related Read and Recall Questions below.

LEARNING OBJECTIVE
After studying this section of the chapter, you should be able to:
1. Explain the role of stock in the capital structure of a corporation.

BUSINESS BACKGROUND

What can the popularity of the corporate form of doing business be attributed to? What are two primary sources of stockholders' equity? How is each generated?

OWNERSHIP OF A CORPORATION

What is the only business form recognized by the law as a separate entity? What does this mean? How are corporations created? What is another name for a charter? Who governs a corporation? What is a stockholder (or shareholder)? What three benefits are received by owners of common stock? What can owners do that creditors cannot do?

AUTHORIZED, ISSUED, AND OUTSTANDING SHARES

What information is specified by the corporate charter? What term describes the maximum number of shares that can be sold (issued) to the public? What term describes stock that has been sold to the public?

What term is used to describe stock that has already been sold to the public that is bought back by the corporation? What term describes shares currently held by individual stockholders (as opposed to those that are held by the company)? How is the number of outstanding shares determined?

> **LEARNING OBJECTIVE**
> *After studying this section of the chapter, you should be able to:*
> 2. Analyze the earnings per share ratio.

KEY RATIO ANALYSIS: EARNINGS PER SHARE (EPS)

How is the earnings per share (EPS) ratio computed? What does it measure? What are two ways in which this ratio is useful? Why might the EPS ratio be misleading?

> **LEARNING OBJECTIVE**
> *After studying this section of the chapter, you should be able to:*
> 3. Describe the characteristics of common stock and analyze transactions affecting common stock.

COMMON STOCK TRANSACTIONS

What is common stock? Why are common stockholders often thought of as the "owners" of the corporation? Who determines the dividend rate for common stock?

What is par value? What is legal capital? What is no-par value stock?

INITIAL SALE OF STOCK

What is an initial public offering (IPO)? What is a seasoned new issue?

What entry would be used to record the sale of 100,000 shares of $0.01 par value stock for $22 per share? How would this entry impact the accounting equation?

Account	Debit	Credit

Assets	=	Liabilities	+	Stockholders' Equity

Refer to your entry above. How would you describe the amount that is credited to the common stock account? If the common stock does not have a stated par value, how would the amount that is credited to the common stock account be determined? What is the normal balance of this account? What happens if there is no par or stated value?

SALE OF STOCK IN SECONDARY MARKETS

If one investor subsequently sells the stock of a corporation to another investor, how are the accounting records of the corporation affected? What is the purpose of the secondary markets? What are three secondary markets?

CAPITAL STOCK SOLD AND ISSUED FOR NONCASH ASSETS OR SERVICES

When a company issues stock to acquire assets or services, what measurement is used to determine the amount used to record the acquired items? If that amount cannot be determined, what amount should be used instead?

What entry would be used to record the issuance of 10,000 shares of $0.01 par value stock in exchange for legal services that were rendered if the stock was selling for $15 per share? How would this entry impact the accounting equation?

Account	Debit	Credit

Assets _____ = _____ Liabilities _____ + _____ Stockholders' Equity _____

STOCK ISSUED FOR EMPLOYEE COMPENSATION

Why do some companies offer compensation packages that include stock options? What problem might be overcome with this strategy? What are stock options? Why can a stock option be thought of as a risk-free investment?

REPURCHASE OF STOCK

What is a common reason for a corporation's purchase of its own stock from existing stockholders? What is treasury stock? Do shares held as treasury stock have voting, dividend or other stockholder rights?

What entry would be used to record a corporation's purchase of 100,000 shares of its own stock for $20 per share? How would this entry impact the accounting equation?

Account	Debit	Credit

Assets _____ = _____ Liabilities _____ + _____ Stockholders' Equity _____

Refer to your entry above. What type of account is the Treasury Stock account? How does an increase in the balance of this account impact total stockholders' equity?

If a company sells its treasury stock for more or less than it paid for it, is a profit (gain) or loss recorded? Why or why not?

What entry would be used to record the resale of the treasury stock described above at $30 per share? How would this entry impact the accounting equation?

Account	Debit	Credit

_____ Assets _____ = _____ Liabilities _____ + _____ Stockholders' Equity _____

Refer to your entry above. How would it change if the treasury stock were sold at a price less than its purchase price?

LEARNING OBJECTIVE
After studying this section of the chapter, you should be able to:
4. Discuss dividends and analyze transactions.

DIVIDENDS ON COMMON STOCK

What two types of returns do investors in common stock expect on their investment? Why do wealthy investors in high tax brackets prefer to receive their return on stock investments in the form of higher stock prices? Why do other investors, such as retirees, prefer to receive their return in the form of dividends?

LEARNING OBJECTIVE
After studying this section of the chapter, you should be able to:
5. Analyze the dividend yield ratio.

KEY RATIO ANALYSIS: DIVIDEND YIELD

How is the dividend yield ratio computed? What does it measure? Why does the dividend yield ratio often tell only part of the story? What is often a more important consideration?

Are corporations legally obligated to pay dividends on common stock? What is created when the board formally declares a dividend? What is a "declaration date?" What is a "record date?" What is a "date of payment?"

What entry would be used to record the declaration of a cash dividend of six cents per share if 1,000,000 shares are outstanding? How would this entry impact the accounting equation?

Account	Debit	Credit

_____ = _____ + _____
        Assets   Liabilities   Stockholders' Equity

What entry would be used to record the subsequent payment of the dividend described above? How would this entry impact the accounting equation?

Account	Debit	Credit

_____ = _____ + _____
        Assets   Liabilities   Stockholders' Equity

What are the two fundamental requirements for payment of a cash dividend?

FINANCIAL ANALYSIS
IMPACT OF DIVIDENDS ON STOCK PRICE

What is an ex-dividend date? Who receives the dividend if you buy stock before the ex-dividend date? Who receives the dividend if you buy the stock after the ex-dividend date? What often happens to the stock's price on the ex-dividend date?

LEARNING OBJECTIVE

After studying this section of the chapter, you should be able to:

6. Discuss the purpose of stock dividends and stock splits, and report transactions.

STOCK DIVIDENDS AND STOCK SPLITS
STOCK DIVIDENDS

What is a stock dividend? What does pro rata basis mean? Why does a stock dividend have no economic value (that is, why isn't an investor who has received a stock dividend wealthier as a result)?

How does the stock market immediately react when a stock dividend is issued? In some cases, why does a stock dividend make the stock more attractive to new investors?

What does the company need to do when a stock dividend occurs? How is a large stock dividend distinguished from a small stock dividend?

If a stock dividend is classified as large, how is the amount that is transferred to the Common Stock account determined? When a small stock dividend occurs, how is the amount that is transferred determined? If the amount exceeds the par value of the additional shares issued, to which account should the excess be transferred?

What entry would be used to record the issuance of 1,000,000 shares of $0.01 par value stock as a large stock dividend? How would this entry impact the accounting equation?

Account	Debit	Credit

_____ Assets _____ = _____ Liabilities _____ + _____ Stockholders' Equity _____

STOCK SPLITS

What is a stock split? What happens to the total number of authorized shares in a stock split? What must happen to the par or stated value so that the total par or stated value of all authorized shares is unchanged?

Why doesn't a stock split result in a transfer from the retained earnings account to the common stock account? If no entry is made, how are users of the financial statements made aware of the stock split?

LEARNING OBJECTIVE
After studying this section of the chapter, you should be able to:
7. Describe the characteristics of preferred stock and analyze transactions affecting preferred stock.

PREFERRED STOCK

What is preferred stock? What are the three most significant differences between preferred stock and common stock?

DIVIDENDS ON PREFERRED STOCK

What are the two most common types of dividend preferences made available to preferred stockholders?

What does a current dividend preference require? If there is preferred stock outstanding, what must happen before dividends can be paid to common stockholders?

Cumulative Dividend Preference

What does a cumulative dividend preference require? What are dividends in arrears? If preferred stock is not cumulative, can dividends be in arrears? Why or why not? Why is preferred stock usually cumulative?

©*The McGraw-Hill Companies, Inc., 2004*

FINANCIAL ANALYSIS
IMPACT OF DIVIDENDS IN ARREARS

Why are analysts interested in information concerning dividends in arrears?

Restrictions on Retained Earnings

Why would restrictions be placed on retained earnings? What does the full disclosure principal require in this regard? Why are analysts interested in information concerning restrictions on retained earnings?

LEARNING OBJECTIVE

After studying this section of the chapter, you should be able to:
8. Discuss the impact of capital stock transactions on cash flows.

FOCUS ON CASH FLOWS
FINANCING ACTIVITIES

Does an inflow or an outflow of cash result from the sale (issuance) of stock? Does an inflow or an outflow of cash result when the issuing corporation repurchases stock? Does an inflow or an outflow of cash result from the payment of cash dividends? How are each of these cash flows reported on the statement of cash flows (that is, as operating, investing or financing activities)?

CHAPTER SUPPLEMENT A (*Determine whether you are responsible for this supplement.*)

Accounting for Owners' Equity for Sole Proprietorships and Partnerships

OWNER'S EQUITY FOR A SOLE PROPRIETORSHIP

What is a sole proprietorship? What are the two owner's equity accounts that are needed? What are the two purposes of the capital account of a sole proprietorship? What is the purpose of the drawing account? After the closing process is complete, what does the capital account reflect at the end of the accounting period?

Why don't the financial statements of a sole proprietorship report income tax expense or income taxes payable? Is the owner's salary recognized as an expense in a sole proprietorship? Why or why not?

OWNERS' EQUITY FOR A PARTNERSHIP

What is the definition of a partnership? How is a partnership formed? What five matters should be specified in a partnership agreement?

What are the three primary advantages of a partnership? What is the primary disadvantage?

How does the accounting for partners' equity (for a partnership) differ from that of owner's equity (for a sole proprietorship)? After the closing process is complete, what is reflected in each partner's capital account?

CHAPTER TAKE-AWAYS

1. *Explain the role of stock in the capital structure of a corporation.*

   The law recognizes corporations as separate legal entities. Owners invest in a corporation and receive capital stock that can be traded on established stock exchanges. Stock provides a number of rights, including the right to receive dividends.

2. *Analyze the earnings per share ratio.*

   The earnings per share ratio facilitates the comparison of a company's earnings over time or with other companies' at a single point in time. By expressing earnings on a per share basis, differences in the size of companies becomes less important.

3. *Describe the characteristics of common stock and analyze transactions affecting common stock.*

   Common stock is the basic voting stock issued by a corporation. Usually it has a par value, but no-par stock can be issued. Common stock offers some special rights that appeal to certain investors.

   A number of key transactions involve capital stock: (1) initial sale of stock, (2) treasury stock transactions, (3) cash dividends, and (4) stock dividends and stock splits. Each is illustrated in this chapter.

4. *Discuss dividends and analyze transactions.*

   The return associated with an investment in capital stock comes from two sources: appreciation and dividends. Dividends are recorded as a liability when they are declared by the board of directors (i.e., on the date of declaration). The liability is satisfied when the dividends are paid (i.e., on the date of payment).

5. *Analyze the dividend yield ratio.*

The dividend yield ratio measures the percentage of return on an investment from dividends. For most companies, the return associated with dividends is very small.

6. *Discuss the purpose of stock dividends, stock splits, and report transactions.*

Stock dividends are pro rata distributions of a company's stock to existing owners. The transaction involves transferring an additional amount into the common stock account. A stock split also involves the distribution of additional shares to owners but no additional amount is transferred into the common stock account. Instead, the par value of the stock is reduced.

7. *Describe the characteristics of preferred stock and analyze transactions affecting preferred stock.*

Preferred stock provides investors certain advantages including dividend preferences and a preference on asset distributions in the event the corporation is liquidated.

8. *Discuss the impact of capital stock transactions on cash flows.*

Both inflows (e.g., the issuance of capital stock) and outflows (e.g., the purchase of treasury stock) are reported in the Financing Activities section of the statement of cash flows. The payment of dividends is reported as an outflow in this section.

KEY RATIOS

The earnings per share ratio states the income of a corporation on a per share basis. The ratio is computed as follows:

Earnings per Share = Income ÷ Average Number of Shares of Common Stock Outstanding

The dividend yield ratio measures the dividend return on the current price of the stock. The ratio is computed as follows:

Dividend Yield Ratio = Dividend per share ÷ Market price per share

FINDING FINANCIAL INFORMATION

Balance Sheet	Income Statement

Under Current Liabilities
Dividends, once declared by the board of directors, are reported as a liability (usually current).
Under Noncurrent Liabilities
Transactions involving capital stock do not generate noncurrent liabilities.
Under Stockholders Equity
Typical accounts include:
  Preferred stock
  Common stock
  Capital in excess of par
  Retained earnings
  Treasury stock
	Capital stock is never shown on the income statement. Dividends paid are not an expense. They are a distribution of income and are, therefore, not reported on the income statement.

Statement of Cash Flows	Statement of Stockholders' Equity
Under Financing Activities + Cash inflows from initial sale of stock + Cash inflows from sale of treasury stock − Cash outflows for dividends − Cash outflows for purchase of treasury stock	This statement reports detailed information concerning stockholders' equity, including (1) amounts in each equity account, (2) number of shares outstanding, (3) impact of transactions such as earning income, payment of dividends, and purchase of treasury stock.

Notes
Under Summary Of Significant Accounting Policies Usually, very little information concerning capital stock is provided in this summary. **Under A Separate Note** Most companies report information about their stock option plans and information about major transactions such as stock dividends or significant treasury stock transactions. An historical summary of dividends paid per share is typically provided.

SELF-TEST QUESTIONS AND EXERCISES

MATCHING

Match each of the key terms listed below with the appropriate textbook definition:

____ Authorized Number of Shares
____ Common Stock
____ Cumulative Dividend Preference
____ Current Dividend Preference
Dividend Dates:
____ Declaration Date
____ Payment Date
____ Record Date
____ Dividends in Arrears

____ Issued Shares
____ Legal Capital
____ No-Par Value Stock
____ Outstanding Shares
____ Par Value
____ Preferred Stock
____ Stock Dividend
____ Stock Split
____ Treasury Stock

A. A legal amount per share established by the board of directors; it establishes a minimum amount a stockholder must contribute and has no relationship to the market price of the stock.
B. Capital stock that has no par value specified in the corporate charter.
C. Maximum number of shares of capital stock of a corporation that can be issued as specified in the charter.
D. A corporation's own stock that has been issued but was subsequently reacquired and is still being held by the corporation.
E. Distribution of additional shares of a corporation's own stock.
F. Date on which the corporation prepares the list of current stockholders as shown on its records; dividends can be paid only to the stockholders who own stock on that date.
G. Preferred stock feature that requires specified current dividends not paid in full to accumulate for every year in which they are not paid. These cumulative preferred dividends must be paid before any common dividends can be paid.
H. Stock that has specified rights over common stock.
I. The feature of preferred stock that grants priority on preferred dividends over common dividends.
J. Date on which the board of directors officially approves a dividend.

K. The basic, normal, voting stock issued by a corporation; called *residual equity* because it ranks after preferred stock for dividend and liquidation distributions.

L. An increase in the total number of authorized shares by a specified ratio; does not decrease retained earnings.

M. Date on which a cash dividend is paid to the stockholders of record.

N. Total number of shares of stock that are owned by stockholders on any particular date.

O. Dividends on cumulative preferred stock that have not been declared in prior years.

P. Total number of shares of stock that have been issued; shares outstanding plus treasury shares held.

Q. The permanent amount of capital defined by state law that must remain invested in the business; provides a "cushion" for creditors.

TRUE-FALSE QUESTIONS

For each of the following, enter a T or F in the blank to indicate whether the statement is true or false.

___1. (LO 1) The number of authorized shares in a corporation refers to the original number of shares issued when that company "went public."

___2. (LO 1) Unlimited liability refers to the fact that creditors of a liquidated corporation can put claims on the assets of shareholders for debts that corporate assets are insufficient to pay.

___3. (LO 3) The EPS ratio is computed by dividing income by average number of common shares issued.

___4. (LO 3) If a corporation only has one class of stock, it is common stock.

___5. (LO 3) Legal capital is a permanent amount of capital that owners cannot withdraw.

___6. (LO 3) Contributed capital from the sale of stock with a par value is usually divided between amounts received equal to par value of the shares sold, and amounts received in excess of par.

___7. (LO 3) When shareholders in a corporation sell all or part of their holdings to other private individuals, no entry is required on the part of the corporation.

___8. (LO 3) Treasury stock consists of unissued shares of the company's stock.

___9. (LO 4) When no other qualifying statements are made, the term "dividend" can mean either a cash or a stock dividend.

___10. (LO 5) Common stock with a low dividend yield would not appeal to potential investors who need steady income from dividends.

___11. (LO 6) A large stock dividend is recorded at the par value of the shares distributed.

___12. (LO 6) A stock split results in a decrease in the par value of the stock, and a proportionate increase in the number of shares outstanding.

___13. (LO 7) The full disclosure principle requires that any restrictions on retained earnings must be reported on the face of the balance sheet.

___14. (LO 7) The chief advantage of preferred stock is that its dividends must be paid before any dividends can be given to common shareholders.

MULTIPLE CHOICE QUESTIONS

Choose the best answer or response by placing the identifying letter in the space provided.

___1. (LO 1) A stockholder of a corporation is

   a. one of the owners of the corporation.
   b. a creditor of the corporation.
   c. both an owner and a creditor of the corporation.
   d. a manager of the corporation.
   e. both c and d.

___2. (LO 1) In order to create a corporation, it is necessary to apply to

   a. the federal government.
   b. the appropriate office in the state in which the corporation will be organized.
   c. the SEC.
   d. the FASB.
   e. the IRS.

___3. (LO 1) Outstanding shares of stock are those which

   a. have been issued to investors.
   b. have been issued, and have not been bought back by the company.
   c. the company is permitted by its charter to issue.
   d. are authorized, but have not yet been issued.
   e. have been repurchased by the company.

___4. (LO 3) Compact Corporation has 50,000,000 shares of common stock, par value $.01, authorized, and 16,697,000 shares issued and outstanding. Its total paid in capital is $199,623,000. If Compact rounds all dollar amounts on its financial statements to the nearest thousandth, the dollar amount reported as common stock on its balance sheet would be

   a. $500
   b. $200
   c. $167
   d. $199
   e. $333

___5. (LO 3) Refer to the information in the preceding question. The average price received by Compact for a share of its stock was

   a. $.01
   b. $3.99
   c. $11.96
   d. $21.13
   e. cannot be calculated from the information given.

___6. (LO 3) Quinn had one hundred shares of Compact common stock that she had purchased for $21 per share. She sold the shares to Randy for $28 per share. On Compact's books this would

    a. be shown as an increase in stockholders' equity of $2,800.
    b. be shown as an increase in stockholders' equity of $700.
    c. be shown as an increase in retained earnings of $700.
    d. be shown as an increase to additional paid-in capital of $700.
    e. not be shown at all.

___7. (LO 3) Cosmic Treats Co. purchased 40,000 shares of its own $1 par common stock on the open market for $600,000. Cosmic intends to hold the stock for employee bonuses. This stock would be carried on Cosmic's books in

    a. a contra equity account.
    b. the common stock account.
    c. an asset account, at cost.
    d. an asset account, at par value.
    e. a liability account.

___8. (LO 4) On December 31, 1995, the board of directors of Ardent Inc. issued a press release to the newspapers stating that the company planned to pay a dividend of $.12 per share on its common stock. The date of this announcement is known as the date of _____; the company must record a liability _____.

    a. record; on the date of declaration.
    b. record; on the date of record.
    c. declaration; in the year in which the dividend will be paid.
    d. declaration; on the date of declaration.
    e. dividend; when the books are closed for the fiscal year.

___9. (LO 5) The dividend yield ratio is

    a. calculated by dividing dividends per share by market price per share.
    b. calculated by dividing total cash dividends by market price per share.
    c. calculated by dividing market price per share by dividends per share.
    d. is calculated by dividing dividends by net income.
    e. a measure of the portion of current earnings that is paid to owners in the form of dividends.

___10. (LO 6) A stock split, unlike a stock dividend,

    a. requires no journal entry.
    b. does not change total stockholders' equity.
    c. reduces the par value of the stock.
    d. increases the total number of shares outstanding.
    e. both a and c.

___11. (LO 7) Ardent Inc. had 1,000 shares of $100 par, 6% preferred stock outstanding, as well as 100,000 shares of $.01 par common stock. On March 31, 1996, their year-end, the board of directors declared a dividend of $9,500. In the past, they have tried to maintain a minimum dividend of $.10 per share on common stock. For the March 31 dividend, preferred stockholders would receive a total of _____ and common stockholders a total of _____.

   a. $6,000; $10,000
   b. $0; $9,500
   c. $4,750; $4,750
   d. $0; $10,000
   e. $6,000; $3,500

___12. (LO 7) Refer to the information in the preceding question. Suppose the preferred stock is cumulative, and Ardent, having had a slow year, was unable to pay any dividends last year. In that case, preferred stockholders would receive _____ and common stockholders would receive _____ on March 31 of this year.

   a. $6,000; $3,500
   b. $12,000; 0
   c. $9,500; 0
   d. $12,000; $10,000
   e. $4,750; $4,750

EXERCISES

Record your answers to each part of these exercises in the space provided. Show your work.

Exercise 1

Tyler Corporation was organized in 20A. Its corporate charter authorized the issuance of 50,000 shares of common stock, par value $5 per share, and 10,000 shares of 8% preferred stock, par value $25 per share.

Part A (LO 3, 4, and 7)

Prepare journal entries for each of the following transactions:

January 1

Sold and issued 40,000 shares of common stock for cash at $25 per share and sold and issued 5,000 shares of preferred stock for cash of $75 per share.

Transaction	Account	Debit	Credit
1/1/20A			
1/1/20A			

Exercise 1, Part A, continued

February 1

Issued 5,000 shares of common stock in exchange for a tract of land. Assume the stock was selling at $26 per share at the time of this transaction.

Transaction	Account	Debit	Credit
2/1/20A			

June 1

Purchased 7,500 shares of common stock in the open market at $24 per share.

Transaction	Account	Debit	Credit
6/1/20A			

August 1

Sold 1,000 shares of the treasury stock at $26 per share.

Transaction	Account	Debit	Credit
8/1/20A			

October 1

Sold another 1,500 shares of the treasury stock at $23 per share.

Transaction	Account	Debit	Credit
10/1/20A			

Exercise 1, Part A, continued

December 1

Declared dividends totaling $100,000.

Allocation of dividend to preferred and common stockholders:

Transaction	Account	Debit	Credit
12/1/20A			

December 31

Paid the dividends that were declared.

Transaction	Account	Debit	Credit
12/31/20A			

Part B (LO 3)

Compute the number of shares of common stock issued and outstanding at December 31, 20A.

Part C (LO 5)

Assuming that the market price of the common stock was $22.50 per share on December 31, 20A, calculate the dividend yield ratio.

Exercise 2 (LO 6)

Core Corporation had 400,000 shares of common stock, par value $2 per share, authorized and 200,000 shares issued and outstanding on December 31, 20A. The market value of its common stock on that date was $100 per share. Prepare journal entries for each of the following independent transactions.

Part A

Core Corporation declared a two-for-one stock split that will be accounted for as a 100% stock dividend.

Transaction	Account	Debit	Credit
12/31/20A			

If you did __not__ prepare a journal entry, provide an explanation and indicate how this transaction would affect the financial statements:

Part B

Assume instead that Core Corporation declared a 25% stock dividend.

Calculations:

Transaction	Account	Debit	Credit
12/31/20A			

If you did __not__ prepare a journal entry, provide an explanation and, indicate how this transaction would affect the financial statements:

Part C

Assume instead that Core Corporation declared a five-to-four stock split (i.e., a 25% increase in the number of shares).

Calculations:

Exercise 2, Part C, continued

Transaction	Account	Debit	Credit
12/31/20A			

If you did __not__ prepare a journal entry, provide an explanation and indicate how this transaction would affect the financial statements:

SOLUTIONS TO SELF-TEST QUESTIONS AND EXERCISES

MATCHING

C	Authorized Number of Shares	P	Issued Shares
K	Common Stock	Q	Legal Capital
G	Cumulative Dividend Preference	B	No-Par Value Stock
I	Current Dividend Preference	N	Outstanding Shares
	Dividend Dates:	A	Par Value
J	Declaration Date	H	Preferred Stock
M	Payment Date	E	Stock Dividend
F	Record Date	L	Stock Split
O	Dividends in Arrears	D	Treasury Stock

TRUE-FALSE QUESTIONS

1. F – The number of authorized shares is the maximum number of shares the corporation is permitted to offer for sale (as set forth in its corporate charter).
2. F – Unlimited liability applies to the owners of sole proprietorships and partnerships; not to corporations.
3. F – The EPS ratio is computed by dividing income by the average number of common shares outstanding.
4. T
5. T
6. T
7. T
8. F – Treasury stock consists of shares of company stock that the company has repurchased.
9. F – Without a qualifier, "dividend" means a cash dividend.
10. T
11. T

12. T
13. F – Restrictions on retained earnings may be disclosed either on the financial statements themselves *or* in the footnotes to the financial statements.
14. T

MULTIPLE CHOICE QUESTIONS

1.	a	3.	b	5.	c	7.	a	9.	a	11.	e
2.	b	4.	c	6.	e	8.	d	10.	e	12.	c

EXERCISES

Exercise 1
Part A

Transaction	Account	Debit	Credit
1/1/20A	Cash (40,000 x $25)	1,000,000	
	Common stock (40,000 x $5)		200,000
	Capital in excess of par value		800,000
	(40,000 x $20)		
1/1/20A	Cash (5,000 x $75)	375,000	
	Preferred stock (5,000 x $25)		125,000
	Capital in excess par value		250,000
	(5,000 x $50)		
2/1/20A	Land (5,000 x $26)	130,000	
	Common stock (5,000 x $5)		25,000
	Capital in excess of par value		105,000
	(5,000 x $21)		
6/1/20A	Treasury stock	180,000	
	Cash (7,500 x $24)		180,000
8/1/20A	Cash (1,000 x $26)	26,000	
	Treasury stock (1,000 x $24)		24,000
	Contributed capital from		
	treasury stock transactions		2,000
	(1,000 x $2)		
10/1/20A	Cash (1,500 x $23)	34,500	
	Contributed capital from treasury		
	treasury stock transactions	1,500	
	(1,500 x $1)		
	Treasury stock (1,500 x $24)		36,000

Exercise 1, Part A, continued

Transaction	Account	Debit	Credit
12/1/20A	Retained earnings	100,000	
	Dividends payable - preferred		10,000
	(5,000 x $25 x .08)		
	Dividends payable - common		90,000
	($100,000 - $10,000)		
12/31/20A	Dividends payable - preferred	10,000	
	Dividends payable - common	90,000	
	Cash		100,000

Part B

Issued:
Jan. 1		40,000
Feb. 1		5,000	45,000

Less shares in treasury:
Purchased:
June 1		(7,500)

Sold:
Aug. 1	1,000		
Oct. 1	1,500	2,500	(5,000)
Issued and outstanding			40,000

Part C

Common dividends ÷ Shares issued and outstanding = Common dividend per share
$90,000 ÷ 40,000 = $2.25

Dividends per share ÷ market value per share = Dividend yield
$2.25 ÷ $22.50 = 10.0%

Exercise 2
Part A

Transaction	Account	Debit	Credit
12/31/20A	Retained earnings	400,000	
	Common stock		400,000
	(200,000 shares x $2 par value)		

Part B

Transaction	Account	Debit	Credit
12/31/20A	Retained earnings	5,000,000	
	Common stock		5,000,000
	((200,000 shares x .25) x $100)		

Exercise 2, continued
Part C

No journal entry is required. In a stock split, the total number of authorized shares is increased by a specified amount and the par or stated value per share of all authorized shares is reduced so that the total par value of all authorized shares is unchanged. Core Corporation's authorized shares would increase to 500,000 (400,000 + (400,000 x .25)) and its par value per share would decrease to $1.60 ($2 ÷ 1.25)).

Before the stock split, the total par value of all authorized shares was $800,000 (400,000 shares x $2 par value per share). After the stock split, the total par value of all authorized shares is still $800,000 (500,000 shares x $1.60 par value per share). On the balance sheet, the amount of common stock would remain unchanged.

AN IDEA FOR YOUR STUDY TEAM

Get together with the other members of your study team. Each member should choose a well known publicly held company and then assume that s/he has owned 10,000 shares of the chosen company's common stock for at least one year. After developing a research strategy, obtain answers to the following questions and compare the results.

1. What is the par value of each of your 10,000 shares?

2. What is the market value of one share of common stock? What is the total market value of your 10,000 shares?

3. How many shares of common stock were reported as authorized, issued and outstanding in the latest financial statements issued by the company?

4. What percentage of the company does your block of shares represent? That is, how much influence would you have if you were to vote at the next annual meeting of stockholders?

5. Does your company have treasury stock? (If so, did you properly compute the amount of your influence? Ask you teammates to check your answer.)

6. Does your company have any outstanding preferred stock? Were there any dividends in arrears at the end of the company's last year-end?

7. What is the total amount of cash dividends that you would have received on your 100 shares during the past year? What were the dividend yield and dividend payout ratio during this period?

8. Was any information about future dividends provided in the company's latest Annual Report?

9. Were any stock dividends or stock splits declared? If so, how many shares of stock would you have owned one year ago?

10. Was a prior period adjustment reported in the latest financial statements issued by the company? What reason was given?

Financial Accounting

ORGANIZATION OF THE CHAPTER

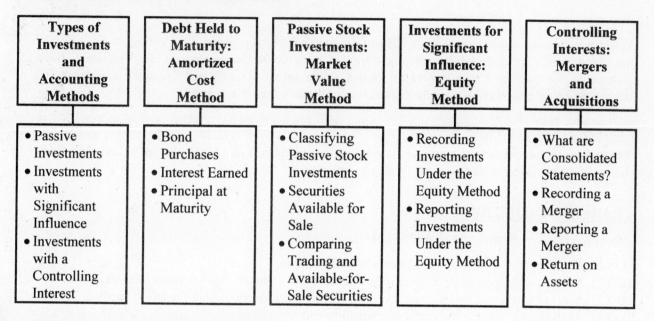

Types of Investments and Accounting Methods	Debt Held to Maturity: Amortized Cost Method	Passive Stock Investments: Market Value Method	Investments for Significant Influence: Equity Method	Controlling Interests: Mergers and Acquisitions
• Passive Investments • Investments with Significant Influence • Investments with a Controlling Interest	• Bond Purchases • Interest Earned • Principal at Maturity	• Classifying Passive Stock Investments • Securities Available for Sale • Comparing Trading and Available-for-Sale Securities	• Recording Investments Under the Equity Method • Reporting Investments Under the Equity Method	• What are Consolidated Statements? • Recording a Merger • Reporting a Merger • Return on Assets

CHAPTER FOCUS SUGGESTIONS

Overview

This chapter covers the reporting issues relating to investments. You will be expected to classify investments, and analyze and report transactions using the appropriate method (i.e., the market value, equity, or consolidated statement method).

Bond Investments Held to Maturity

When a bond in acquired with the intent of holding it until maturity, the investment is recorded at cost. It is reported at amortized cost on the balance sheet. Interest earned is reported on the income statement.

Passive Investments in Stock

An investment is presumed passive if the investing company owns less than 20% of another company's outstanding voting stock. The market value method is used to measure and report these investments. The investment is initially recorded at cost. Thereafter, the investment is reported based on the current market value of the stock. Such investments in common stock must be classified as securities available for sale or trading securities. Unrealized gains and losses on securities available for sale are reported on the balance sheet as a component of stockholders' equity; unrealized gains and losses on trading securities are reported on the income statement. The calculation of the gain or loss realized at the time of the sale then depends on whether the security sold was classified as a security available for sale or a trading security.

Investments in Stock for Significant Influence

Although other factors may indicate significant influence, it is presumed if the investing company owns from 20% to 50% of another company's outstanding voting stock. The equity method is used to measure and report these investments. The investment is initially recorded at cost. Thereafter, the investment account is increased by the investor's proportionate share of the net income reported by the investee company and decreased by its proportionate share of the dividends declared by the investee company. The proportionate share of net income is reported on the income statement.

Investments in Stock for Control

When a company acquires more than 50% of another company's outstanding voting stock, control is presumed. Rules for consolidation are then applied to combine the companies; the separate financial statements are combined each period to form a single set of consolidated financial statements. The consolidation process must include the elimination of the investment account.

Financial Statement Analysis Matters

You will need to know how to compute the return on assets ratio. You should attempt to understand what this ratio is measuring so that you will be able to interpret it.

LEARNING OBJECTIVES

After studying this chapter, you should be able to:

(LO 1) Analyze and report bond investments held to maturity.
(LO 2) Analyze and report passive investments in securities using the market value method.
(LO 3) Analyze and report investments involving significant influence using the equity method.
(LO 4) Analyze and report investments in controlling interests.
(LO 5) Analyze and interpret the return on assets ratio.

READ AND RECALL QUESTIONS

After you read each section of the chapter, answer the related Read and Recall Questions below.

TYPES OF INVESTMENTS AND ACCOUNTING METHODS

What are the four categories of investments? What are the characteristics of each?

DEBT HELD TO MATURTY: AMORTIZED COST METHOD
BOND PURCHASES

What account should be debited when a company acquires bonds and intends and is able to hold the bonds until maturity? How should incidental acquisition costs, such as transfer fees and broker commissions, be recorded?

What entry would be used to record the purchase of $100,000 of 8% bonds that mature in five years if management plans and is able to hold the bonds to maturity? How would this entry impact the accounting equation?

Account	Debit	Credit

Assets _____ = _____ Liabilities _____ + _____ Stockholders' Equity _____

INTEREST EARNED

How much interest will be received on a semiannual basis on the bonds described above? What entry would be used to record the semiannual receipt of interest on these bonds? How would this entry impact the accounting equation?

Account	Debit	Credit

Assets _____ = _____ Liabilities _____ + _____ Stockholders' Equity _____

PRINCIPAL AT MATURITY

What entry would be used to record the receipt of the principal payment when the bonds described above mature? How would this entry impact the accounting equation?

Account	Debit	Credit

Assets _____ = _____ Liabilities _____ + _____ Stockholders' Equity _____

If the bond investment must be sold before maturity, how is any difference between the market value (i.e., the proceeds from the sale) and the book value reported? On the other hand, if management simply *intends* to sell the bonds before maturity, in what manner should they be treated?

LEARNING OBJECTIVE
After studying this section of the chapter, you should be able to:
2. Analyze and report passive investments in securities using the market value method.

When is an investment considered to be passive? What reporting method should be used for passive investments? What accounting principal is violated by this method? Why does the reporting of passive investments at market value enhance the relevance of financial statements? Why are the market values of passive investments deemed to be measurable?

When the fair market value of a passive investment changes, what accounts are impacted? What does unrealized mean? What accounting principal is violated when an unrealized holding gain is recorded?

CLASSIFYING PASSIVE STOCK INVESTMENTS

What is the objective when a trading securities portfolio is managed? What is the objective when a securities available for sale portfolio is managed?

SECURITIES AVAILABLE FOR SALE
Purchase of Stock

Assume that Dow Jones purchases 10,000 shares of IFNews common stock for $60 per share; there are 100,000 shares of IFNews common stock outstanding. Assuming the investment will be classified as securities available for sale, what entry would be used to record this transaction? How would this entry impact the accounting equation?

Account	Debit	Credit

Assets	=	Liabilities	+	Stockholders' Equity

Dividends Earned

Assume that Dow Jones receives a $10,000 dividend check from IFNews. What entry would be used to record the receipt of the dividend? How would this entry impact the accounting equation? How is the dividend reported on the financial statements? Would this entry be different if Dow Jones had classified the securities as trading securities rather than as securities available for sale?

Account	Debit	Credit

_____ Assets _____ = _____ Liabilities _____ + _____ Stockholders' Equity _____

Year-End Valuation

At the end of the accounting period, how are passive investments reported on the balance sheet? What two accounts are affected when a passive investment is adjusted to market value?

If the Allowance to Value at Market – SAS account has a debit balance, is it added to or subtracted from the Investment in SAS account when the balance sheet is prepared? What if it has a credit balance?

How is the Unrealized Gains and Losses – SAS account reported in the financial statements? Is the unrealized loss/gain reported as part of net income?

Assume that the IFNews stock, which Dow Jones holds as securities available for sale, has a cost of $600,000 (10,000 shares at $60 per share) and a market value of $580,000 (10,000 shares at $58 per share) at the end of the accounting period. What adjusting entry would be used to adjust the investment to market value? How would this entry impact the accounting equation?

Account	Debit	Credit

_____ Assets _____ = _____ Liabilities _____ + _____ Stockholders' Equity _____

Assume that Dow Jones holds the IFNews stock described above through the end of the next accounting period and that the market value had increased from $580,000 (as described above) to $610,000 (10,000 shares at $61 per share). What adjusting entry would be used to adjust the investment to market value? How would this entry impact the accounting equation?

Account	Debit	Credit

_____ Assets _____ = _____ Liabilities _____ + _____ Stockholders' Equity _____

Sale of Stock

When securities available for sale are sold, what three balance sheet accounts are affected?

Assume that Dow Jones sells all 10,000 shares of IFNews stock for $62.50 per share. What are the two entries that would be used to record this transaction? How would each impact the accounting equation?

Account	Debit	Credit

_____ Assets _____ = _____ Liabilities _____ + _____ Stockholders' Equity _____

Account	Debit	Credit

_____ Assets _____ = _____ Liabilities _____ + _____ Stockholders' Equity _____

COMPARING TRADING AND AVAILABLE FOR SALE SECURITIES
Available for Sale Securities:

How is the balance in the Net Unrealized Gains and Losses – SAS account reported in the financial statements? At the time of the sale of an SAS investment, how is the gain or loss on the sale determined? What is then eliminated in the second entry that is used to record the sale transaction?

Trading Securities:

How is the balance in the Net Unrealized Gains and Losses – TS account (that is, the amount of the adjustment to record unrealized gains and losses) reported in the financial statements? What happens to this account balance at the end of the accounting period as part of the closing process?

When a TS investment is sold, what two (rather than three) balance sheet accounts are affected? How is the gain or loss on the sale determined? Is a second entry required to record the sale transaction? Why or why not?

FINANCIAL ANALYSIS
EQUITY SECURITIES AND EARNINGS MANAGEMENT

Why do most managers prefer to treat their passive investments as securities available for sale? How do diligent analysts see through this strategy?

LEARNING OBJECTIVE
After studying this section of the chapter, you should be able to:
3. Analyze and report investments involving significant influence using the equity method.

INVESTMENTS FOR SIGNIFICANT INFLUENCE: EQUITY METHOD

Why would a company want to exert influence over another company without becoming the controlling shareholder? When is significant influence presumed (in terms of ownership percentages)?

What method should be used when an investor can exert significant influence over an investee? What account name would be used for such investments? Would these investments be classified as short-term or long-term on the balance sheet?

RECORDING INVESTMENTS UNDER THE EQUITY METHOD

If significant influence is presumed and the investee reports positive results of operations for the year, what does the investor record? On the other hand, if the investee declares and pays dividends, what does the investor do?

Purchase of Stock

If Dow Jones purchases 40,000 shares (or 40% of the outstanding voting stock) of IFNews for $400,000 in cash, what method must it use to account for this investment? What entry would be used to record the purchase? How would this entry impact the accounting equation?

Account	Debit	Credit

_____ = _____ + _____
        Assets   Liabilities   Stockholders' Equity

Investee Earnings

Assume that IFNews reported net income of $500,000 for the year. As noted above, Dow Jones owns 40% of the outstanding IFNews stock; what is its equity in (or share of) the IFNews income? What entry would be used to record the equity in investee earnings? How would this entry impact the accounting equation?

Account	Debit	Credit

_____ = _____ + _____
        Assets   Liabilities   Stockholders' Equity

If the investee reports a net loss, how does the investor record its equity in (or share of) the loss? How is the Equity in Investee Earnings (or Loss) account balance reported in the financial statements?

Dividends Received

Assume that IFNews declared and paid a cash dividend of $2 per share to stockholders. As noted above, Dow Jones owns 40,000 shares of IFNews stock. What entry would be used to record the receipt of the dividend? How would this entry impact the accounting equation?

Account	Debit	Credit

Assets	=	Liabilities	+	Stockholders' Equity

Assuming that it had a zero beginning balance, what would the balance in the Investments in Associated Companies account be after Dow Jones recorded the three transactions described above (i.e., the purchase of the 40,000 shares of IFNews stock, its equity in the net income reported by IFNews and the dividend received from IFNews)?

Investment in Associated Companies

Beginning
balance
0

REPORTING INVESTMENTS UNDER THE EQUITY METHOD

How is the Investment in Associated Companies account reported in the financial statements? Does this investment account reflect either cost or market value? What does the account balance reflect? At the end of the accounting period, is the investment account adjusted to reflect changes in the market value of the securities that are held? When the securities are sold, how is the amount of the gain or loss that is realized in the sale determined? How is it reported in the financial statements?

QUESTION OF ETHICS
IMPROPER INFLUENCE

What does "arm's length" mean? When one corporation is able to exert a significant influence over another (i.e., it owns 20% to 50% of the common stock), is it reasonable to assume that transactions between the two corporations' are at arm's length? What method is designed to overcome this problem? How does this method prevent manipulation?

Can managers choose between the market value method and equity method? Why or why not? Why might managers want to avoid using the equity method?

FOCUS ON CASH FLOWS
INVESTMENTS

How should the proceeds from the sale of passive investments or investments held for significant influence be reported in the statement of cash flows (as an operating, investing or financing activity)? Assuming that the indirect method is used, should a gain from the sale of passive investments or investments held for significant influence be added back to or subtracted from net income in the operating activities section of the statement of cash flows? How should a loss from such a sale be handled?

Assume that the equity method is used to account for an investment. Assuming that the indirect method is used, should the dividends be added back to or subtracted from net income in the operating activities section of the statement of cash flows? Again, assuming that the indirect method is used, should the equity in the earnings of the investee be added back to or subtracted from net income in the operating activities section of the statement of cash flows? How would equity in investee losses be handled?

CONTROLLING INTERESTS: MERGERS AND ACQUISITIONS

What is vertical integration? What is horizontal growth? What is synergy?

WHAT ARE CONSOLIDATED FINANCIAL STATEMENTS

What is a parent company? What is a subsidiary? What are consolidated financial statements? What are intercompany items?

Why must intercompany items be eliminated when consolidated financial statements are prepared?

RECORDING A MERGER

What is a merger? What principle applies to the recording of the net assets of the target company in a merger?

What is goodwill? How is the amount of goodwill that is acquired computed? What method is required by U.S. GAAP to record mergers and acquisitions? When can goodwill be reported on the balance sheet?

REPORTING A MERGER
Post-Merger Balance Sheet

When the post-merger balance sheet is prepared, are the assets and liabilities of the subsidiary reflected at their original book values or their fair market values?

Post-Merger Income Statement

Would the post-merger income statement reflect all of the revenues and expenses of the combined company? What expense might change as a result of a merger? *(Hint: If the fair market value of the plant and equipment of the subsidiary company exceeded its book value at the time of the merge and the plant and equipment were then reported at fair market value, what expense would need to be recalculated as a result?)*

Does goodwill have a definite or indefinite life? *(You should review the coverage of goodwill, an intangible asset, in Chapter 8; the related concepts apply here.)* Is this intangible asset amortized? Why or why not?

Must goodwill be reviewed annually for possible impairment of value? Why or why not? How would an impairment loss that arose from an annual review of goodwill impact the income statement and balance sheet?

FINANCIAL ANALYSIS
ACCOUNTING FOR GOODWILL

Before 2001, what did GAAP require with regards to goodwill? Beginning in 2002, what was required? For companies with large goodwill balances, how did this change impact earnings reported in 2002 (and thereafter)? How must analysts react?

LEARNING OBJECTIVE
After studying this section of the chapter, you should be able to:
5. Analyze and interpret the return on assets ratio.

How is the return on assets (ROA) ratio computed? What does it measure? All other things equal, what is suggested by a high return on assets? How is this measure used to evaluate the performance of division managers?

Complete top row of boxes by (1) inserting the names of each of the two return on asset (ROA) factors in the top row of boxes and (2) writing out the related formulas in the bottom row of boxes.

ROA		

_____	=	_____	x	_____

PREPARING CONSOLIDATED STATEMENTS

What are consolidated statements?

RECORDING ACQUISITION OF A CONTROLLING INTEREST

When both companies retain their separate legal identities after one company acquires the other, what type of relationship exists? In such cases, do both companies' accounting systems continue to record their respective transactions or are the accounting systems combined into one?

Assume that Dow Jones acquires all of the stock of IFNews for $100 million. What entry would be used to record the acquisition? How would this entry impact the accounting equation of Dow Jones? What entry would be made on the books of IFNews?

Account	Debit	Credit

Assets	=	Liabilities	+	Stockholders' Equity

PREPARING CONSOLIDATED FINANCIAL STATEMENTS AFTER ACQUISITION
The Balance Sheet

Why does the Investment in IFNews account need to be eliminated in order to prepare a consolidated balance sheet? What does the investment account balance represent? When the investment account is eliminated, what is it replaced with? What five steps are performed in the consolidation process?

The Income Statement

What three steps must be performed (ignoring taxes) to prepare the consolidated income statement?

CHAPTER TAKE-AWAYS

1. *Analyze and report bond investments held to maturity.*

   - To exert significant influence over the investee firm's operating and financing policies (presumed if owning between 20 and 50 percent of the outstanding voting shares of the investee).

   - To control the operating and financing policies of another company (presumed if owning more than 50 percent of the outstanding voting shares of the investee).

   When management intends to hold a bond investment until it matures, the held-to-maturity bond is recorded at cost when acquired and reported at amortized cost on the balance sheet. Any interest earned during the period is reported on the income statement.

2. *Analyze and report passive investments in stock using the market value method.*

   Acquiring less than 20 percent of the outstanding voting shares of an investee's common stock is presumed to be a passive stock investment. Passive investments may be classified as trading securities (actively traded to maximize return) or securities available for sale (earn a return but are not as actively traded), depending on management's intent. The investments are recorded at cost and adjusted to market value at year-end. A valuation allowance is increased or decreased to arrive at market value with the resulting unrealized holding gain or loss recorded. For trading securities, the net unrealized gains and losses are reported in net income; for securities available for sale, the net unrealized gains and losses are reported as a component of stockholders' equity in other comprehensive income. Any dividends earned are reported as revenue and any gains or losses on sales of passive investments are reported on the income statement.

3. *Analyze and report investments involving significant influence using the equity method.*

   If between 20 and 50 percent of the outstanding voting shares are owned, significant influence over the investee firm's operating and financing policies is presumed, and the equity method is applied. Under the equity method, the investor records the investment at cost on the acquisition date. Each period thereafter, the investment amount is increased (or decreased) by the proportionate interest in the income (or loss) reported by the investee corporation and decreased by the proportionate share of the dividends declared by the investee corporation. Each period the investor recognizes as revenue its proportionate share of the income (or loss) reported by the investee company.

   The investing section of the statement of cash flows discloses purchases and sales of investments. In the operating section, net income is adjusted for any gains or losses on sales of investments and equity in the earnings of associated companies (net of dividends received).

4. *Analyze and report investments in controlling interests.*

   Mergers occur when one company purchases all of the net assets of another and the target company ceases to exist as a separate legal entity. Mergers and ownership of a controlling interest of another corporation (more than 50 percent of the outstanding voting shares) must be accounted for using the purchase method. The acquisition is accounted for in conformity with the cost principle, with the investee's assets and liabilities measured at their market values. Any amount paid above the market value of the net assets is reported as goodwill by the investor. The concept of consolidation is based on the view that a parent company and its subsidiaries constitute one economic entity. Therefore, the separate income statements, balance sheets, and statements of cash flows should be combined each period on an item-by-item basis as a single set of consolidated financial statements. Consolidated statements are the same as those that result from a merger when all of the assets and liabilities are acquired and the target company ceases to exist.

5. *Analyze and interpret the return on assets ratio.*

The return on assets ratio measures how much the company earned for each dollar of assets. It provides information on profitability and management's effectiveness, with an increasing ratio over time suggesting increased efficiency. ROA is computed as net income divided by average total assets.

KEY RATIO

Return on assets (ROA) measures how much the company earned on every dollar of assets during the period. A high or rising ratio suggests that the company is managing its assets and efficiently. It is computed as follows:

Return on Assets = Net Income ÷ Average Total Assets

Average Total Assets is determined as follows:

(Total Assets, beginning of the year + Total Assets, end of year) ÷ 2

FINDING FINANCIAL INFORMATION

Balance Sheet
Current Assets
Investment in trading securities (net of valuation allowance)
Investment in securities available for sale (net of valuation allowance)
Noncurrent Assets
Investment in securities available for sale (net of valuation allowance)
Investment in associated companies
Stockholders' Equity
Accumulated Other Comprehensive Income
Net unrealized loss/gain on securities-available-for-sale

Income Statement
Under "Other Items"
Investment income
Loss or gain on sale of investments
Net unrealized gains and losses on trading securities
Equity in investee earnings or losses

Statement of Cash Flows
Operating Activities
Net income adjusted for:
Gains/losses on sale of investments
Equity in earnings/losses of associated companies
Dividends received from associated companies
Net unrealized gains/losses on trading securities

Notes
In Various Notes
Accounting policies for investments
Details on securities held as trading and available for sale securities and investments in associated companies

SELF-TEST QUESTIONS AND EXERCISES

MATCHING

Match each of the key terms listed below with the appropriate textbook definition:

____ Consolidated Financial Statements   ____ Merger
____ Equity Method   ____ Parent Company
____ Goodwill (Cost in Excess of Net Assets   ____ Purchase Method
        Acquired)   ____ Securities Available for Sale
____ Held-to-Maturity Investments   ____ Subsidiary Company
____ Investments in Associated (Affiliated)   ____ Trading Securities
        Companies   ____ Unrealized Holding Gains and Losses
____ Market Value Method

A. The company that gains a controlling influence over another company (the subsidiary).
B. All investments in stocks or bonds that are held primarily for the purpose of active trading (buying and selling) in the near future (classified as short-term assets).
C. The difference between the purchase price of a company and the fair market value of the net assets (assets minus liabilities) that were acquired.
D. The entity that is acquired by the parent company.
E. Used when an investor can exert significant influence over an investee. It permits recording of investor's share of investee's income.
F. Reports securities at their current market value.
G. An acquisition that is completed by purchasing the subsidiary company's voting common stock for cash.
H. Amounts associated with price changes of securities that are currently held.
I. All passive investments other than trading securities (classified as either short-term or long-term).
J. The financial statements of two or more companies that have been combined into a single set of financial statements as if the companies were one.
K. A long-term investment in bonds that management has the ability and intent to hold until maturity.
L. Occurs when one company purchases all of the net assets of another and the target company goes out of existence.
M. A long-term investment in which the investor owns between 20 and 50 percent of the investee's outstanding voting stock.

TRUE-FALSE QUESTIONS

For each of the following, enter a T or F in the blank to indicate whether the statement is true or false.

____1. (LO 1) Passive investments are made to earn a high rate of return on funds that may be needed for short-term or long-term purposes in the future.

____2. (LO 1) Significant influence occurs when the investing company has the ability to determine the operating and financial policies of another company in which it own shares of voting stock.

____3. (LO 1) Investments made with the intent to exert control over another corporation can achieve diversification so that a company does not depend on the economic fortunes of a single area of business.

___4. (LO 2) The reporting of passive investments on the balance sheet is an exception to the cost principle.

___5. (LO 2) The SAS portfolio is managed with the objective of generating profits on short-term differences in the price of the securities.

___6. (LO 2) Net unrealized gains/losses on the SAS portfolio are reported as Other Comprehensive Income in the stockholders' equity section of the balance sheet.

___7. (LO 2) Realized gains and losses on the SAS are reported as Investment Income on the income statement.

___8. (LO 3) Under the equity method, if the investee reports positive net income for the year, the investor decreases its Investment in Associated Companies account.

___9. (LO 3) Under the equity method, if the investee declares and pays dividends during the year, the investor records Investment Income when it receives its share of the dividends.

___10. (LO 4) In simple terms, a consolidation is an adding together of the separate financial statements of the parent company and the subsidiary to make it appear as if a single company exists.

___11. (LO 4) In a combination by purchase, the stock of the subsidiary is acquired from its current owners with cash by the parent, or acquiring company.

___12. (LO 5) The return on assets (ROA) ratio allows analysts to company management's investment performance against alternative investment options with differing levels of risk.

MULTIPLE CHOICE QUESTIONS

Choose the best answer or response by placing the identifying letter in the space provided.

___1. (LO 1) The difference between significant influence and control in a long-term investment is mainly

    a. one of intent.

    b. whether the investor company owns between 20% and 50% of the investee company's stock or more than 50%.

    c. a matter of how much control of the board of directors is achieved.

    d. a matter of how many management personnel it is possible to insert into the investee company.

    e. a question of the type of securities held.

___2. (LO 2) A company ordinarily makes short-term investments in order to

    a. minimize investment risk.

    b. earn a higher return on funds that are often to be used for operating purposes in the near future.

    c. accumulate funds for future investments in assets.

    d. have at least a small say in the management of another company.

    e. all of the above.

___3. (LO 2) When there is neither significant influence nor control, the proper way to measure and report an investment in the voting stock of a company and the income from that investment is

    a. the market value method.

    b. the equity method.

    c. the consolidation method.

    d. either (b) or (c).

    e. either (a) or (b) or (c). ·

___4. (LO 2) *(Hint: The answer to this question appears in a footnote.)* All investments in nonvoting stock are accounted for under

   a. the cost method.
   b. the equity method.
   c. the market value method.
   d. the investment method.
   e. the consolidation method.

___5. (LO 2) Trading securities are held primarily for

   a. influence in the management of another entity.
   b. their desirability to other companies, giving them a guaranteed high resale value.
   c. accumulating funds for the purchase of long-lived assets.
   d. sale in the near future.
   e. earning a return on funds that may be required for operating purposes in the future.

___6. (LO 2) When a trading security increases in value during the accounting period,

   a. an entry is required to record investment income on the income statement.
   b. an entry is required to record investment income on the balance sheet.
   c. an entry is required to record an unrealized gain/loss – TS as a separate component of stockholders' equity on the balance sheet.
   d. an entry is required to record an unrealized gain/loss – TS as a component of net income on the income statement.
   e. An entry is not required at the end of the accounting period

___7. (LO 2) Securities available for sale differ from trading securities in that any net unrealized gains or losses are recognized

   a. as a separate component of stockholders' equity, rather than on the income statement.
   b. on the income statement, rather than as a separate component of stockholders' equity on the balance sheet.
   c. only when the security is sold.
   d. differently; losses are recorded, but gains are not.
   e. as other income rather than as regular revenue items.

___8. (LO 3) The equity method presumes an investment was made

   a. to put temporarily excess cash to work in a high-return investment.
   b. as a sinking fund for bond retirement.
   c. for a long-term strategic purpose.
   d. for the purchase of a major asset.
   e. as a first step in purchasing another company.

Use the following information to answer the next three questions:

On January 2, 20A, Northeast Outdoor, Inc., a retailer, acquired 10,000 of the 40,000 outstanding voting common stock (par value $1 per share) of St. Charles Camping Equipment Company, a manufacturer, on the open market for $220,000. On December 31, 20A, the market value of the 10,000 shares of St. Charles common stock was $265,000. St. Charles Camping Equipment declared and paid a dividend of 10¢ per share on December 31, 20A. St. Charles reported a net income of $1,200,000 for the year ending December 31, 20A.

___9. (LO 3) At the end of 20A, as a result of the increase in the market value of its investment in St. Charles common stock, Northeast would

    a. record a net unrealized gain, which would be reported on the income statement.
    b. record a net unrealized gain, which would be reported as a separate item in stockholders' equity.
    c. record a net unrealized gain as an addition to retained earnings on the balance sheet.
    d. make no entry at all.
    e. Record a net unrealized gain, which would be reported as a contra-equity account on the balance sheet.

___10. (LO 3) Northeast would record the dividend it receives from St. Charles Camping Equipment as

    a. a decrease in the related investment account.
    b. an increase in the related investment account.
    c. dividend revenue.
    d. an increase in retained earnings.
    e. an increase in the Net Unrealized Gains/Losses account.

___11. (LO 4) Northeast hopes at some point to purchase a controlling interest in St. Charles Camping Equipment. If they achieve this goal, it would be an example of

    a. vertical integration.
    b. diversification.
    c. horizontal growth.
    d. synergy.
    e. all of the above.

___12. (LO 4) Large Company paid $150,000 cash for 100% of the outstanding stock of Small Company. Small Company's machinery had a book value of $40,000, but an appraisal revealed that the equipment had a fair market value of $50,000. Small Company also had a small but very strong, loyal customer base. For these reasons, Large was willing to pay $150,000 for the net book value of Small's stockholders' equity of $128,000. The amount of goodwill reported on Large's consolidated balance sheet would be

    a. $10,000.
    b. $12,000.
    c. $22,000.
    d. $128,000.
    e. Nothing; goodwill is not recorded in a combination by purchase.

___13. (LO 4) Goodwill is considered a(n)

    a. asset with a definite life.
    b. asset with an indefinite life.
    c. separate component of stockholders' equity with a definite life.
    d. separate component of stockholders' equity with an in definite life.
    e. liability until disposed of.

___14. (LO 5) Many financial analysts use the return on asset ratio to evaluate

    a. the overall dividend rate of a company's investments.
    b. the effectiveness of the management of a company.
    c. how quickly assets are turned into cash.
    d. how efficiently long-lived assets are being used.
    e. how carefully a company controls expenses.

EXERCISES

Record your answers to each part of these exercises in the space provided. Show your work.

Exercise 1 (LO 1)

On January 1, 20A, the Aurora Star purchased a 7% bond with a maturity value of $400,000 at par. The bond will mature in five years (on December, 31, 20E). Management intends to hold the bond until maturity. Interest is paid semiannually on June 30 and December 31.

Prepare the journal entries to record the purchase of the bond on January 1, 20A, and the receipt of interest on June 30, 20A.

Transaction	Account	Debit	Credit
1/1/20A			
6/30/20A			

Exercise 2 (LO 2 and 3)

Parker, Inc. periodically makes passive investments for the purpose of earning a return on funds that may be required for operating purposes in the near future; Parker does not intend to actively trade these investments. Parker makes other investments because it wants to exert influence without becoming a majority owner. During 20A, Parker acquired interests in two companies by purchasing 10,000 shares of the voting common stock of Broderick, Inc. and 100,000 shares of the voting common stock of Chadwick, Inc. Broderick has 100,000 shares of common stock outstanding, par value $2 per share. Chadwick has 250,000 shares of common stock outstanding, par value $10 per share. All three companies have calendar year-ends.

Part A

How should the investments in Broderick and Chadwick be classified? Why? What accounting method(s) should Parker use for its investments? Why?

Investment in Broderick Common Stock:

Investment in Chadwick Common Stock:

Part B

Prepare journal entries for each of the following transactions. If you do <u>not</u> prepare a journal entry for a given transaction, provide an explanation.

January 1

Purchased 10,000 shares of Broderick common stock at $35 per share.

Transaction	Account	Debit	Credit
1/1/20A			

Exercise 2, Part B, continued

January 2

Purchased 100,000 shares of Chadwick common stock at $50 per share.

Transaction	Account	Debit	Credit
1/2/20A			

December 29

Broderick declared and paid a cash dividend of $1.00 per share.

Transaction	Account	Debit	Credit
12/29/20A			

December 30

Chadwick declared and paid a cash dividend of $2.00 per share.

Transaction	Account	Debit	Credit
12/30/20A			

December 31

Received the 20A annual financial statements of Broderick, Inc. that reported net income of $100,000.

Transaction	Account	Debit	Credit
12/31/20A			

December 31

Received the 20A annual financial statements of Chadwick, Inc. that reported net income of $1,000,000.

Transaction	Account	Debit	Credit
12/31/20A			

Exercise 2, Part B, continued

December 31

Market price of Broderick stock was $40 per share.

Transaction	Account	Debit	Credit
12/31/20A			

December 31

Market price of Chadwick stock was $75 per share.

Transaction	Account	Debit	Credit
12/31/20A			

Part C

How would the various transactions relating to the investment in the voting common stock of Broderick be reported in Parker's balance sheet and income statement? (Specify how the various amounts that would be reported on each financial statement.)

Balance Sheet:

Income Statement:

Part D

How would the various transactions relating to the investment in the voting common stock of Chadwick be reported in Parker's balance sheet and income statement? (Specify how the various amounts that would be reported on each financial statement.)

Exercise 2, Part D, continued

Balance Sheet:

Income Statement:

Exercise 3 (LO 2)

On January 1, 20A, Davido Company purchased 5,000 shares of Venus Inc. voting common stock for $30 per share. The price of Venus common stock was $29 per share on December 31, 20A. Davido sold all of its shares of Venus stock on January 31, 20B at $32 per share.

Part A

Assume that Davido purchased the voting common stock of Venus for inclusion in its securities available for sale (SAS) portfolio. Prepare the journal entries that are required by the information presented above.

Transaction	Account	Debit	Credit
1/1/20A			
12/31/20A			
1/31/20B			
1/31/20B			

Exercise 3, continued
Part B

Again, assuming that Davido purchased the voting common stock of Venus for inclusion in its SAS portfolio, how would the investment in the Venus' common stock be reported in the 20A and 20B financial statements?

Effect on 20A Financial Statements:

Effect on 20B Financial Statements:

Part C

Assume that Davido purchased the voting common stock of Venus for inclusion in its trading securities (TS) portfolio. Prepare the journal entries that are required by the information presented above.

Transaction	Account	Debit	Credit
1/1/20A			
12/31/20A			
1/31/20B			

Exercise 3, continued
Part D

Again, assuming that Davido purchased the voting common stock of Venus for inclusion in its trading securities, how would the investment in the Venus' common stock be reported in the 20A and 20B financial statements?

Effect on 20A Financial Statements:

Effect on 20B Financial Statements:

Part E

During the time that a passive investment security is held, how does the reporting of net unrealized gains/losses on securities in the SAS portfolio differ from that of securities in the TS portfolio?

Exercise 3, continued
Part F

When a passive investment security is sold, how does the reporting of realized gains/losses on securities in the SAS portfolio differ from that of securities in the TS portfolio?

Part G

Summarize the total income that would be reported on the income statement during the years ended December 31, 20A and 20B assuming that the Venus common stock is classified as SAS (Securities Available for Sale) or TS (Trading Securities). *(Hint: Look at Part B of Exhibit 12.3 for an example of how to format a comparison of income statement reporting for TS and SAS.)*

Exercise 4 (LO 4 and Supplement A)

On January 1, 20B, DPK Enterprises acquired all 250,000 shares of the outstanding stock of JMF Companies for $5 cash per share. An appraisal revealed that the market values of JMF's assets were the same as their book values at the date of acquisition. On that date (prior to the acquisition), the separate balance sheets (summarized) of the companies reported the following book values.

	DPK Enterprises	JMF Companies
Assets		
Cash and other current assets	$1,525,000	$200,000
Property, plant and equipment, net	50,000	150,000
Total assets	$1,575,000	$350,000
Liabilities and Stockholders' Equity		
Current liabilities	$ 100,000	$ 40,000
Stockholders' equity	1,475,000	310,000
Total liabilities and stockholders' equity	$1,575,000	$350,000

Exercise 4, continued
Part A

Prepare the journal entry that would be recorded by DPK at the date of acquisition.

Transaction	Account	Debit	Credit
1/1/20B			

Part B

Determine the amount of goodwill that should be recognized in this transaction.

Part C

Complete the following worksheet to obtain the numbers for the consolidated balance sheet immediately after the acquisition. (The entry to record DPK's investment in JMF is already reflected.)

	DPK Enterprises	JMF Companies	Eliminations	Consolidated
Assets				
Cash and other current assets	$ 275,000	$200,000		
Investment in JMF	1,250,000			
Property, plant and equipment, net	50,000	150,000		
Goodwill				
Total assets	$1,575,000	$350,000		
Liabilities and Stockholders' Equity				
Current liabilities	$ 100,000	$ 40,000		
Stockholders' equity	1,475,000	310,000		
Total liabilities and stockholders' equity	$1,575,000	$350,000		

SOLUTIONS TO SELF-TEST QUESTIONS AND EXERCISES

MATCHING

J	Consolidated Financial Statements	L	Merger
E	Equity Method	A	Parent Company
C	Goodwill (Cost in Excess of Net Assets Acquired)	G	Purchase Method
		I	Securities Available for Sale
K	Held-to-Maturity Investments	D	Subsidiary Company
M	Investments in Associated (Affiliated) Companies	B	Trading Securities
		H	Unrealized Holding Gains and Losses
F	Market Value Method		

TRUE-FALSE QUESTIONS

1. T
2. F – Controlling another company when the investing company has the ability to determine the operating and financial policies of another company in which it own shares of voting stock
3. T
4. T
5. F – The trading securities portfolio is managed with the objective of generating profits on short-term differences in the price of the securities.
6. T
7. F – Realized gains and losses on the securities-held-for-sale portfolio are reported as Gains or Losses on Sale of Investments on the income statement.
8. F – Under the equity method, if the investee reports positive net income for the year, the investor increases its Investment in Associated Companies account.
9. F – Under the equity method, if the investee declares and pays dividends during the year, the investor reduces its Investment in Associated Companies account when it receives its share of the dividends.
10. T
11. T
12. T

MULTIPLE CHOICE QUESTIONS

1.	b	4.	c	7.	a	10.	a	13.	b
2.	b	5.	d	8.	c	11.	a	14.	b
3.	a	6.	d	9.	d	12.	b		

EXERCISES

Exercise 1

Transaction	Account	Debit	Credit
1/1/20A	Held-to-maturity investment	400,000	
	Cash		400,000
6/30/20A	Cash ($400,000 x .07 x 6/12)	14,000	
	Interest revenue		14,000

Exercise 2
Part A

Parker's investment in Broderick would be considered a passive investment because it owns 10% (10,000 ÷ 100,000) of Broderick's outstanding stock. It was noted that Parker periodically makes passive investments for the purpose of earning a return on funds that may be required for operating purposes in the near future. As such, the passive investment in Broderick would be classified as securities available for sale (SAS). Parker should account for its investment in Broderick using the market value method.

Parker's investment in Chadwick would be considered an investment made with the intent of exerting significant influence over another corporation because it owns 40% (100,000 ÷ 250,000) of Chadwick's outstanding stock. Parker should account for its investment in Chadwick using the equity method.

Part B

Transaction	Account	Debit	Credit

Purchase of Securities – Market Value Method:

Transaction	Account	Debit	Credit
1/1/20A	Investment in SAS	350,000	
	Cash (10,000 x $35)		350,000
	Purchased 10,000 shares of Broderick common stock @ $35/share.		

Purchase of Securities – Equity Method:

Transaction	Account	Debit	Credit
1/2/20A	Investments in associated companies	5,000,000	
	Cash (100,000 x $50)		5,000,000
	Purchased 100,000 shares of Chadwick common stock @ $50 per share.		

Receipt of Dividends – Market Value Method:

Transaction	Account	Debit	Credit
12/29/20A	Cash (10,000 x $1)	10,000	
	Investment income		10,000
	Received cash dividend from Broderick.		

Receipt of Dividends – Equity Method:

Transaction	Account	Debit	Credit
12/30/20A	Cash (100,000 x $2)	200,000	
	Investments in associated companies		200,000
	Received cash dividend from Chadwick.		

Exercise 2, Part B, continued

Transaction	Account	Debit	Credit

Earnings of Investee – Market Value Method:

Transaction	Account	Debit	Credit
12/31/20A	No entry; under the market value method equity in investee's net income is not recorded.		
	Received the 20A annual financial statements from Broderick; net income of $100,000 reported.		

Earnings of Investee – Equity Method:

Transaction	Account	Debit	Credit
12/31/20A	Investments in associated companies	400,000	
	Equity in investee earnings ($1,000,000 x .4)		400,000
	Received the 20A annual financial statements from Chadwick; net income of $1,000,000 reported.		

Year-End Valuation – Market Value Method:

Transaction	Account	Debit	Credit
12/31/20A	Allowance to value at market – SAS	50,000	
	Net unrealized gains/losses – SAS (10,000 x ($40 - $35))		50,000
	Determined market price of Broderick common stock was $40 per share.		

Year-End Valuation – Equity Value Method:

Transaction	Account	Debit	Credit
12/31/20A	No entry; under equity method, unrealized gains and losses are not recorded.		
	Determined market price of Chadwick common stock was $75 per share.		

Part C

Investment in Broderick:

Recall that the investment in Broderick's voting common stock is a passive investment classified as securities available for sale (SAS). As such, the market value method is used for reporting purposes. This investment would be reported as an Investment in SAS under current assets on the balance sheet. The unrealized gain of $50,000 (which is the Allowance to Value at Market – SAS account balance) would be added to the cost of $350,000 (which is the Investment in SAS account balance) to arrive at the carrying value of $400,000 (which equals the market value of the investment at year-end). In addition, the Net Unrealized Gains/Losses – SAS account balance of $50,000 (a gain) would be reported as a separate component of stockholders' equity (under Other Comprehensive Income) on the balance sheet.

The $10,000 of investment income would be reported as investment income on the income statement.

Exercise 2, continued
Part D

Investment in Chadwick:

Recall that the investment in Chadwick's voting common stock is a significant influence investment. As such, the equity method is used for reporting purposes. The long-term Investments in Associated Companies account balance would be reported on the balance sheet. The amount would be determined as follows:

Investment in Associated Companies				
(A)	5,000,000			(A) Purchase of investment (see 1/1/20A entry above).
(C)	400,000	200,000	(B)	(B) Receipt of dividends (see 12/30/20A entry above).
balance 5,200,000				(C) Equity in net income (see 12/31/20A entry above).

The Equity in Investee Earnings account balance of $400,000 would be reported under in the Other Items section of the income statement.

Exercise 3
Part A *(Assuming Venus common stock is classified as SAS.)*

Transaction	Account	Debit	Credit
1/1/20A	Investment in SAS	150,000	
	Cash (5,000 x $30)		150,000
	Purchased 5,000 shares of Venus' common stock @ $30 per share.		
12/31/20A	Net unrealized gains/losses – SAS (5,000 x ($30 - $29))	5,000	
	Allowance to value at market – SAS		5,000
	Determined market price of Venus' common stock was $29 per share.		
1/31/20B	Cash (5,000 x $32)	160,000	
	Investment in SAS (5,000 x $30)		150,000
	Gain on Sale of Investment (5,000 x ($32 - $30))		10,000
1/31/20B	Allowance to value at market - SAS	5,000	
	Net unrealized gains/losses – SAS (5,000 x ($30 - $29))		5,000
	Sold 5,000 shares of Venus' common stock @ $32 per share.		

Financial Accounting

Exercise 3, continued

Part B *(Assuming Venus common stock is classified as SAS.)*

Effect on 20A Financial Statements:

This investment would be reported as an Investment in SAS under current assets on the balance sheet at December 31, 20A. The unrealized loss of $5,000 (which is the Allowance to Value at Market account balance) would be subtracted from the cost of $150,000 (which is the Investment in SAS account balance) to arrive at the carrying value of $145,000 (which equals the market value of the investment at year-end). The Net Unrealized Gains/Losses – SAS account balance of $5,000 (a loss) would be reported as a separate component of stockholders' equity (accumulated other comprehensive income) on the balance sheet at December 31, 20A.

No transactions relating to this investment would be reported on the income statement for the year ended December 31, 20A.

Effect on 20B Financial Statements:

Because it was sold prior to year-end, this investment would not be reported on the balance sheet at December 31, 20B.

The gain on sale of investments of $10,000 would be reported on the income statement for the year ended December 31, 20B.

Part C *(Assuming Venus common stock is classified as TS.)*

Transaction	Account	Debit	Credit
1/1/20A	Investment in TS	150,000	
	Cash (5,000 x $30)		150,000
	Purchased 5,000 shares of Venus' common stock @ $30 per share.		
12/31/20A	Net Unrealized Gains/Losses – TS (5,000 x ($30 - $29))	5,000	
	Allowance to Value at Market – TS		5,000
	Determined market price of Venus' common stock was $29 per share.		
1/31/20B	Cash (5,000 x $32)	160,000	
	Allowance to Value at Market – TS (5,000 x ($30 - $29))	5,000	
	Investment in TS (5,000 x $30)		150,000
	Gain on Sale of Investment (5,000 x ($32 - $29))		15,000
	Sold 5,000 shares of Venus' common stock @ $32 per share.		

Exercise 3, continued
Part D *(Assuming Venus common stock is classified as TS.)*

Effect on 20A Financial Statements:

This investment would be reported as an Investment in TS under current assets on the balance sheet at December 31, 20A. The unrealized loss of $5,000 (which is the Allowance to Value at Market – TS account balance) would be subtracted from the cost of $150,000 (which is the Investment in TS account balance) to arrive at the carrying value of $145,000 (which equals the market value of the investment at year-end).

The Net Unrealized Gains/Losses – TS account balance of $5,000 would be reported on the income statement (that is, the loss would decrease net income) for the year ended December 31, 20A.

Effect on 20B Financial Statements:

Because it was sold prior to year-end, this investment would not be reported on the balance sheet at December 31, 20B.

The gain on sale of investments of $15,000 would be reported on the income statement for the year ended December 31, 20B.

Part E

While the investment securities are held:
Securities Available for Sale:
- The Net Unrealized Gains/Losses – SAS would be reported under as a separate component of stockholders' equity (Accumulated Other Comprehensive Income) on the balance sheet.

Trading Securities:
- The Net Unrealized Gains/Losses – TS would be reported under Nonoperating items on the income statement.

Part F

During the year that the investment securities are sold:
Securities Available for Sale:
- The securities were sold during the year and the related Allowance to Value at Market - SAS was eliminated when the sale was recorded.
- The gain or loss on sale of investments would be determined by comparing the sales proceeds with the original cost of the securities. That gain or loss would be reported on the income statement.

Trading Securities:
- The securities are no longer held; however, the related Net Unrealized Gains/Losses – TS was *not* eliminated when the sale was recorded (since that account balance would have been closed to Retained Earnings at the end of the preceding accounting period).
- The gain or loss on sale of investments would be determined by comparing the sales proceeds with the market value of the securities at the beginning of the accounting period. That gain or loss on sale of investments would be reported on the income statement.

Exercise 3, continued
Part G

Impact on income statement:

	Classified as SAS		Classified as TS	
	20A	**20B**	**20A**	**20B**
Investment income	None reported (1)	None reported (1)	None reported (1)	None reported (1)
Net unrealized gains/losses	Not applicable (2)	Not applicable (2)	($5,000)	–
Gain on sale	–	$10,000	–	$15,000

$10,000 (over both years) $10,000 (over both years)

(1) No dividends were declared by Venus in this exercise.
(2) The Net Unrealized Gains/Losses – SAS account balance is reported as a separate component of stockholders' equity on the balance sheet.

Exercise 4
Part A

Transaction	Account	Debit	Credit
1/1/20B	Investment in JMF Companies	1,250,000	
	Cash (250,000 x $5)		1,250,000

Part B

Purchase price		$1,250,000
Net assets acquired, at market value:		
Market value of assets acquired	$350,000	
Less book value of liabilities assumed	40,000	310,000
Goodwill		$ 940,000

Part C

	DPK Enterprises	JMF Companies	Eliminations	Consolidated
Assets				
Cash and other current assets	$ 275,000	$200,000		$ 475,000
Investment in JMF	1,250,000		$(1,250,000)	
Property, plant and equipment, net	50,000	150,000		200,000
Goodwill			940,000	940,000
Total assets	$1,575,000	$350,000	$ (310,000)	$1,615,000
Liabilities and Stockholders' Equity				
Current liabilities	$ 100,000	$ 40,000		$ 140,000
Stockholders' equity	1,475,000	310,000	$ (310,000)	1,475,000
Total liabilities and stockholders' equity	$1,575,000	$350,000	$ (310,000)	$1,615,000

AN IDEA FOR YOUR STUDY TEAM

Euro Disney operates the Disneyland Paris theme park and resort near Paris, France. Obtain a recent annual report for The Walt Disney Company and answer the following questions:

1. Does The Walt Disney Company "own" Euro Disney? Is Euro Disney a subsidiary? Explain your answer. What is the corporate relationship?

2. What method of accounting does The Walt Disney Company use to account for its investment in Euro Disney? How can you tell?

3. What effect, if any, do the operating results of Euro Disney have on the financial statements of The Walt Disney Company?

ORGANIZATION OF THE CHAPTER

Classification of the Statement of Cash Flows	Reporting and Interpreting Cash Flows from Operating Activities	Reporting and Interpreting Cash Flows from Investing Activities	Reporting and Interpreting Cash Flows from Financing Activities	Additional Cash Flow Disclosures
• Cash Flows from Operating Activities • Cash Flows from Investing Activities • Cash Flows from Financing Activities • Net Increase (Decrease) in Cash • Relationships to the Balance Sheet and Income Statement	• **Part A**: Reporting Cash Flows from Operating Activities– Indirect Method **OR** • **Part B**: Reporting Cash Flows from Operating Activities– Direct Method • Interpreting Cash Flows from Operating Activities • Quality of Income Ratio	• Reporting Cash Flows from Investing Activities • Interpreting Cash Flows from Investing Activities • Capital Acquisitions Ratio	• Reporting Cash Flows from Financing Activities • Interpreting Cash Flows from Financing Activities	• Noncash Investing and Financing Activities • Supplemental Cash Flow Information

CHAPTER FOCUS SUGGESTIONS

Overview

This chapter covers the preparation and interpretation of the statement of cash flows. This required financial statement provides cash flow information in a manner that maximizes its usefulness to decision-makers.

Classifying Cash Flows

The statement of cash flows has three main sections: cash flows from operating activities which are related to earning income from normal operations; cash flows from investing activities which are related to the acquisition and sale of productive assets; and cash flows from financing activities which are related to financing the enterprise.

Preparing the Statement

To develop the information to be reported in each section it is necessary to analyze the changes in selected accounts. The purpose of this analysis is to determine the cash flow effects of the transactions reflected in those accounts. You will need to be able to identify the accounts that must be analyzed to prepare each of the three sections of the statement.

Determining Cash Flows from Operating Activities

The cash flows from operating activities section of the statement can be prepared using either the direct or indirect method. The amount of cash flows from operating activities reported is the same whether the direct or indirect method is used. Although the FASB prefers the direct method, most companies use the indirect method.

The direct method reports the components of the cash flows from operating activities as gross receipts (such as cash received from customers) and gross payments (such as cash paid for salaries and wages).

The indirect method starts with net income and adjusts it to cash flows from operating activities. The adjustments are necessary because net income is an accrual basis amount. Revenues are recorded when earned, and expenses when incurred without regard to when the related cash flows occur. For the most part, the adjustments convert net income to a cash basis amount.

Financial Statements Analysis Matters

You will need to know how to compute the quality of income and capital acquisitions ratios. You should attempt to understand what these ratios are measuring so that you will be able to interpret them.

LEARNING OBJECTIVES

After studying this chapter, you should be able to:

(LO 1)   Classify cash flow statement items as part of net cash flows from operating, investing, and financing activities.
(LO 2A) Report and interpret cash flows from operating activities using the indirect method.
(LO 2B) Report and interpret cash flows from operating activities using the direct method.
(LO 3)   Analyze and interpret the quality of income ratio.
(LO 4)   Report and interpret cash flows from investing activities.
(LO 5)   Analyze and interpret the capital acquisitions ratio.
(LO 6)   Report and interpret cash flows from financing activities.
(LO 7)   Explain the impact of additional cash flow disclosures.

READ AND RECALL QUESTIONS

After you read each section of the chapter, answer the related Read and Recall Questions below.

BUSINESS BACKGROUND

Why is cash flow critical to a company's success? In what three ways does the statement of cash flows focus management's attention?

> **LEARNING OBJECTIVE**
> *After studying this section of the chapter, you should be able to:*
> 1. Classify cash flow statement items as part of net cash flows from operating, investing, and financing activities.

CLASSIFICATIONS ON THE STATEMENT OF CASH FLOWS

What is the basic purpose of the statement of cash flows? What are cash equivalents? What two criteria must be met for an investment to be considered a cash equivalent? Does the original maturity date impact whether the criteria are met? What three types of investments are examples of cash equivalents?

CASH FLOWS FROM OPERATING ACTIVITIES

What are cash flows from operating activities? What two typical types of cash inflows and four typical types of cash outflows are classified as cash flows from operating activities? What are the two alternative approaches for presenting the operating activities section of the statement of cash flows?

What is the direct method? Why have many financial executives reported that they do not use this method?

What is the indirect method? Why do net income and cash flows from operating activities usually differ in amount?

CASH FLOWS FROM INVESTING ACTIVITIES

What are cash flows from investing activities? What two typical types of cash inflows and two typical types of cash outflows are classified as cash flows from investing activities?

CASH FLOWS FROM FINANCING ACTIVITIES

What are cash flows from financing activities? What two typical types of cash inflows and three typical types of cash outflows are classified as cash flows from financing activities?

NET INCREASE (DECREASE) IN CASH

What do you get when you combine the net cash flows from operating activities, investing activities and financing activities? How does this amount relate to the other financial statements?

RELATIONSHIPS TO THE BALANCE SHEET AND INCOME STATEMENT

Why can't companies prepare the statement of cash flows by using amounts recorded in T-accounts? What data is required to prepare the statement of cash flows?

What is the simple algebraic manipulation of the balance sheet equation that can be used to explain the change in cash?

> **LEARNING OBJECTIVE**
> *After studying this section of the chapter, you should be able to:*
> 2A. Report and interpret cash flows from operating activities using the indirect method.

Does the method used to prepare the cash flows from operating activities section of the statement of cash flows (i.e., indirect or direct method) impact the amount of cash flows that are generated by operating activities? Why or why not?

PART A: REPORTING AND INTERPRETING CASH FLOWS FROM OPERATING ACTIVITIES – INDIRECT METHOD

When the indirect method is used to prepare the cash flows from operating activities section of the statement of cash flows, what is the starting point? What is this amount converted to?

What is the first step that should be preformed when using the indirect method? Which types of balance sheet accounts relate to earning income (i.e., operating activities)?

What is the second step that should be performed when using the indirect method? What is the third step?

The table below lists the adjustments that are most frequently encountered when the indirect method is used to convert net income to cash flows from operating activities. Complete the table by inserting "added" or "subtracted" in the second column of each row.

Income Statement Amounts or Balance Sheet Changes	Impact on the Statement of Cash Flows
Net income	Starting point for completion
Depreciation expense	
Decreases in current assets	
Increases in current liabilities	
Increases in current assets	
Deceases in current liabilities	

Why must depreciation and amortization expense be added back to convert net income to cash flows from operations?

In terms of adding or subtracting items to convert net income to cash flows from operating activities, what is the general rule for current assets? What is the general rule for current liabilities?

Change in Accounts Receivable

When there is a net decrease in accounts receivable for the period, should the decrease be added to, or subtracted from, net income to convert net income to cash flows from operating activities? When there is a net increase in accounts receivable for the period, should the increase be added or subtracted?

Change in Inventory

When there is a net decrease in inventory for the period, should the decrease be added to, or subtracted from, net income to convert net income to cash flows from operating activities? When there is a net increase in inventory for the period, should the increase be added or subtracted?

Change in Prepaid Expenses

When there is a net decrease in prepaid expenses for the period, should the decrease be added to, or subtracted from, net income to convert net income to cash flows from operating activities? When there is a net increase in prepaid expenses for the period, should the increase be added or subtracted?

Change in Accounts Payable

When there is a net increase in accounts payable for the period, should the increase be added to, or subtracted from, net income to convert net income to cash flows from operating activities? When there is a net decrease in accounts payable for the period, should the decrease be added or subtracted?

Change in Accrued Expenses

When there is a net increase in accrued expenses for the period, should the increase be added to, or subtracted from, net income to convert net income to cash flows from operating activities? When there is a net decrease in accrued expenses for the period, should the decrease be added or subtracted?

LEARNING OBJECTIVE
After studying this section of the chapter, you should be able to:
2B. Report and interpret cash flows from operating activities using the direct method.

PART B: REPORTING AND INTERPRETING CASH FLOWS FROM OPERATING ACTIVITIES – DIRECT METHOD

What is presented when the direct method is used to prepare the operating activities section of the statement of cash flows? How is this section of the statement prepared when this method is used?

Converting Revenues to Cash Inflows

What is the formula that can be used to convert sales revenue to cash collected from customers?

Converting Cost of Goods Sold to Cash Paid to Suppliers

What is the formula that can be used to convert cost of goods sold to cash paid to suppliers?

Converting Operating Expenses to a Cash Outflow

What is the formula that can be used to convert operating expenses to cash paid for these expenses?

INTERNATIONAL PERSPECTIVE
AUSTRALIAN PRACTICES

What does Australian GAAP require in terms of the presentation of the operating activities section of the statement of cash flows?

INTERPRETING CASH FLOWS FROM OPERATIONS

What is working capital? Why do many analysts believe that the operating activities section of the cash flow statement is the most important section? What common rule of thumb do financial and credit analysts follow regarding net income and cash flows from operating activities?

Increase in Receivables: A Warning Sign?

Increases in accounts receivable can cause net income to be greater than cash flows from operating activities. Why do many financial analysts view this situation as a warning sign?

Analyzing Inventory Changes

Why is an unexpected increase in inventory a possible cause for concern? What does a decline in inventory suggest? Why didn't beverage industry analysts interpret Boston Beer's decrease in inventory as a warning sign?

LEARNING OBJECTIVE
After studying this section of the chapter, you should be able to:
3. Analyze and interpret the quality of income ratio.

KEY RATIO ANALYSIS: QUALITY OF INCOME RATIO

How is the quality of income ratio computed? What does it measure? All other things equal, what are two scenarios indicated by a higher quality of income ratio?

When the quality of income ratio does not equal 1, what are four potential causes of any difference?

A QUESTION OF ETHICS
FRAUD AND CASH FLOWS FROM OPERATIONS

How might an astute analyst interpret a growing difference between net income and cash flows from operating activities?

LEARNING OBJECTIVE
After studying this section of the chapter, you should be able to:
4. Report and interpret cash flows from investing activities.

REPORTING AND INTERPRETING CASH FLOWS FROM INVESTING ACTIVITIES
REPORTING CASH FLOWS FROM INVESTING ACCTIVITIES

Which types of balance sheet accounts must normally be analyzed when the cash flows from investing activities section is prepared? What are four typical investing activities?

Does the sale of equipment result in a cash inflow or a cash outflow? Does the purchase of equipment result in a cash inflow or a cash outflow? What three lines (or items) on the statement of cash flows will explain the change (increase or decrease) in the equipment account?

Does the purchase of short-term investments result in a cash inflow or outflow? Should the proceeds from the sales of short-term investments be reported as a cash inflow or outflow? What two lines (or items) on the statement of cash flows will explain the change (increase or decrease) in the equipment account?

LEARNING OBJECTIVE
After studying this section of the chapter, you should be able to:
5. Analyze and interpret the capital acquisitions ratio.

KEY RATIO ANALYSIS: CAPITAL ACQUISITIONS RATIO

How is the capital acquisitions ratio computed? What does it measure? Why is this ratio often computed over longer periods of time than one year? *(Hint: The answer to this question is in a footnote.)* What does a high capital acquisitions ratio indicate?

Boston Beer Company's capital acquisitions ratio increased from 0.71 (in 1995–1997) to 3.47 (in 1998–2000). How might beverage industry analysts interpret this information?

Why should a particular firm's capital acquisitions ratio be compared only with its prior years' figures or with other firms in the same industry?

FINANCIAL ANALYSIS
FREE CASH FLOW

How is free cash flow computed? Why is free cash flow considered a positive sign? Why might it represent a hidden cost to shareholders?

REPORTING AND INTERPRETING CASH FLOWS FROM FINANCING ACTIVITIES

Which types of balance sheet accounts must normally be analyzed when the cash flows from financing activities section is prepared? What are seven typical financing activities?

If debt or stock is issued for other than cash, is the issuance included in the financing activities section of the statement of cash flows? If the company makes payments on long-term debt, how is the amount associated with interest classified on the statement of cash flows?

How are dividend payments classified on the statement of cash flows?

INTREPRETING CASH FLOWS FROM FINANCING ACTIVITIES

What are three sources of funds that are normally used to finance the long-term growth of a company?

ADDITIONAL CASH FLOW DISCLOSURES

If a company uses the indirect method to present cash flows from operating activities, what other information must be provided?

Noncash Investing and Financing Activities

What are noncash investing and financing activities? How should they be reported?

Supplemental Cash Flow Information

When companies use the indirect method to present cash flow from operating activities, what two other figures must be provided?

CHAPTER SUPPLEMENT A (*Determine whether you are responsible for this supplement.*)

Adjustment for Gains and Losses

How should transactions that cause gains and losses be classified on the statement of cash flows?

Assuming that a transaction that causes a gain or loss will be classified as an investing or financing activity, why must an adjustment be made for the gain or loss in the operating activities section of the statement of cash flows? Should gains be added to, or subtracted from, net income to convert net income to cash flows from operating activities? Should losses be added or subtracted?

CHAPTER SUPPLEMENT B (*Determine whether you are responsible for this supplement.*)

Spreadsheet Approach – Statement of Cash Flows, Indirect Method

How do most companies organize the data that is required to prepare a statement of cash flows? What are the benefits of this approach? When a spreadsheet approach is used to prepare the statement of cash flows, how is the spreadsheet organized?

CHAPTER TAKE-AWAYS

1. *Classify cash flow statement items as part of net cash flows from operating, investing, and financing activities. p. 683*

   The statement has three main sections: Cash Flows from Operating Activities, which are related to earning income from normal operations; Cash Flows from Investing Activities, which are related to the acquisition and sale of productive assets; and Cash Flows from Financing Activities, which are related to external financing of the enterprise. The net cash inflow or outflow for the year is the same amount as the increase or decrease in cash and cash equivalents for the year on the balance sheet. Cash equivalents are highly liquid investments with original maturities of less than three months.

2a. *Report and interpret cash flows from operating activities—Indirect method. p. 687*

   The indirect method for reporting cash flows from operating activities reports a conversion of net income to net cash flow from operating activities. The conversion involves additions and subtractions for (1) noncurrent accruals including expenses (such as depreciation expense) and revenues which do not affect current assets or current liabilities and (2) changes in each of the individual current assets (other than cash and short-term investments) and current liabilities (other than short-term debt to financial institutions and current maturities of long-term debt, which relate to financing), which reflect differences in the timing of accrual basis net income and cash flows.

2b. *Report and interpret cash flows from operating activities—Direct method. p. 687*

   The direct method for reporting cash flows from operating activities accumulates all of the operating transactions that result in either a debit or a credit to cash into categories. The most common inflows are cash received from customers and dividends and interest on investments. The most common outflows are cash paid for purchase of services and goods for resale, salaries and wages, income taxes, and interest on liabilities. It is prepared by adjusting each item on the income statement from an accrual basis to a cash basis.

3. *Analyze and interpret the quality of income ratio. p. 697*

   Quality of income ratio (Cash Flow from Operating Activities ÷ Net Income) measures the portion of income that was generated in cash. A higher quality of income ratio indicates greater ability to finance operating and other cash needs from operating cash inflows. A higher ratio also indicates that it is less likely that the company is using aggressive revenue recognition policies to increase net income.

4. *Report and interpret cash flows from investing activities. p. 699*

   Investing activities reported on the cash flow statement include cash payments to acquire fixed assets and short- and long-term investments and cash proceeds from the sale of fixed assets and short- and long-term investments.

5. *Analyze and interpret the capital acquisitions ratio. p. 701*

   The capital acquisitions ratio (Cash Flow from Operating Activities ÷ Cash Paid for Property, Plant, and Equipment) reflects the portion of purchases of property, plant, and equipment financed from operating activities without the need for outside debt or equity financing or the sale of other investments or fixed assets. A high ratio benefits the company because it provides the company with opportunities for strategic acquisitions.

6. **Report and interpret cash flows from financing activities. p. 702**

Cash inflows from financing activities include cash proceeds from issuance of short- and long-term debt and common stock. Cash outflows include cash principal payments on short- and long-term debt, cash paid for the repurchase of the company's stock, and cash dividend payments. Cash payments associated with interest are a cash flow from operating activities.

7. **Explain the impact of additional cash flow disclosures. p. 704**

Noncash investing and financing activities are investing and financing activities that do not involve cash. They include, for example, purchases of fixed assets with long-term debt or stock, exchanges of fixed assets, and exchanges of debt for stock. These transactions are disclosed only as supplemental disclosures to the cash flow statement along with cash paid for taxes and interest under the indirect method.

KEY RATIOS

Quality of income ratio indicates what portion of income was generated in cash. It is computed as follows:

Quality Of Income Ratio = Cash Flow from Operating Activities ÷ Net Income

Capital acquisitions ratio measures the ability to finance purchases of plant and equipment from operations. It is computed as follows:

Cash Acquisitions Ratio =
Cash Flow from Operating Activities ÷ Cash Paid For Property, Plant, and Equipment

FINDING FINANCIAL INFORMATION

Balance Sheet
Changes In Assets, Liabilities, and Stockholders' Equity

Income Statement
Net Income and Noncurrent Accruals

Statement of Cash Flows

Cash Flows From Operating Activities
Cash Flows From Investing Activities
Cash Flows From Financing Activities
Separate Schedule (Or Note)
  Non-cash investing and financing activities
  Interest and taxes paid

Notes

Under Summary of Significant Accounting Policies
  Definition of cash equivalents
Under A Separate Note
If not listed on cash flow statement:
  Non-cash investing and financing activities
  Interest and taxes paid

Financial Accounting

SELF-TEST QUESTIONS AND EXERCISES

MATCHING

Match each of the key terms listed below with the appropriate textbook definition:

____ Cash Equivalent
____ Cash Flows from Financing Activities
____ Cash Flows from Investing Activities
____ Cash Flows from Operating Activities
     (Cash Flows from Operations)

____ Direct Method
____ Free Cash Flow
____ Indirect Method
____ Noncash Investing and Financing Activities

A. Short-term investments with original maturities of three months or less that are readily convertible to cash and whose value is unlikely to change.

B. Cash Flows from Operating Activities less dividends less capital expenditures.

C. Cash inflows and outflows related to external sources of financing (owners and creditors) for the enterprise.

D. The method of presenting the operating activities section of the statement of cash flows that adjusts net income to compute cash flows from operating activities.

E. Cash inflows and outflows related to the acquisition or sale of productive facilities and investments in the securities of other companies.

F. Transactions that do not have direct cash flow effects; reported as a supplement to the statement of cash flows in narrative or schedule form.

G. Cash inflows and outflows directly related to earnings from normal operations.

H. The method of presenting the operating activities section of the statement of cash flows that reports components of cash flows from operating activities as gross receipts and gross payments.

TRUE-FALSE QUESTIONS

For each of the following, enter a T or F in the blank to indicate whether the statement is true or false.

____1. (LO 1) The sum of the individual increases or decreases for all three sections of the statement of cash flows equals the change in cash and cash equivalents during the year.

____2. (LO 2) The amount of the cash flows from operating activities that is reported under the direct method is usually less than the amount reported under the indirect method, as a result, more companies use the indirect method.

____3. (LO 2) When the indirect method is used to preparing the operating activities section of the statement of cash flows, net income is reported first as a positive amount.

____4. (LO 2A) When the indirect method is used, an increase in accounts receivable is added to convert net income to cash flows from operating activities.

____5. (LO 2A) When the indirect method is used, a decrease in inventory is added to convert net income to cash flows from operating activities.

____6. (LO 2A) When the indirect method is used, an increase in accounts payable is subtracted to convert net income to cash flows from operating activities.

____7. (LO 2A) When the indirect method is used, a decrease in accrued liabilities is subtracted to convert net income to cash flows from operating activities.

___8. (LO 2A) When the indirect method is used, depreciation expense should be added to convert net income to cash flows from operating activities.

___9. (LO 2A) When the indirect method is used, gains from the sales of operating assets should be subtracted to convert net income to cash flows from operating activities.

___10. (LO 3) A low quality of income ratio can be due to normal seasonal changes.

___11. (LO 4) The balance sheet accounts that must be analyzed to prepare the section of the statement of cash flows that reports cash flows from investing activities section are the long-term asset accounts.

___12. (LO 5) Positive free cash flow is a positive sign.

___13. (LO 6) Interest expense related to bonds payable would be reported in the cash flows from financing activities section.

___14. (LO 6) The declaration of a dividend would be reported in the cash flows from financing activities section.

MULTIPLE CHOICE QUESTIONS

Choose the best answer or response by placing the identifying letter in the space provided.

___1. (LO 1) A significant amount of net income is not a guarantee of future success because net income is a(n) _____ number, and does not necessarily reflect the company's ability to generate _____.

   a. accrual basis; cash.
   b. cash; sales.
   c. cumulative; cash.
   d. deceptive; sales.
   e. estimated; actual income.

___2. (LO 1) The statement of cash flows is divided into the following sections:

   a. current and noncurrent.
   b. inflows and outflows.
   c. operating, investing, and financing.
   d. operating and non-operating.
   e. assets, liabilities, and equity.

___3. (LO 2) Cash flows from operating activities represent

   a. cash inflows from sales of goods or services.
   b. purchases and disposals of operating assets.
   c. ordinary income items.
   d. cash inflows and outflows from normal operations.
   e. cash income before accounting changes and taxes.

___4. (LO 2B) The direct method and the indirect method are alternative methods of preparing

    a. cash inflows.
    b. the operating activities section of the statement of cash flows.
    c. the worksheet for the statement of cash flows.
    d. the net income calculation.
    e. all of the above.

___5. (LO 2B) A company's sales for its latest fiscal year were $1,500,000, all on account. Beginning accounts receivable for the year were $180,000. Accounts receivable at the end of the year totaled $200,000. Collections from customers were

    a. $1,500,000.
    b. $1,520,000.
    c. $1,480,000.
    d. $1,300,000.
    e. $180,000.

___6. (LO 2B) The beginning balance of salaries payable was $5,000. The company paid $200,000 cash for salaries during the year. At the end of the year, salaries payable had a balance of $8,000. Salaries expense reported on the income statement was

    a. $203,000.
    b. $200,000.
    c. $197,000.
    d. $208,000.
    e. $192,000.

___7. (LO 2B) Office supplies expense amounted to $322,000 for the year. The office supplies account had a beginning balance of $20,000, and an ending balance of $28,500. Purchases of office supplies amounted to

    a. $322,000.
    b. $313,500.
    c. $342,000.
    d. $330,500.
    e. $293,500.

___8. (LO 2B) Interest receivable decreased from $5,000 to $3,000 during the year, and the company reported interest revenue of $35,000 for the year. Cash collections of interest totaled

    a. $33,000.
    b. $35,000.
    c. $32,000.
    d. $37,000.
    e. $38,000.

___9. (LO 2B) Accrued income taxes payable at the end of the year amounted to $30,000. Income tax expense was reported to be $52,000, and payments for the year for income taxes were $40,000. The beginning balance of income taxes payable was

    a. $10,000.
    b. $12,000.
    c. $18,000.
    d. $42,000.
    e. indeterminable from the information given.

___10. (LO 2A) Depreciation expense for a company was $215,000 for the year. Using the indirect method for cash flows from operating activities, this expense would be

    a. added back to net income.
    b. subtracted from net income.
    c. not listed on the statement of cash flows.
    d. reported in the investing section as a deduction.
    e. reported in the investing section as an inflow.

___11. (LO 2A) A company with a calendar year end purchased an asset for $90,000 on January 1, 20A. On January 1, 20D, when accumulated depreciation was $52,000, the company sold the asset, reporting a gain of $5,000 on the income statement. If the company used the indirect method for cash flows from operating activities, it would need to _____ to reconcile net income to cash flows from operating activities.

    a. add $5,000
    b. add $43,000
    c. deduct $5,000
    d. deduct $43,000
    e. exclude this item

___12. (LO 4) Refer to the information in the preceding question. This transaction should be recorded in the _____ section, as an _____ of _____.

    a. operating; outflow; $5,000.
    b. investing; inflow; $5,000.
    c. investing; outflow; $5,000.
    d. supplementary schedule; inflow; $43,000.
    e. investing; inflow; $43,000.

___13. (LO 6) Debt with a net book value of $20,500,000 was retired early at a loss of $250,000. The company would report this item on the statement of cash flows in the _____ section as a(n) _____ of _____.

    a. investing; outflow; $20,250,000
    b. financing; outflow; $20,250,000
    c. financing; outflow; $20,750,000
    d. financing; inflow; $20,250,000
    e. financing, inflow; $250,000

___14. (LO 4) Cash flows from investing activities are normally determined by analyzing

    a. all non-cash asset accounts.
    b. long-lived asset accounts.
    c. long-term liability accounts.
    d. shareholders' equity accounts.
    e. both (a) and (b).

___15. (LO 5) All of the following would be reported as cash flows from financing activities except the

    a. sale of additional shares of the company's stock.
    b. income for the period.
    c. payment of a cash dividend.
    d. repayment of the principal of a bond payable.
    e. borrowing of cash on a long-term note payable.

___16. (LO 7) The purchase of a machine in exchange for a 5-year note payable would

    a. not be reported on the statement of cash flows, because it involves no cash.
    b. be included in investing activities as a cash outflow.
    c. be included in financing activities as a cash inflow.
    d. be reported in a footnote or supplemental schedule to the statement of cash flows.
    e. both (b) and (c).

EXERCISES

Record your answers to each part of these exercises in the space provided. Show your work.

Exercise 1 (LO 1, 2, 4, and 6)

Complete the first two columns in the following table by indicating:

1.   Whether each transaction would appear in the operating activities (O), investing activities (I), or financing activities (F) section of the statement or, if necessary, indicate that the transaction would not appear in any of these three sections of the statement (none), and

2.   If the transaction would be reported on the statement of cash flows as a positive number (+) or a negative number (−).

Strategy – Determining if a Transaction does not Affect Cash Flow
Determine the journal entry recorded for the transaction.
The transaction affects cash flows if, and only if, the Cash account is included in the journal entry.

Operating (O), Investing (I), Financing (F), or Not in These Sections (None)	Reported as a Positive (+) or Negative (−) Number	Transaction
		Recording and payment of salaries and wages.
		Proceeds from sale of bonds for cash.
		Purchase of equipment for cash.

Exercise 1, continued

Operating (O), Investing (I), Financing (F), or Not in These Sections (None)	Reported as a Positive (+) or Negative (−) Number	Transaction
		Cash purchases of office supplies.
		Cash interest payments to bondholders.
		Prepayment of insurance for first six months of year.
		Payment of principal to bondholders.
		Cash sales.
		Purchase of long-term investment for cash.
		Payment of dividends to stockholders.
		Receipt of cash upon signing long-term note payable to bank.
		Issuance of common stock for cash.
		Recording and payment of interest due on note payable.
		Issuance of common stock for land.
		Repurchase of common stock on open market for cash.
		Payment of principal amount due on long-term note payable.
		Acquisition of land in exchange for note payable.
		Recorded adjusting entry for expiration of prepaid insurance.
		Receipt of dividend income on long-term investment.
		Proceeds from sale of long-term investment.

Exercise 2 (LO 2A)

Assume that a company chooses the indirect method to determine net cash flows from operating activities.

Part A

Why is net income the starting point when the indirect method is used to determine cash flows from operating activities? Why is a company's net income different than its cash flows from operating activities?

Exercise 2, continued
Part B

Indicate whether each of the following would be added to or subtracted from net income to reconcile net income to cash flows from operating activities.

Added or Subtract from	Item Required to Convert Net Income to Cash Flows From Operating Activities
	Increase in accounts receivable
	Decrease in accounts payable
	Decrease in inventory
	Increase in accrued expenses
	Gain on sale of investments
	Depreciation expense
	Loss on retirement of bonds
	Increase in prepaid expenses
	Increase in deferred tax liability
	Equity in net income of investee

Exercise 3 (LO 2A)

Use the indirect method to compute the amount of net cash flows from operating activities using the information provided below.

Net income	$500,000	Loss on sale of investments	$42,000
Increase in accounts receivable	14,000	Amortization expense	12,000
Increase in accounts payable	32,000	Gain on retirement of bonds	25,000
Decrease in inventory	35,000	Decrease in prepaid expenses	5,000
Decrease in accrued expenses	16,000	Equity in net loss of investee	2,000

Exercise 4 (LO 2B)

Use the direct method to compute the amount of net cash flows from operating activities using the information provided below.

Income Statement Information:		*Other Information Compiled from Financials:*	
Revenues	$200,000		
Cost of sales	60,000	Increase in receivables	$ 200
Gross margin	140,000	Decrease in inventories	600
Salary expense	60,000	Increase in prepaid expense	700
Depreciation and amortization	30,000	Decrease in accounts payable	2,200
Other expense	20,000	Decrease in accrued liabilities	800
Net income before tax	30,000	Increase in income taxes payable	1,900
Income tax expense	9,000	Reduction of long-term debt	13,700
Net income	$ 21,000	Additions to equipment	29,000

Exercise 5

Consider the following information:

Proceeds from sale of bonds for cash	$1,000,000
Cash interest payments to bondholders	25,000
Conversion of bonds into preferred stock	1,000,000
Purchase of long-term investment for cash	300,000
Payment of dividends to stockholders	75,000
Proceeds from long-term note payable	500,000
Issuance of common stock for cash	5,000,000
Payment of interest due on long-term note payable	50,000
Issuance of common stock for land	250,000
Repurchase of common stock on open market for cash	125,000
Payment of principal amount due on long-term note payable	250,000
Acquisition of land in exchange for note payable	900,000
Receipt of dividend income on long-term investment	40,000
Proceeds from sale of building	525,000
Proceeds from sale of long-term investment	2,500,000
Purchases of equipment	125,000

Part A (LO 4)

Compute the amount of net cash flows from investing activities.

Part B (LO 4)

Compute the amount of net cash flows from financing activities.

Exercise 5, continued
Part C (LO 4 and 6)

If you did not use any of the items listed in Parts A or B, explain why and indicate, if appropriate, how each item would be reported on the Statement of Cash Flows.

SOLUTIONS TO SELF-TEST QUESTIONS AND EXERCISES

MATCHING

A	Cash Equivalent		H	Direct Method
C	Cash Flows from Financing Activities		B	Free Cash Flow
E	Cash Flows from Investing Activities		D	Indirect Method
G	Cash Flows from Operating Activities (Cash Flows from Operations)		F	Noncash Investing and Financing Activities

TRUE-FALSE QUESTIONS

1. T
2. F – The amount of cash flows from operating activities that is reported under the direct method is the same as that reported under the indirect method.
3. T
4. F – When the indirect method is used, an increase in accounts receivable is subtracted from net income.
5. T
6. F – When the indirect method is used, an increase in accounts payable is added to net income.
7. T
8. T
9. T
10. T
11. F – The balance sheet accounts that must be analyzed to prepare the cash flows from investing activities section are the short-term investment and long-term asset accounts.
12. F – While positive free cash flow is considered a positive sign of financial flexibility, it also can represent a hidden cost to shareholders. Sometimes managers use positive free cash flow to pursue unprofitable investments just for the sake of growth or for perks for management use (such as fancy offices and corporate jets).
13. F – Interest expense related to bonds payable would be reported in the cash flows from operating activities section.
14. T

MULTIPLE CHOICE QUESTIONS

1. a
2. c
3. d
4. b
5. c ($180,000 + $1,500,000 - x = $200,000, x = $1,480,000)
6. a ($5,000 + x - $200,000 - $8,000, x = $203,000)
7. d ($20,000 + x - $322,000 = $28,500, x = $330,500)
8. d ($5,000 + $35,000 - x = $3,000, x = $37,000)
9. c (x + $52,000 - $40,000 = $30,000, x = $18,000)
10. a
11. c
12. e ($43,000 is the amount of cash received)
13. c ($20,500,000 + $250,000 = $20,750,000)
14. b
15. b
16. d

EXERCISES
Exercise 1

Operating (O), Investing (I), Financing (F), or Not in These Sections (None)	Reported as a Positive (+) or Negative (–) Number	Transaction
O	–	Recording and payment of salaries and wages.
F	+	Proceeds from sale of bonds for cash.
I	–	Purchase of equipment for cash.
O	–	Cash purchases of office supplies.
O	–	Cash interest payments to bondholders.
O	–	Prepayment of insurance for first six months of year.
F	–	Payment of principal to bondholders.
O	+	Cash sales.
I	–	Purchase of long-term investment for cash.
F	–	Payment of dividends to stockholders.
F	+	Receipt of cash upon signing long-term note payable to bank.
F	+	Issuance of common stock for cash.
O	–	Recording and payment of interest due on note payable.
None	Not applicable	Issuance of common stock for land.
F	–	Repurchase of common stock on open market for cash.
F	–	Payment of principal amount due on long-term note payable.
None	Not applicable	Acquisition of land in exchange for note payable.
None	Not applicable	Recorded adjusting entry for expiration of prepaid insurance.
O	+	Receipt of dividend income on long-term investment.
I	+	Proceeds from sale of long-term investment.

Exercise 2
Part A

The cash flows from operating activities section of the statement of cash flows reports both the cash inflows and cash outflows that directly relate to income from normal operating activities reported on the income statement. As a result, net income is a natural starting point for this section of the statement of cash flows when the indirect method is used. However, the income statement is prepared using the accrual basis.

When the accrual basis is used, cash is not necessarily received when revenues are recorded, and cash is not necessarily disbursed when expenses are recorded. By its very nature, the statement of cash flows is a cash basis statement. As a result, certain adjustments must be made to convert net income from an accrual basis number to a cash basis number when preparing cash flows from operating activities section. In addition, other adjustments must be made to ensure that the amounts reported in this section relate only to "normal" operating activities.

Part B

Add or Subtract	Item Required to Convert Net Income to Cash Flows From Operating Activities
Subtract	Increase in accounts receivable
Subtract	Decrease in accounts payable
Add	Decrease in inventory
Add	Increase in accrued expenses
Subtract	Gain on sale of investments
Add	Depreciation expense
Add	Loss on retirement of bonds
Subtract	Increase in prepaid expenses
Add	Increase in deferred tax liability
Subtract	Equity in net income of investee

Exercise 3
Cash Flows from Operating Activities—Indirect Method

Net income	$500,000
Adjustments:	
Change in accounts receivable	(14,000)
Change in inventory	35,000
Change in prepaid expenses	5,000
Change in accounts payable	32,000
Change in accrued expenses	(16,000)
Amortization expense	12,000
Gain on retirement of bonds	(25,000)
Loss on sale of investments	42,000
Equity in net loss of investee	2,000
Net cash flow from operating activities	$573,000

Exercise 4
Cash Flows from Operating Activities—Direct Method

Cash collected from customers (1)	$199,800
Cash payments to employees	(60,000)
Cash payments to suppliers (2)	(61,600)
Cash payments for other expenses (3)	(21,500)
Cash payments for income tax (4)	(7,100)
Net cash flow from operating activities	$ 49,600

(1) Cash collected from customers: $200,000 – 200 = 199,800
(2) Cash payments to suppliers: 60,000 – 600 + 2,200 = 61,600
(3) Cash payments for other expenses: 20,000 + 700 + 800 = 21,500
(4) Cash payments for income taxes: 9,000 – 1,900 = 7,100

The additions to equipment would be classified as an investing activity and the reduction of long-term debt would be classified as a financing activity; as such, this information was not used in the calculation above.

Exercise 5
Part A – Investing Activities

Proceeds from sale of building	$ 525,000
Purchases of equipment	(125,000)
Proceeds from sale of long-term investment	2,500,000
Purchase of long-term investment	(300,000)
Net Cash Flows from Investing Activities	$2,600,000

Part B – Financing Activities

Financing Activities

Proceeds from long-term note payable	$ 500,000
Payment of long-term note payable	(250,000)
Proceeds from sale of bonds	1,000,000
Proceeds from issuance of common stock	5,000,000
Repurchase of common stock on open market for cash	(125,000)
Payment of dividends to stockholders	(75,000)
Net Cash Flows from Financing Activities	$6,050,000

Part C

The following items would be classified as cash flows from operating activities:

Cash interest payments to bondholders	$25,000
Payment of interest due on long-term note payable	50,000
Receipt of dividend income on long-term investment	40,000

The following items would be reported as noncash investing and financing activities:

Conversion of bonds into preferred stock	$1,000,000
Issuance of common stock for land	250,000
Acquisition of land in exchange for note payable	900,000

©The McGraw-Hill Companies, Inc., 2004

AN IDEA FOR YOUR STUDY TEAM

Get together with the other members of your study team and locate two or three publicly held companies that have recently fallen into financial difficulties. Locate recent copies of their annual reports to stockholders. Look carefully at the statements of cash flows. What items can you list that seem to be indicators of potential cash flows problems?

ORGANIZATION OF THE CHAPTER

The Investment Decision

Understanding a Company's Strategy	Financial Statement Analysis	Ratio and Percentage Analysis	Component Percentages
Tests of Profitability 1. Return on Equity (ROE) 2. Return on Assets (ROA) 3. Financial Leverage Percentage 4. Earnings per Share (EPS) 5. Quality of Income	Tests of Liquidity 8. Cash Ratio 9. Current Ratio 10. Quick Ratio (Acid Test) 11. Receivable Turnover 12. Inventory Turnover	Tests of Solvency 13. Times Interest Earned 14. Cash Coverage Ratio 15. Debt-to-Equity Ratio Market Tests 16. Price/Earnings (PE) Ratio 17. Dividend Yield	Interpreting Ratios and Other Analytical Considerations Other Financial Information Information in an Efficient Market

CHAPTER FOCUS SUGGESTIONS

Overview

This chapter emphasizes the analytical uses of information contained in financial statements. You should be familiar with each of the five categories of commonly used financial ratios. You will need to know how to compute each of the ratios that are set forth in the chapter, and understand what each ratio measures. Although many ratios are often calculated for a given company, not all of the ratios may be relevant to the decision being made. You should be familiar with the various types of standards that are used to evaluate the results of relevant ratios, and be able to identify situations in which further investigation and evaluation are required.

LEARNING OBJECTIVES

After studying this chapter, you should be able to:

(LO 1) Explain how a company's business strategy affects financial analysis.
(LO 2) Discuss how analysts use financial statements.
(LO 3) Compute and interpret component percentages.
(LO 4) Compute and interpret profitability ratios.
(LO 5) Compute and interpret liquidity ratios.
(LO 6) Compute and interpret solvency ratios.
(LO 7) Compute and interpret market test ratios.

READ AND RECALL QUESTIONS

After you read each section of the chapter, answer the related Read and Recall Questions below.

> **LEARNING OBJECTIVE**
> *After studying this section of the chapter, you should be able to:*
> 1. Explain how a company's business strategy affects financial analysis.

BUSINESS BACKGROUND

When considering an investment in stock, what three factors should investors consider as they evaluate the company's future income and growth potential?

UNDERSTANDING A COMPANY'S STRATEGY

The DuPont model (introduced in chapter 5) helps analysts understand that a number of business strategies affect the profitability of a business. Demonstrate your understanding of this model by: (1) inserting the names of each of the three return on equity (ROE) factors in the top row of boxes and (2) writing out the related formulas in the bottom row of boxes.

ROE	=		X		X	
_____	=	_____	X	_____	X	_____

What are the two fundamental strategies that companies follow to earn a high rate of return?

What is the best way to start your financial statement analysis? Why? Where can you find information about a company's strategy?

FINANCIAL STATEMENT ANALYSIS

What are two methods for making financial comparisons? Why is it difficult to use the second method?

RATIO AND PERCENTAGE ANALYSES

What does a ratio or percent express? Why do decision makers use ratio analysis or percentage analysis?

COMPONENT PERCENTAGES

What does a component percentage express? What is the base amount for the income statement? What is the base amount for the balance sheet?

When an income statement account is compared with a balance sheet amount, what should be done to the balance sheet amount? When is it appropriate to simply use data from the ending balance sheet?

What are five categories of commonly used financial ratios? *(Hint: The categories are listed in Exhibit 14.3 in the text.)*

After studying this section of the chapter, you should be able to:
4. Compute and interpret profitability ratios.

TESTS OF PROFITABILITY

What does profitability measure? How do tests of profitability measure the adequacy of income?

1. Return on Equity (ROE)

How is the return on equity ratio computed? What does it measure? What should be used, if applicable, in the numerator (that is, in lieu of simply using income)?

2. Return on Assets (ROA)

How is the return on assets ratio computed? What does it measure? Why is the ROA ratio usually considered to be a better measure (compared to ROE) of management's ability to utilize assets more effectively? What should be used, if applicable, in the numerator (that is, in lieu of simply using income plus interest expense (net of tax))?

3. Financial Leverage Percentage

What is financial leverage? How is the financial leverage ratio computed? What does it measure? When does positive leverage occur?

Why do most companies obtain a significant amount of resources from creditors rather than obtaining resources only from the sale of their capital stock? How can financial leverage be enhanced?

4. Earnings per Share (EPS)

In simple situations, how is earnings per share computed? What does it measure?

5. Quality of Income

How is the quality of income ratio computed? What does it measure? What does a quality of income ratio above one indicate? What does a ratio below one represent?

6. Profit Margin

How is the profit margin percentage computed? What does it measure? Why is it difficult to compare profit margins for companies in different industries? Is a larger profit margin percentage always better?

7. Fixed Asset Turnover

What are fixed assets? How is the fixed asset turnover ratio computed? What does it measure? When is this ratio widely used? How is the asset turnover ratio computed? What does it measure?

LEARNING OBJECTIVE
After studying this section of the chapter, you should be able to:
5. Compute and interpret liquidity ratios.

TESTS OF LIQUIDITY

What is liquidity? What is the focus of the various tests of liquidity?

8. Cash Ratio

How is the cash ratio computed? What does it measure? Why should a company be careful not to have a cash ratio that is too high? Why do analysts become very concerned if this ratio deteriorates over a period of time? Why do some analysts choose not to use the cash ratio?

9. Current Ratio

How is the current ratio computed? What does it measure? What is another name for this ratio? What current ratio would analysts consider to be conservative? When is a current ratio of just a little higher than 1 acceptable? When is a current ratio closer to 2 desirable? Is it possible to have a current ratio that is too high?

10. Quick Ratio (Acid Test)

How is the quick ratio computed? What are quick assets? What does it measure? How is this ratio a measure of a company's safety margin?

11. Receivable Turnover

How is the receivable turnover ratio computed? Why is this ratio called a turnover ratio? What does the receivable turnover ratio measure? What does a high receivable turnover ratio usually suggest about a company? Why might a high ratio suggest the opposite? What would cause the receivable turnover ratio to be too low? What problem will cause a very high ratio?

How is the average age of receivables computed? What does it measure? What is the rule of thumb for the relationship between the average age of receivables and the credit terms granted to customers?

12. Inventory Turnover

How is the inventory turnover computed? What does it measure? Why is an increase in this ratio usually considered to be favorable? Why might a high inventory turnover ratio indicate a problem?

How is the average days' supply in inventory computed? What does it measure?

LEARNING OBJECTIVE
After studying this section of the chapter, you should be able to:
6. Compute and interpret solvency ratios.

TESTS OF SOLVENCY

What is solvency? What do tests of solvency measure?

13. Times Interest Earned Ratio

How is the times interest earned ratio computed? What does it measure? What does a very high ratio indicate? How do some analysts modify this ratio? Why do other analysts still believe that this ratio is flawed?

14. Cash Coverage

How is the cash coverage ratio computed? What does it measure? Why might interest payments be a better measure of the company's obligation than accrued interest expense?

15. Debt-to-Equity

How is the debt/equity ratio computed? What does it measure? Why is equity capital usually less risky than debt for a company?

MARKET TESTS

What do market tests measure?

16. Price/Earnings (P/E) Ratio

How is the price/earnings ratio computed? What does it measure? What does a high P/E multiple indicate? How is the capitalization ratio computed? What does it measure? What is related to the value of a company's stock?

17. Dividend Yield Ratio

How is the dividend yield ratio computed? What does it measure? Would stocks of companies with high or low growth potential offer higher dividend yields?

INTERPRETING RATIOS AND OTHER ANALYTICAL CONSIDERATIONS

What should analysts do before using ratios computed by others? What should a ratio be compared to when it is being interpreted? When are comparisons of ratios for different companies appropriate?

How might ratios obscure underlying factors that are of interest? What should be done in this situation?

In general, what knowledge do you now have that will enable you to more effectively analyze the information contained in financial statements?

OTHER FINANCIAL INFORMATION

What were three special factors that might affect the analysis of a company (such as Home Depot)?

QUESTION OF ETHICS
INSIDER INFORMATION

What is insider information? What can happen if you buy or sell stock based on insider information? What approach can you take to decide if information that comes to your attention is insider information? What have many public accounting firms done to uphold the highest ethical standard in this regard?

Information in an Efficient Market

What is an efficient market? What does the price of a security reflect in an efficient market? What should not be possible in an efficient market?

CHAPTER TAKE-AWAYS

1. **Explain how a company's business strategy affects financial analysis.**

   In simple terms, a business strategy establishes the objectives a business is trying to achieve. Performance is best evaluated by comparing the financial statements to the objectives that the business is working to achieve. In other words, an understanding of a company's strategy provides the context for conducting financial statement analysis.

2. **Discuss how analysts use financial statements.**

   Analysts use financial statements to understand present conditions and past performance as well as to predict future performance. Financial statements provide important information to help users understand and evaluate corporate strategy. The data reported on statements can be used for either time-series analysis (evaluating a single company over time) or in comparison with similar companies at a single point in time. Most analysts compute component percentages and ratios when using statements.

3. **Compute and interpret component percentages.**

   To compute component percentages for the income statement, the base amount is net sales revenue. Each expense is expressed as a percentage of net sales revenue. On the balance sheet, the base amount is total assets; each balance sheet account is divided by total assets. Component percentages are evaluated by comparing them over time for a single company or by comparing them with percentages for similar companies.

4. **Compute and interpret profitability ratios.**

   Several tests of profitability focus on measuring the adequacy of income by comparing it to other items reported on the financial statements. Exhibit 14.3 lists these ratios and shows how to compute them. Profitability ratios are evaluated by comparing them over time for a single company or by comparing them with ratios for similar companies.

5. **Compute and interpret liquidity ratios.**

   Tests of liquidity focus on measuring a company's ability to meet is current maturing debt. Exhibit 14.3 lists these ratios and shows how to compute them. Profitability ratios are evaluated by comparing them over time for a single company or by comparing them with ratios for similar companies.

6. **Compute and interpret solvency ratios.**

   Solvency ratios measure a company's ability to meet its long-term obligations. Exhibit 14.3 lists these ratios and shows how to compute them. Profitability ratios are evaluated by comparing them over time for a single company or by comparing them with ratios for similar companies.

7. **Compute and interpret market test ratios.**

   Market test ratios relate the current price of a stock to the return that accrues to investors. Exhibit 14.3 lists these ratios and shows how to compute them. Profitability ratios are evaluated by comparing them over time for a single company or by comparing them with ratios for similar companies.

FINDING FINANCIAL INFORMATION

Balance Sheet	Income Statement
Ratios are not reported on the balance sheet but analysts will use balance sheet information to compute many ratios. Most analysts use an average of the beginning and ending amounts for balance sheet accounts when comparing the account to an income statement account.	Earnings per share is the only ratio that is required to be reported on the financial statements. It is usually reported at the bottom on the income statement.

Statement of Cash Flows	Statement of Stockholders' Equity
Ratios are not reported on the SCF but some ratios use amounts from this statement.	Ratios are not reported on this statement but some ratios use amounts from this statement.

Notes

Under summary of significant accounting policies
This note has no information pertaining directly to ratios, but it is important to understand accounting differences if you are comparing two companies.

Under a separate note
Most companies include a 10-year financial summary as a separate note. These summaries include data for significant accounts, some accounting ratios and non-accounting information.

SELF-TEST QUESTIONS AND EXERCISES

MATCHING

Match each of the key terms listed below with the appropriate textbook definition:

____	Component Percentage	____	Ratio (Percentage) Analysis
____	Efficient Markets	____	Tests of Liquidity
____	Market Tests	____	Tests of Solvency
____	Tests of Profitability		

A. An analytical tool designed to identify significant relationships; measures the proportional relationship between two financial statement amounts.
B. Expresses each item on a particular financial statement as a percentage of a single base amount.
C. Ratios that tend to measure the market worth of a share of stock.
D. Ratios that measure a company's ability to meet its currently maturing obligations.
E. Securities markets in which prices fully reflect available information.
F. Ratios that measure a company's ability to meet its long-term obligations.
G. Compare income with one or more primary activities.

TRUE-FALSE QUESTIONS

For each of the following, enter a T or F in the blank to indicate whether the statement is true or false.

___1.   (LO 1) The past performance of a company can be useful in forecasting future results.

___2.   (LO 1) Economy-wide factors affect all companies in the same way.

___3.   (LO 2) Time series analysis involves comparing information for a single company for the current and the previous year.

___4.   (LO 2) The standard industrial classification codes established by the government are a source of potentially comparable companies to be used for analytical purposes.

___5.   (LO 2) All decisions are future oriented.

___6.   (LO 2) When considering a stock investment, the investor should consider the company's future income and growth potential on the basis of economy-wide, industry and individual company factors.

___7.   (LO 3) Component percentages express each item on a particular financial statement as a percentage of a single base amount.

___8.   (LO 4) The return on equity (ROE) ratio equals the net profit margin ratio times the asset turnover ratio times financial leverage ratio.

___9.   (LO 4) Return on equity relates the company's net income (or, if applicable, its income before extraordinary items) to the average amount of capital invested by the owners of the company.

___10. (LO 4) Return on assets is the same as return on equity.

___11. (LO 4) Financial leverage is the advantage, or disadvantage, that occurs as the result of earning a return on owners' investment that is different from the return earned on total investment.

___12. (LO 7) There is much evidence to support the assumption that the stock markets react very quickly to new information in an unbiased manner.

MULTIPLE CHOICE QUESTIONS

Choose the best answer or response by placing the identifying letter in the space provided.

___1.   (LO 1) An example of an economy-wide factor that might affect any company is

   a.   a hurricane.
   b.   the price of wheat.
   c.   gross national product.
   d.   increased import tariffs on automobiles.
   e.   a winter with relatively little snow.

___2.   (LO 3) When the balance sheet is expressed in component percentages, all amounts are stated as a percentage of

   a.   working capital.
   b.   total assets.
   c.   cash.
   d.   sales.
   e.   total equity.

___3. (LO 4) Despite the risks of debt financing, companies obtain significant resources from creditors because of the

    a. benefits of financial leverage.
    b. ease of selling bonds.
    c. ability to deduct interest from taxes, but not dividends.
    d. convertibility of debt.
    e. both a and c.

___4. (LO 4) Return on equity is a test of

    a. profitability.
    b. liquidity.
    c. solvency.
    d. market strength.
    e. capital structure.

___5. (LO 4) Equity capital is considered to be less risky than debt capital because

    a. there is no legal requirement to declare and pay dividends, and it has no maturity date.
    b. equity ownership can be purchased by investors in smaller quantities.
    c. stock can be repurchased more easily.
    d. equity capital distributes ownership of the company more widely.
    e. equity provides more opportunities for financial leverage.

___6. (LO 6) Solvency tests are designed to forecast the company's ability to

    a. avoid bankruptcy.
    b. meet long-term obligations.
    c. meet currently maturing obligations
    d. avoid running short of cash.
    e. both (b) and (c).

___7. (LO 7) The dividend yield ratio is meant to measure the

    a. average dollar amount of dividends that the company pays.
    b. return based on the current market price of the stock.
    c. proportion of earnings per share paid out in dividends.
    d. proportion of dividends to interest on debt.
    e. growth in the value of the stock.

___8. (LO 7) An efficient market

    a. responds immediately to new information.
    b. uses automated systems to update information.
    c. reacts to new information quickly and in an unbiased manner.
    d. takes into account old as well as new information.
    e. processes transactions as quickly as possible.

EXERCISES

Record your answers to each part of these exercises in the space provided. Show your work.

Exercise 1 (LO 1, 2, 3 and 4)

You were introduced to Pixar in chapter 3 of this Study Guide. The income statements and balance sheets set forth below were compiled (with classifications added as deemed necessary using reasonable assumptions) using information included in the Forms 10-K that were filed by Pixar with the SEC for fiscal 2001 (year ending December 29, 2001), fiscal 2000 (year ending December 30, 2000) and fiscal 1999 (year ending January 1, 2000). All dollar amounts shown below are in thousands.

Pixar
Statement of Operations
for the years ended December 29, 2001 (referred to as fiscal 2001)
and December 30, 2000 (referred to as fiscal 2000)

	Fiscal 2001	Fiscal 2000
Revenue:		
Film and animation services	$63,365	$ 163,154
Software	6,858	9,113
Total revenue	**70,223**	**172,267**
Cost of revenue:		
Film and animations services	11,769	36,433
Software	549	571
Total cost of revenue	**12,318**	**37,004**
Gross profit	**57,905**	**135,263**
Operating expenses:		
Research and development	6,341	5,562
Sales and marketing	1,991	1,615
General and administrative	8,057	7,686
Total operating expenses	**16,389**	**14,863**
Income from continuing operations	**41,516**	**120,400**
Other income, net	14,355	12,978
Income from continuing operations before taxes	**55,871**	**133,378**
Income tax expense	19,865	55,351
Net income from continuing operations	**36,006**	**78,027**
Income from discontinued operations		
(includes income tax expense)	211	406
Net income	**$36,217**	**$ 78,433**

Exercise 1, continued

Pixar
Balance Sheets
As of December 29, 2001, December 30, 2000 and January 2, 2000

	12/29/01	12/30/00	1/2/00
Assets:			
Current Assets (see note below):			
Cash and cash equivalents	$ 56,289	$ 63,241	$ 31,170
Short-term investments	222,310	139,514	163,779
Trade accounts receivable, net of allowance	1,516	1,136	714
Due from Disney	13,512	73,850	
Other receivables	5,632	3,121	16,026
Prepaid expenses and other assets	3,528	4,903	3,888
Deferred income taxes	21,673	25,915	34,533
Total Current Assets	**324,460**	**311,680**	**250,110**
Property and equipment, net	111,995	110,891	60,266
Capitalized film production costs	86,839	57,032	64,529
Total Assets	**$523,294**	**$479,603**	**$374,905**
Liabilities and Shareholders' Equity:			
Current Liabilities:			
Accounts payable	4,843	1,622	$ 458
Income taxes payable	1,808	9,650	12,230
Accrued liabilities	8,844	12,229	16,475
Unearned revenue	2,113	15,382	1,299
Total Current Liabilities	**17,608**	**43,883**	**30,462**
Shareholders' equity:			
Common stock	325,362	293,209	281,274
Accumulated other comprehensive income	1,845	249	(660)
Retained earnings	178,479	142,262	63,829
Total Shareholders' Equity	**505,686**	**435,720**	**344,443**
Total Liabilities and Shareholders' Equity	**$523,294**	**$479,603**	**$374,905**

Exercise 1, continued

Other information reported in those Forms 10-K included the following:

- Net cash provided by operating activities amounted to $100,925 and $84,640 during fiscal 2001 and 2000, respectively.
- Pixar did not declare any dividends during fiscal 2001, 2000 or 1999.
- Shares used in computing basic net income per share (that is, basic earnings per share) were 48,276,000 and 47,280,000 (not in thousands) during fiscal 2001 and 2000, respectively.
- Shares outstanding at December 29, 2001 and December 30, 2000 were 49,445,956 and 47,633,372 (not in thousands), respectively.

Part A (LO 4)

Compute the following ratios for fiscal 2001 and fiscal 2000 using the information set forth above.

TESTS OF PROFITABILITY

Return on Equity

Formula

2001

2000

Return on Assets

Formula

2001

2000

Exercise 1, Part A, continued

TESTS OF PROFITABILITY

Financial Leverage Percentage

Formula

2001

2000

Earnings per Share (EPS)

Formula

2001

2000

Quality of Income

Formula

2001

2000

Exercise 1, Part A, continued

TESTS OF PROFITABILITY

Profit Margin

Formula

2001

2000

Fixed Asset Turnover Ratio

Formula

2001

2000

Part B (LO 5)

Compute the following ratios for fiscal 2001 and fiscal 2000 using the information set forth above.

TESTS OF LIQUIDITY

Cash Ratio

Formula

2001

2000

Financial Accounting

Exercise 1, Part B, continued

TESTS OF LIQUIDITY

Current Ratio

Formula

2001

2000

Quick Ratio (Acid Test)

Formula

2001

2000

Receivable Turnover

Formula

2001

2000

Exercise 1, Part B, continued

TESTS OF LIQUIDITY

Average Age of Receivables

Formula

2001

2000

Part C (LO 6)

Compute the following ratio for fiscal 2001 and fiscal 2000 using the information set forth above.

TEST OF SOLVENCY

Debt-to-Equity

Formula

2001

2000

Part D (LO 4, 5, 6 and 7)

Look through the list of ratios set forth in Parts A, B, and C, and list any commonly used ratios that were not included in that list. Indicate why each ratio was excluded from the list, identify its type (profitability, liquidity, etc.) and give the formula for each.

Exercise 1, continued
Part E (LO 4)

Comment on the results of Pixar's tests of profitability.

Part F (LO 5)

Comment on the results of Pixar's tests of liquidity.

Part G

What other information is required to interpret Pixar's ratios?

Exercise 2 (LO 5)

Allied American had inventories totaling $4,300, $4,800, and $4,700 at the end of 20A, 20B, and 20C, respectively. Allied's net credit sales were $117,000, $123,000, and $115,000 during 20A, 20B, and 20C, respectively. Allied's cost of goods sold were $70,000, $73,000, and $69,000 during 20A, 20B, and 20C, respectively.

Part A

Compute the following tests of liquidity ratios for 20C and 20B for Allied:

Inventory Turnover

Formula

20C

20B

Average Days' Supply in Inventory

Formula

20C

20B

Exercise 2, continued
Part B

How would you interpret the results of the ratios calculated above?

SOLUTIONS TO SELF-TEST QUESTIONS AND EXERCISES

MATCHING

B	Component Percentage	A	Ratio (Percentage) Analysis
E	Efficient Markets	D	Tests of Liquidity
C	Market Tests	F	Tests of Solvency
G	Tests of Profitability		

TRUE-FALSE QUESTIONS

1. T
2. F – Economy-wide factors may affect all companies, but not necessarily at the same time or to the same extent. (For example, increases in interest rates often slow economic growth because consumers are less willing to buy merchandise on credit when interest rates are high. Retailers may suffer the effects well before firms that provide services to businesses.)
3. F – In time series analysis, information for a single company is compared over time (e.g., a time series analysis might reveal that a ratio has declined each year for the past five years).
4. T
5. T
6. T
7. T
8. T
9. T
10. F – Return on assets is computed by dividing the sum of net income (or, if applicable, income before extraordinary items) and interest expense (net of tax) by average total assets. Return on equity is computed by dividing the sum of net income (or, if applicable, income before extraordinary items) and interest expense (net of tax) by average total stockholders' equity.
11. T
12. T

MULTIPLE CHOICE QUESTIONS

1.	c	3.	e	5.	a	7.	b
2.	b	4.	a	6.	b	8.	e

EXERCISES

Exercise 1 - Part A -TESTS OF PROFITABILITY

Return on Equity

Income before extraordinary items ÷ Average owners' equity
2001
$36,006 ÷ [($435,720 + $505,686) ÷ 2] = $36,006 ÷ $470,703 = 7.7%
2000
$78,027 ÷ [($344,443 + $435,720) ÷ 2] = $78,027 ÷ $390,081.5 = 20.0%

Exercise 1 - Part A -TESTS OF PROFITABILITY, continued

Return on Assets

(Income before extraordinary items + Interest expense (net of tax)) ÷ Average total assets
2001
($36,006+ $0) ÷ [($479,603 + $523,294) ÷ 2] = $36,006 ÷ $501,448.5 = 7.2%
2000
($78,027 + $0) ÷ [($374,905 + $479,603) ÷ 2] = $78,027 ÷ $427,254 = 18.3%

Financial Leverage

Return on equity – Return on assets
2001
7.7% (from above) – 7.2% (from above) = 0.5%
2000
20.0% (from above) – 18.3% (from above) = 1.7%

Earnings per Share (EPS)

Income before extraordinary items ÷ Average number of shares of common stock outstanding
Note: Dollar amounts are not in thousands in the calculations shown below for this ratio.
2001
$36,006,000 ÷ 48,276,000 = $0.75
2000
$78,027,000 ÷ 47,280,000 = $1.65

Quality of Income

Cash flows from operating activities ÷ Net income
2001
$100,925 ÷ $36,217 = 2.8
2000
$84,640 ÷ $78,433 = 1.1

Profit Margin

Income before extraordinary items ÷ Net sales revenue
2001
$36,006 ÷ 70,223 = 51.3%
2000
$78,027 ÷ 172,267 = 45.3%

Fixed Asset Turnover

Net sales revenue ÷ Average net fixed assets
2001
$70,223 ÷ [($110,891 + $111,995) ÷ 2] = $70,223 ÷ $111,443 = 0.6
2000
$172,267 ÷ [($60,266 + $110,891) ÷ 2] = $172,267 ÷ $85,578.5 = 2.0

©The McGraw-Hill Companies, Inc., 2004

396   *Financial Accounting*

Exercise 1, continued

Part B -TESTS OF LIQUIDITY

Cash Ratio

(Cash + cash equivalents) ÷ Current liabilities
2001
$56,289 ÷ $17,608 = 3.2
2000
$63,241÷ $43,883 = 1.4

Current Ratio

Current assets ÷ Current liabilities
2001
$324,460 ÷ $17,608 = 18.4 to 1
2000
$311,680 ÷ $43,883 = 7.1 to 1

Quick Ratio (Acid Test)

Quick assets (cash, short-term investments and accounts receivable) ÷ Current liabilities
2001
($56,289 + $222,310 + $1,516) ÷ $17,608 = 280,115 ÷ $17,608 = 15.9 to 1
2000
($63,241 +$139,514+ $1,136) ÷ $43,883 = $203,891 ÷ $43,883 = 4.6 to 1
Note that the "Due from Disney" and "Other Receivables" were excluded from quick assets because they were not categorized as trade receivables on Pixar's balance sheet.

Receivable Turnover

Net credit sales (or total sales if net credit sales is not known) ÷ Average net trade receivables
2001
$70,223 ÷ [($1,136 + $1,516) ÷ 2] = $70,223 ÷ $1,326 = 53.0
2000
$172,267 ÷ [($714 + $1,136) ÷ 2] = $172,267 ÷ $925 = 186.2

Average Age of Receivables

Days in year (365) ÷ Receivable turnover ratio
2001
365 ÷ 53.0 (from above) = 6.9 days
2000
365 ÷ 186.2 (from above) = 2.0 days

Exercise 1, continued

Part C -TEST OF SOLVENCY

Debt-to-Equity Ratio

Total liabilities ÷ Owners' equity
2001
$17,608 ÷ $505,686 = 3.5%
2000
$43,883 ÷ $435,720 = 10.1%

Part D

The **inventory turnover ratio** (computed by dividing cost of goods sold by average inventory) and average days' supply in inventory (computed by dividing 365 by the inventory turnover ratio) were not listed under the tests of liquidity. Pixar does not have inventory.

The **times interest earned ratio** (computed by dividing the sum of net income, interest expense and income tax expense by interest expense) and **cash coverage ratio** (computed by dividing the sum of cash flow from operating activities, interest expense and income tax expense by interest expense paid) were not listed under tests of solvency. Pixar did not report any notes payable on its balance sheets, nor did it separately report the amount of interest expense, if any, on its income statement.

The **price/earnings (P/E) ratio** (computed by dividing current market price per share by earnings per share) and the **dividend yield ratio** (computed by dividing dividends per share by market price per share) were not listed under market tests. *(Note that the 2001 and 2000 dividend yields would be zero; Pixar did not declare any dividends during these fiscal years.)*

Part E

Pixar's return on equity decreased from 20.0% to 7.7%. Thus, in 2001, the company earned 7.7%, after income taxes, on the investment provided by its owners. The company's return on assets also decreased from 18.3% to 7.2%. Management earned 7.2% on the total resources it used during the year. Pixar's financial leverage was slightly positive during 2000 at 1.7%; its financial leverage was a bit less positive during 2001 as it decreased to 0.5%. Pixar does not currently borrow money (i.e., there are no notes payable on its balance sheet) and so it cannot borrow more effectively (by paying a low rate of interest since it currently has a borrowing rate of zero), however, it could make further improvements in its financial leverage by investing effectively (i.e., earning a high rate of return on investment).

Earnings per share declined significantly from $1.65 during fiscal 2000 to $0.75 during fiscal 2001. However, Pixar's quality of income improved from 1.1 during fiscal 2000 to 2.8 during fiscal 2001. Both ratios, which were higher than 1, imply higher-quality earnings because each dollar of income is supported by at least one dollar of cash flow.

Pixar's revenues earned an average of 51.3 cents of profit per revenue dollar during fiscal 2001 versus 45.3 cents of profit during fiscal 2000.

Exercise 1, Part E, continued

Pixar's fixed asset turnover ratio, which measures the company's ability to generate revenues from its investment in fixed assets (or plant and equipment in Pixar's case) decreased from 2.0 during fiscal 2000 to 0.6 during fiscal 2001, indicating that the company was less effective in its utilization of fixed assets to generate revenue.

Part F

Tests of liquidity measure a company's ability to meet its currently maturing debts. Pixar's cash ratio increased from 1.4 to 3.2, its current ratio increased from 7.1 to 1 to 18.4 to 1and its quick ratio also increased from 4.6 to 1 to 15.9 to 1 as of the end of fiscal 2001 versus the end of fiscal 2000. All three ratios seem to indicate that the company has a high margin of safety in terms of its liquidity.

Comparing 2000 with 2001, Pixar's receivable turnover ratio decreased from 186.2 to 53.0 and the average age of its receivables increased from 2.0 to 6.9. However, Pixar's net trade receivables are less than 1% of its total assets; as such, these ratios may not be meaningful in terms of measuring the company's liquidity.

Part G

Analysts must understand Pixar's operations and the accounting policies that it uses. They might use rules of thumb to interpret the meaning of some ratios. Other ratios might be evaluated using a time series analysis (comparing this year's ratios to those of previous years). Analysts would also compare Pixar's ratios to those of its direct competitors (which may be difficult if its competitors are different in terms of size, are owned by other companies, have subsidiaries, operate in other lines of business, and/or use alternative accounting policies) and industry averages (which also may be difficult for the same reasons). Because many of the ratios represent averages, analysts need to be aware of any underlying factors that might be of interest.

Exercise 2
Part A

Inventory Turnover

20C
($69,000 / [($4,800 + $4,700) / 2] = $69,000 / $4,750 = 14.5
20B
($73,000 / [($4,300 + $4,800) / 2] = $73,000 / $4,550 = 16.0

Average Days' Supply in Inventory

20C
365 / 14.5 (from above) = 25.2 days
20B
365 / 16.0 (from above) = 22.8 days

©The McGraw-Hill Companies, Inc., 2004

Exercise 2, continued
Part B

The decrease in Allied's inventory turnover and increase in its average days' supply in inventory during 20C both appear to be unfavorable. However, further investigation may be warranted. For example, the company may have decided to keep higher levels of inventory on hand so that sales are not lost because of items that are out of stock. In addition, these ratios represent averages. As such, they may obscure underlying factors that are of interest.

AN IDEA FOR YOUR STUDY TEAM

Now that the course is over, take a few minutes to "recap." List at least ten things that you learned in this course that you truly believe you will use sometime in the future (in another course, during an internship you have lined up, when you are succeeding in the career that you are striving for, or in your life outside of work). Maybe you are already using some of the things that you have learned! Be specific; indicate *how* you will use what you have learned (don't just jot down, "how to read financial statements"). Then, get together with the other members of your study team, and compare your lists.

Financial Accounting